Quotes and Testi

CH00602511

From earliest times, man has imparted wisdom
This book is in the best of that tradition, showin
have found the path to strategic leadership.
leader, but it's also a great read.

Simon Burke
Executive Chairman, Superquinn, Chairman, Majestic Wines plc

Freedom from Fear will inspire you to stop just thinking good strategy, and to start putting it into practice. This book is rare in acknowledging the business fundamental, that strategic thinking only gets your business airborne. It's decisive and dynamic action that gets you down safely!

Neil Boote
Managing Director, Firebrand Live

Before I met Bob, I thought strategic leadership was something practised only by captains of industry. How wrong was I! This book builds on Bob's previous work and translates the concept of strategic thinking into practical action. With the help of some fascinating stories, Bob convinces us that we have nothing to fear, and that we can all make a difference to our lives and the world around us. In his own words, 'Leadership has no rank... anyone can be a leader.'

Paul Cooper
Deputy Director of Capital Projects, University of Bristol

Bob Gorzynski is unique in his ability to make you think differently. Fearing what we might see around or in us often limits our potential. This book will enable you to look deeper in a more assured way then you have ever done before.

Robert Taylor
Founder of Strategic Negotiation Services (SNS)

A powerful companion to *The Strategic Mind*, rich in stories of strategic leadership – a 'must read' book for strategy and leadership courses at all levels.

Claire Wellings
Head of Department of Services Management,
The Business School, University of Gloucestershire

Bob has gifted us another inspirational book, this time challenging us to engage with the fear that rules our world. Our society lives illusionally, with a self-created complexity, which has abandoned many simple truths. This book is a timely call to action, guiding us eloquently to the conclusion that our destiny is the integration of the individual with the whole. It left me with an unequivocal sense of both personal responsibility for the world we live in and how our thinking can expand positively the place we occupy in it!

June Burrough
Founder and Director, Pierian Centre, Bristol

A refreshing and well illustrated perspective on the connection between strategy and leadership that is thought provoking and highly relevant in these times of disruptive change and economic uncertainty.

Michael Lindsay, COO, Technology based company, United States

Freedom from Fear is an inspirational book written by an inspirational author. The book captures and conveys the essential yet elusive characteristics of strategic leadership and the qualities embodied by strategic leaders. It provides clear insight into the actions that each of us can take to be a strategic leader. It is a book that should be read by all, to find the strategic leader within and to make a difference – however big or small.

Jo Kitney
State Manager, Workplace Health and Safety,
Chamber of Commerce and Industry, Queensland, Australia

A down to earth book, spiced up with many interesting stories, to illustrate the importance of recognizing issues in our lives, and the courage of making discerned decisions to address them accordingly. This is what strategic leadership is all about in our lives. Go ahead and buy this book and your life will be changed forever, for the better of course!

Jerry Guan
Senior Director, Langshaw International Pte Ltd, Singapore

This book – Gorzynski's best yet in my view – combines immense readability with a powerful over-arching narrative that shows how truly effective strategy making engages both the head and the heart. I defy anybody to read this book and not be a better leader as a result.

John Middleton
Senior Lecturer – Business and Management, Bath Spa University

Using wide-ranging case studies, *Freedom from Fear* provides insight and wisdom into the strategic thinking that today's leaders must develop. A captivating read that will inspire potential leaders to overcome their fears and begin their own leadership journey.

Simon Taylor
Account Manager, BP

I believe that dreams are important and the best are contagious. We need dreamers – Bob Gorzynski is a dream catcher!

Rob Parsons,
Executive Chairman, Care for the Family

Rich with insights, human stories and case studies from a wide spectrum of organisations and inspirational leaders, this book clearly demonstrates how we can unleash our capacity for strategic leadership and the personal fulfilment that the journey brings.

Mark Oxton
Head of Human Resources, Ocado

Bob is that rare creature, a strategic thinker possessing human values who also writes well. In one chapter he moves effortlessly from the wisdom of a children's book, to Shakespeare and the horrors of Auschwitz. This is a delight of a book, even when you disagree with him you learn from him.

Dave Snowden,
Founder and Chief Scientific Officer, Cognitive Edge,
Formerly a Director in the IBM Institute for Knowledge Management

For me, it's the journey that Bob takes you on, that enables you to viscerally feel what strategic leadership is all about. It is this feeling that removes the fear and gives one the freedom to act. Another great contribution to the evolution of strategic thinking....

Paul E. Cleveland
Founder and Director, Cleveland Consulting Ltd, Toronto, Canada

Building on *The Strategic Mind* Bob's new insightful look at leadership provides a commonsense approach to turning a humble leader into a strategic one.

Bob Bosshard
Partner, PricewaterhouseCoopers, Toronto, Canada

Inspiring and very readable. Spirituality has traditionally been the preserve of the few. In his new book, *Freedom from Fear*, Bob Gorzynski demonstrates that the development of spiritual qualities like compassion, awareness and non-attachment are no longer 'optional extras'. Personal development is now vital to success in any endeavour or leadership role.

John Preston
Meditation Teacher

Alive with literary, factual examples and poignant anecdotes, this book is a very valuable addition to undergraduate and postgraduate reading lists. Bob Gorzynski, with his fresh yet grounded view of the world, inspires us to undertake our own creative journey into strategic leadership, the importance of which is all too evident in the current climate.

Yvonne Ellis
Course Leader, Music and Music Management, University of Gloucestershire

Freedom from Fear provides valuable lessons not just for business leaders, but for all individuals who want to leverage their skills and passion to make a difference in our ever changing and demanding world.

Jamie Macdonald, former COO, Commercial Sector, Toronto, Canada

Freedom from Fear has a number of compelling messages. Bob Gorzynski holds a mirror up to show how the ways we traditionally think and act have created many of the problems that the world faces today. However, drawing on perennial wisdom and using riveting case studies from across business and not-for-profit sectors he demonstrates that there can be a new way of leading. The book is not addressed solely at leaders at the top of large organisations but is actually pointing the finger and offering a hand to all of us to make a difference, demonstrate a new type of leadership and become part of the solution.

Mike Green, Visiting Executive Fellow, Henley Business School

FREEDOM FROM FEAR

The mantle of strategic leadership

Bob Gorzynski

2000

Also by Bob Gorzynski
and published by Management Books 2000*:

The Strategic Mind

*For further details and a complete list of Management Books 2000 titles
visit our web-site on http://www.mb2000.com*

First published in 2010 by Management Books 2000 Ltd
Forge House, Limes Road
Kemble, Cirencester
Gloucestershire, GL7 6AD, UK
Tel: 0044 (0) 1285 771441
Fax: 0044 (0) 1285 771055
Email: info@mb2000.com
Web: www.mb2000.com

British Library Cataloguing in Publication Data is available

ISBN 9781852526375

To my wife, Tracy, and my two teenage boys, Scott and Jamie.
You are my world.

To Andrew Carter, whose tremendous courage and
acceptance in death taught me that great leaders are found in
all walks of life.
You were – and are – an inspiration to us all.

'Darkness cannot drive out darkness
Only light can do that.
Hate cannot drive out hate,
Only love can do that.'

Dr Martin Luther King Jr.

CONTENTS

ACKNOWLEDGEMENTS

I'm sure that writers are eternal optimists at heart. We are confident that there are so many people 'out there' just *waiting* to read a book like this one. If we were more reasonable (and possibly sane) we would undoubtedly think twice before beginning the venture at all. Certainly, our families, friends and colleagues are inclined to be a good deal more realistic, particularly when our income drops dramatically during the writing process at the very same time as our coffee expense rises exponentially. There have been a good many occasions over the past 18 months when I have been asked, 'How is your book coming on Bob?' Sometimes, this is simply a thinly veiled way of saying, 'Are you still not finished?' or 'How long does it take to write a book anyway?' This is my opportunity to thank some very special people who have gone much further than this and, literally, made this book possible.

I could not possibly have completed *Freedom from Fear* without the support and encouragement of my long suffering wife, Tracy, and my two boys, Scott and Jamie. A very big 'thank you' for putting up with me, yet again, during the writing phase. Likewise, my eternal thanks to my very patient, yet persistent, publisher, Nick Dale-Harris, who has gently cajoled me into meeting my deadlines and making the book a reality. Without your help, support and belief in the project it would never have happened.

I would also like to thank those very special people who have shared this journey with me and contributed in a way that is beyond measure. June Burrough, Simon Burke and John Tucker, for travelling the same road and being there with constant support, encouragement and insight along the way. Rob Parsons, for giving me the courage to begin my journey as a writer. I will always be indebted to you. And, Simon Taylor, for your help and support when I needed it most, when my confidence was at its lowest ebb. You are a true friend. Finally to all the many others who have given me the space and time to complete *Freedom from Fear*. You know who you are! Thank you.

FOREWORD

I have known Bob for almost twenty years, as a friend, a colleague, a teacher and a mentor. In all of those roles there is one thing that shines through, he is a man who genuinely cares. Bob cares about our past, our present and, above all, our future. We meet regularly and every time we meet I get this sense of Bob caring about his fellow man, his great concern for what is happening to our planet and the great sense of responsibility he feels for what we will leave behind for our children's children.

We last met in Marlborough to talk about this book. As is usual with Bob, when he talks about his concerns he gets very emotional and when he gets emotional, he sheds tears. I have never asked him what the tears are about. It could be sadness. It could be anger. It could be just sheer frustration at our unwillingness or inability to see what is happening to our world. It was a huge honour for me when he asked me to write this foreword and I hope I am not betraying this honour by taking a punt and suggesting that the tears I see might just be tears of hope.

Freedom from Fear is about leadership and I believe that leadership in its broadest sense is about being able to paint a picture of hope. Hope is something that resides in all of us at some point in our lives. For me, hope is something with spiritual qualities and is very much linked to dreaming. I know that Bob is a dreamer and this book embodies the possibility of hope through dreaming. This is not simply a book on the academic theories on leadership; there are plenty of those on the bookshelves. It is a book about *real* people, real lives lived and it deserves to be taken seriously. You see, Bob wants to make a difference and he does so by telling stories. He asks us to suspend our view of the world and join him on a journey of discovery, a journey to discover the very essence of leadership.

I believe the journey of great leadership starts in the family. As a parent, I often hoped and dreamed that I had been a good father, that I had been part of a parental team that had created a family environment in which my two daughters felt loved and were secure in the knowledge that they would be loved until the day we died. I am immensely proud of my two daughters, each I believe showing real leadership in the jobs they do. If you happen to be in an accident around the Bristol area, you will want to see leadership in action. The green uniform of a paramedic is a very comforting sight and it might just be my youngest daughter. My eldest daughter runs a preschool nursery in Phuket, Thailand, and has just given us the privilege of seeing parenting up close and personal. As a parent, we do not see our parenting. We *are* the parenting. As a grandparent, we get to observe parenting and, in the observation, you realise how hard it is, and what a great responsibility it is to be in such a position of leadership. It is said by many commentators that developing our children is the biggest leadership challenge of all. Having just spent two weeks with my eldest daughter and our three-year-old grandson, I have observed how difficult this job can be; especially when you are juggling with all of the issues of running a business.

When I was young man growing up one of my greatest heroes was Andy Ripley. Andy George Ripley is now 62. He is blind and dying from cancer. On the 26th May 2010 he was presented with the Blyth Spirit Award. His Wikipedia entry simply says, 'he's a former rugby union international who represented England from 1972-1976'. Writing in the Sunday Times, his friend and writer, Paul Kimmage, suggests that this is a complete travesty. 'This is a man with a brain like Einstein and a pen like Shakespeare. This is a Lion from 1974 who played first class rugby at the age of 41 and who almost made a Boat Race crew at 50. This is a man who might have doubled for Steve McQueen. This is a man who has always made us smile'. What an accolade. Just think about how much the world has been influenced by Einstein and Shakespeare and how many of us have watched Steve McQueen and thought, male and female alike, 'if only'! Paul Kimmage goes on to describe visiting Andy Ripley at his home in Surrey. 'You look better,' he observes, 'the last time I was here you looked really tired.' 'You see,' replies Andy Ripley, 'there is always possibility, isn't there?' He then comments about his family being his fortune. It most certainly is mine.

So, for me, this is a book that has to be read, not because it will be the definitive word on leadership, not because it will impact on academia, and not because it is likely to change the leadership in corporate organisations or government. This book has to be read because it is written by someone who truly cares about you and me and our planet. It has to be read because it paints pictures, it dares to dream of a better way and it creates possibilities. Above all, it has to be read because it creates hope. The last words must go to Andy Ripley:

'Dare we hope? We dare.

Can we hope? We can.

Should we hope? We must.

We must, because to do otherwise is to waste the most precious of gifts, given so freely by God to all of us. So when we do die, it will be with hope and it will be easy and our hearts will not be broken.'

John Tucker,
Founder and Director,
International Centre for Families in Business

PROLOGUE

*'The beauty and genius of a work of art may be reconceived,
though its first material expression be destroyed; a vanished
harmony may yet again inspire the composer, but when the last
individual of a race of living beings breathes no more, another
heaven and another earth must pass before such a one can be
again.'*
William Beebe, American Naturalist

Parable of the bees

Bees are in trouble. Both bumblebees and honeybees have suffered
dramatic declines over the past five years. Traditionally, the biggest
problem has been a parasite known as the Varroa mite, which
affects the immune system of the bee. Once a colony becomes
infected by the parasite it quickly dies out. In 2006, reports started
coming in from the United States of something even more alarming.
Hives were being mysteriously abandoned overnight, putting large
colonies of bees at risk. This event was christened 'Colony Collapse
Disorder' ('CCD') and it has quickly spread to Europe and the United
Kingdom. One third of all bees in the United States died and in
France the death rate was as high as 60%. We don't know for sure
what causes CCD, although parasites, viruses, intensive farming
practices and even mobile phone signals have all been held up as
potential causes. What is far more certain is that the consequences
of steep declines in bee populations could spell disaster. Bees have
a unique place in the world's ecosystem and in human society. A
third of all the food that we eat is pollinated by honeybees and
much of what we wear also depends on it. The relationship between

bees and plants is critical for maintaining biodiversity. Without the pollination of bees, many birds and small mammals that feed on berries and seeds would die, with devastating consequences throughout the food chain. Dr George McGavin, a zoologist and television presenter, is very direct about the potential consequences; 'Without bees, terrestrial ecosystems would be dramatically different, and in the ensuing extinction spasm, the human population would crash.'

The precipitous decline in bees should strike fear into our hearts. Dr McGavin believes that the human race would survive for less than a decade if bees disappear, calling a world without them 'totally catastrophic'. Albert Einstein shared this gloomy prognosis, once reputedly saying that if the bees disappeared 'man would have only four years of life left'. Yet, these statements probably leave us unmoved. We have immunised ourselves from dire predictions, which in any case are uncertain and will play out at some point in the future. Fear works best in the certainty of the present moment. It energises us and helps us to act in the here and now. We are biologically conditioned to be adept at reacting to short-term problems, which require quick, and often innovative, responses. We are much less capable of focusing on issues that unfold over the long term. As a result, we have a natural tendency to procrastinate, especially when the future benefits are uncertain and the present cost, even if tiny, is tangible.

Ted O'Donoghue and Matthew Rabin published a paper on the economics of procrastination in 1999 explaining why we put off unpleasant things rather than do them today. They argue that we are often unrealistically optimistic about the future likelihood of doing things. This is particularly true if there is a mismatch between costs and future benefits. We may recognise that exercise is good for us in the long term but the payment to the gym is due this week. We may be aware that it is sensible to live according to our means but we resist saving this month because we have seen an espresso machine that we would very much like to have today. We can taste the freshly ground coffee in our minds right now. Yet, we all too easily forget that feeling in the pit of our stomach when our credit card bill arrives and we are, once again, unable to pay off the balance. A gap between intention and action develops. We believe that we will act 'tomorrow' but the immediate cost involved means that we do not do so today. When the initial effort involved is unpleasant, this quickly translates into endless procrastination. Rob Parsons uses this understanding to devastating effect in his best-selling book, *The Sixty Minute Father*. He recognises that we would all like to be good parents. We set out with the best intentions. What prevents so many of us from coming good on our aspirations? Rob talks of the three illusions that get in our way, but the third he calls 'the greatest illusion of all' because of its ability to rob us of the time for the things that matter most to us. That illusion is that 'a slower day is coming.' We will spend the time when we are less busy. We *will* do it... only tomorrow.

The biggest challenges that we now face are long term in nature. Environmental and climate related issues obviously fall into this category. But so do many others, including maintaining economic growth and prosperity, reducing income inequality and eradicating poverty. When the gap between intention and action lengthens there are very real costs involved, even if they will be experienced 'tomorrow'. Since thinking long term does not come easily to us it requires practice and discipline. Yet this alone is not enough. If we believe that we are separate, there will always be a limited incentive for us to take on a long-term perspective. Many of us find it difficult to take regular exercise or live within our means, despite the fact that both have direct personal benefits in the future. It is hardly surprising that the idea of paying today for uncertain benefits in the future, which will accrue largely to others, is a non-starter for most people in our society. As long as we are separate, 'us' and 'them', we will always be schoolchildren in the playground crying 'it's not fair, they did it!' Only when the boundaries between 'us' and 'them' finally begin to dissolve, will we be able to take full responsibility and act accordingly. This may sound rather philosophical and idealistic. Or, perhaps, it seems to be just plain unrealistic. But maybe that's the point. It is only when the scale of the problems confronting us become serious enough, and we are *all* affected, that we will be able to make this shift in consciousness. And that point in our history is right now.

The plight of the bee, with its pivotal role in sustaining life, is a symbol for all the challenges that confront us. Matthew Oates, the National Trust's adviser on nature conservation, observes that it 'perfectly illustrates the interconnectivity of living things.' 'Valuing them properly,' he continues, 'will make a huge difference. Bee consciousness is vital!' And, that recognition is happening. Innocent Drinks has partnered with the National Trust in 2010 in the 'buy one get one bee' project, which aims to introduce two million bees across the United Kingdom by funding new colonies at 40 different National Trust properties. The Trust is acting in other areas too. It is deliberately clearing patches of heath in order to provide vital nesting areas and it is promoting both honey and the importance of bees at its sites. Meanwhile, the BBC is actively promoting greater 'Bee Awareness' through its 'Bee Part Of It' project, which aims to create local bee-friendly spaces throughout the country. Some of these initiatives will fail but that is how we learn. We simply pick ourselves up and start again, only this time from a slightly higher place. Nothing is lost.

In December 1884, the 'Tongariro', one of the first refrigerated ships, left London for Wellington, New Zealand, with 282 bumblebee queens on board. The New Zealanders wanted long-tongued bees to pollinate the red clover that they used for sheep pastures, so that they could avoid re-importing and re-seeding the clover each year. 48 bees survived that journey and their descendants are flourishing on New Zealand's South Island today. Ironically, the shorthaired bumblebee has now died out in Britain. As a result, it looks likely that some long distant cousins may be making their journey back 'home'. There is no shortage of creative solutions once we feel that we are not only an important part of the problem but also an essential element in the solution.

The mantle of strategic leadership

The parable of the bees is an unfinished story. How the story turns out depends on us. It will help if we can learn to think more strategically, to see the whole picture and acknowledge our relationship with the world around us. But we also need the capacity to act, which is a central tenet of leadership. Strategic leadership is the capacity to act *wisely*. This book sets out the journey to strategic leadership. We can *all* be strategic leaders. We *all* have a part to play. There are many reasons why we should make the journey. The most important one is that it will make a big difference: to our lives, our organizations and communities and to our world. And, the bees will certainly thank us.

INTRODUCTION

'While those borders crumble every day
The faultlines are showing
And all I thought was here to stay
Slowly is going.'
Karine Polwart

'The intuitive mind is a sacred gift and the rational mind its
faithful servant. We have created a society that honours the
servant and has forgotten the gift.'
Albert Einstein

The journey ahead

We live in a very special time, a unique point in human history. We are in a place between worlds, on the threshold of profound change. In so many ways we are very blessed to be here, at the very lynchpin of human history. Our day-to-day reality reflects the beauty and the pain of the past, both our achievements and the shadow side of those accomplishments, a fragmented and disconnected world. In front of us is a precipice. We cannot scale or surmount it, or will it away. So, the question is 'can we fly?' The answer is emphatically, 'yes we can', but there is a caveat. It is a significant one. We cannot fly alone. For the first time in our history we will need to work together as a species, to move beyond the self-destructive habits of our individualistic culture. We all have a role to play. If you are reading this book you too have heard the call. It is a beautiful calling. The only question is how to respond.

The arts are a wonderful barometer of what's really going on in our world. Blockbuster movies that capture the public imagination are particularly revealing, none more so than *Avatar*, which has taken nearly $2 billion at the box office to become the highest grossing movie of all time. It tells a familiar story, one that has been told in innumerable permutations since the dawn of time. It is ultimately a story of rebirth, but it is also familiar to us as a 'voyage and return' plot where the hero ventures into a new world and emerges from it transformed (the underlying plot in tales as diverse as *Alice in Wonderland*, *Peter Rabbit* and the *Epic of Gilgamesh*, the earliest recorded story in history). At a surface level, we might see *Avatar* as simply a modern morality tale, focused on environmental destruction or the injustices of powerful nations subjugating indigenous cultures. But it is more than this. To understand why the movie has been so astoundingly successful, we must look below the surface at the archetypal plot that it follows.

Avatar is a story of a man, Jake Sully, who is only partly developed, strong in the traditional 'masculine' characteristics of power, structure and control, but largely unaware of the 'feminine' strengths in relationship and understanding the greater whole. His story as an ex marine (the 'masculine' qualities) who enters the world of the indigenous Na'vi people (embodying the 'feminine') is one of transformation. In it he gradually accepts and integrates both sets of characteristics to become a powerful leader representing the fully integrated human being. This is symbolised, of course, by Jake gaining the love of the Na'vi Princess, Neytiri, and his subsequent union with her. They are bonded together, forever, as one. Naturally, our hero suffers various trials and tests but because he possesses the full 'tool kit' of humanity, he emerges successfully as the leader of the Na'vi people and overcomes the vastly superior military might of the human mining settlement (who remain, to their cost, completely ignorant of the relational dimension of the world to the very end). Interestingly, Jake is only able to make this leadership journey because he is open and receptive, capable of taking on new knowledge and perspectives. He is a completely clean sheet, a point made forcibly in the movie when Jake first arrives on Pandora and is asked what training he has undertaken. His answer is 'zip'. That is his salvation.

At one level, *Avatar* is simply a movie, a diverting piece of entertainment. But, at another, it is a clear reflection of the zeitgeist, the spirit of our times. We are at a critical point in our history. Our existing ways of thinking are no longer adequate to resolve the issues and challenges that confront us (which are, of course, largely of our own making). We are being called upon to recognise and integrate the relational aspects of our nature to become fully realised human beings. This is a tough order and we have much to learn. This book is concerned with two aspects of that journey. The first is developing our capability to think strategically (the ability to see the 'big picture', including the perspective of the whole and our relationship to it) and the second is building our leadership capabilities to act upon that knowledge. This is the journey to strategic leadership and it is open to all of us. *Avatar* has one more lesson to give us. It shares much in plot terms with the *Epic of Gilgamesh*, which follows the adventures of the historical King of Uruk in Ancient Sumeria, sometime between 2750 and 2500

BC. We are engaged on a quest that has been with us since the dawn of civilisation.

The leader within us

Do we all have leadership potential or is leadership reserved for the few who are special in some way; those, perhaps, who have exceptional gifts, talents or personal charisma? This is, perhaps, the most important question that we can ask about leadership. I recently attended an evening book presentation by Stephen Cottrell, perhaps better know as the Bishop of Reading. He is a thoroughly engaging speaker, very down to earth and humble enough to describe himself as 'just an oik from Essex'. At one point, he talked about leadership and asked the audience how many of us were parents. After a good show of hands, he remarked that all parents are, by nature, leaders. They are leaders of the most important 'organisation' of them all, the family. This echoes many comments made by the Dalai Lama that the true leaders of the world are not the gurus, business executives or politicians but the women of the world. It is a woman who gives a child its first sense of love, affection and belonging, from which all else springs. I would widen this definition of leadership to include all of us, whether parents or not. We all have the capacity for leadership, which is just as well, as never before has the world been in more need of it.

My definition of leadership is a simple one; the capacity to *influence* the world in some significant way. This certainly includes business executives and public figures but it also includes anyone who is determined to make a difference in any context whatsoever. It is not important whether our actions are considered 'big' or 'small' by the world around us, as we shall see time and time again in this book. The world is full of heroes and heroines who are beating the odds and making a profound difference in their own areas and in their own ways, sometimes recognised, often not. I have learned that it is better not to judge the significance of either our own efforts or those of others for one simple reason. Much of our effect upon the world is invisible to us. Stephen Cottrell mentioned a lovely example of this when he commented that one of the most influential people in his life was his RE teacher at secondary modern school. Her passion, both in teaching and in living her Christianity, turned a light on for him and significantly affected the direction of his life. Did he tell her at the time? Of course not! He was a perfectly healthy and normal 14 year-old boy and he wouldn't have dreamed of doing such a thing. Had he not met her many years later she may never have known the powerful influence that she had on him, just one of her many pupils.

Democracy of pain and suffering

In May 1993 John Tucker lost everything. For fifteen years he had been the founder and Managing Director of a highly successful training and management development business, which counted British Airways, Rolls Royce, British Aerospace and Ford Motor Company as valued customers. When it failed, he was forced into personal bankruptcy and everything went. When John talks of his experience today the emotions are every bit as raw as they were back then. 'We lost absolutely everything and failed in the most horrible way imaginable,' he says, 'the feeling of shame was unbearable.' 'We felt we were branded with a "Big B" on our foreheads,' he continues, 'integrity is absolutely paramount to me and to have it questioned in such a demeaning way was devastating.' Time has not dulled the painful experience in any way and he concludes, 'we were ashamed that we had done something that society found unforgiveable and without the support of very close friends I don't know how I would have got through it. I was very close to suicide at times and even now we really don't know the full impact it has had on the family.'

Today, John Tucker runs the International Centre for Families in Business, which offers family businesses a safe place for learning and education and a venue where the family and other key personnel can gain access to information, attend workshops, seek advice, and above all, meet and share best practice with other families in business. He is widely recognized as a strategic leader in his field and has built a determined and dedicated team around him who specialize in working with family businesses facing change and transition, particularly management and ownership succession. It may seem that the world of personal bankruptcy and failure is a world away. In fact, nothing could be further from the truth. John's current achievements are directly related to his journey, indeed born out of his experience. This is what has so fired his doggedness and determination to really make a difference. Such is the path of true strategic leadership.

We will return to John Tucker's leadership journey later in the book, when we look at how we stay on course when the leadership journey gets rough and the winds of adversity howl in our ears. However, John's experience brings another very important question to our attention at the very beginning of our journey. Are struggle, pain and difficulties, sometimes even life-threatening circumstances, really necessary to shape us as leaders? Surely there must be another way of forging leadership potential, perhaps in seven easy steps? I believe that if you are reading this far you already know the answer. Achieving anything of real value requires effort, sometimes lots of it. When we first fall in love it is easy to maintain a relationship, but after a while we begin to notice character defects in our partner. Worse still, and most unfairly, our partner finds that we are not perfect (how could such a thing be true?). The amazing thing is that we never noticed before! And so the real work begins. We begin to forge a deeper, stronger, bond, based on our real selves, including those parts that we would normally prefer to hide. When we talk to couples who have been together for fifty or sixty years, it is often the trials and tribulations that they remember, and how they made it through, stronger and more determined. It is often the tough times that cement a relationship. So too with leadership.

There are no easy steps to becoming a leader. There are no quick fixes. No 'ten magic points' or 'seven-step' models that can make us a leader overnight. If there were, leadership would not be such a precious commodity. We might all have leadership qualities within us but many of us shy away from the journey of unlocking that potential. It can be very hard work and it is almost certainly going to be quite a rollercoaster ride. Steve Jobs, CEO of Apple, was unceremoniously fired in 1985 from the company he founded and has suffered significant bouts of ill health over the past five years including a diagnosis of incurable liver cancer in 2004. Richard Branson is dyslexic and was written off at school (he was apparently told by his exasperated head teacher that he would either become a millionaire or end up in jail). The Prince of Wales has suffered constant ridicule in the media, despite the fact that many of his ideas are now seen as prescient and well ahead of their time. The path of leadership can be a very demanding one. As Nelson Mandela remarked, 'In my country we go to prison first and then become President.' I am very fortunate to work with social entrepreneurs who are building businesses and enterprises of real value in the community. Yet, I know of two cases where the founder has been ejected from the endeavour after it became successful because non-executives found working with them 'too disruptive'. If you set out to make a difference you will be tested over the years, that's a guarantee. As for those seven step models, Peter Drucker, who is widely regarded as the best management writer of all time, liked to say that people like to use the world 'guru' because the word 'charlatan' is so hard to spell.

The rewards of leadership

'You must be the change you want to see in the world.'
Mahatma Ghandi

A good friend commented to me recently, 'Bob, you make leadership sound like such a burden. Shouldn't you make it appear less onerous, otherwise why would anyone want to do it?' The best answer to this question is that it is a journey worth taking, both for its own sake, and because our world desperately *needs* leaders. There is a lot of work to be done. However, this response requires a leap of faith and we may not be ready for that just yet. So let me put it another way. No matter how hard the leadership journey may be at times, there is magic in it. If you have children you will probably recognise this statement. We all know that being a parent can be tough. But that doesn't mean we would wish to forego the journey of becoming a mother or a father. Sometimes, we may wish we had done things a little differently along the way, but that is the beauty of hindsight! Perhaps, it is just as well that most of us enter into parenthood with so little idea of what is in store for us. It can come as quite a shock. I distinctly remember bringing my first son back home, looking at my wife and thinking, 'now what are we supposed to do?' It's hard to convey the message that being a parent is 90% hard work and 10% pure magic and still make it sound worthwhile. That is, unless we have experienced the magic first. So it is too with leadership.

Leadership is always its own reward. That's why the best leaders of all are largely invisible. What sort of incentive is that to become a leader we may ask? Well, quite a big one actually. It means we can stop worrying about outcomes and get on with the business of being a leader. If we plant an oak tree for our grandchildren we don't expect to see it in its prime. It is enough to know that with due care and nurture it will be there several hundred years from now, providing shade and shelter for future generations. I have worked with many leaders across commercial, voluntary, social and educational areas and none of them questions whether the journey was worthwhile (however much they may wish they had done some things differently along the way). And it's not just leaders in the conventional sense. Just ask a teacher who is told by a former pupil that she has made all the difference in their life, or a drug worker who meets a former client many years later who has made a new life for himself. We thrive when we are given real responsibility and learn to use it wisely. It is also worth remembering that we rarely see more than a small fragment of the full impact we have on others. The most profound aspects of relationship often only emerge years later, sometimes long after we have moved on. In short, we may never know the difference we make.

Strategic leadership

Strategic leadership is the ability to think strategically combined with the *capacity to act*. When I wrote *The Strategic Mind* I explored how we develop the capacity to think strategically, which I define as the *intuitive ability to see the whole*. This book builds on *The Strategic Mind* and goes beyond it by looking in detail at the leadership dimension. To make a real difference in the world we need to be able to think at a deeper level *and* translate this insight into action. *Freedom from Fear* explores how to do just that. It deals explicitly with the translation of strategic thinking into action in a practical context. The many case studies and stories look at leaders who are making a profound difference in the world, not only by thinking differently but also by having the courage and commitment to bring those ideas into reality. We begin by looking at the case for strategic thinking and examining how we develop that ability. In part two, we take a detailed look at *how* we become a leader by examining the core capabilities that underlie leadership. And, finally, in part three, we bring this all together to see just what a dramatic impact on our world strategic leadership can have.

We become strategic leaders by learning how to think at a deeper level and then using this knowledge to have a positive impact in the world. It is a journey that we can *all* make and, given the challenges before us, one that is vitally important for our world and for future generations. Unfortunately, the ability to think strategically does not necessarily come naturally or easily to many of us. Moreover, there is an emphasis on getting things done in our culture and most of us are under constant pressure to 'produce' in the short term. Reflective thinking is not exactly the order of the day. These obstacles, however, do not make it any the less important. If we are to have any hope of resolving the daunting challenges that confront us, it is vital that we become more *conscious* of the way in which we think. As Einstein so aptly commented, 'The significant problems we face cannot be solved at the same level of thinking we were at when we created them'. We need this 'radical' thinking to get down to the root of matters, which is where the word 'radical' actually comes from (as with the word, radish, a root vegetable). When we go back to the root of something we give ourselves the time to absorb the deeper truth that lies within. Leadership without this deeper wisdom may be courageous and well intended but it can also be misguided and even dangerous. Ironically, the more critical the decision, the more important it is to slow down. We can all do with lessons on how to sit on our hands! At the very least, short term thinking can actually take us further in the wrong direction, sapping our commitment and energy along the way. I have a simple four-stage reflective process that helps me remember this before I make any important decision: *Slow Down, Observe, Reflect*, and then *Act*.

It is impossible for anyone to watch the media today without being acutely aware of the severity of the issues that face our world and the difficult choices that lie ahead of us. Many of us are also conscious of the disturbing fact that we do not seem to be making much progress by simply doing more of what we've always done. A man stuck in a hole would be wise to stop digging if he wishes to improve his chances of escape. Yet, under intense pressure to turn things around, spurred on by the alarming predictions that are held up in front of us, our immediate urge is to dig faster, deeper, and of course, to dig more productively. So let's just stop for a moment. Breathe deep and close our eyes. There is another way. If we are willing to don the mantle of strategic leadership we can step into a new world and, much more importantly, we can also guide others into that world with us. Surely that is a challenge that is well worth taking? In the process of doing so we transform not only ourselves but the world around us too. We may begin the journey as intrepid explorers yet end it as something else entirely. As the American writer, Richard Bach, points out, 'What the caterpillar calls the end of the world, the master calls a butterfly.'

The challenge before us

'Man has a genius for survival, often only manifested at the eleventh hour. Now is the time we must act together.'
The Prince of Wales

On the surface, many of the world's biggest challenges do not appear to be related. Economic and financial crises, for example, are not obviously connected to environmental degradation and climate change. Look a little more closely, however, and we begin to see some important common denominators. They are related to the *way* in which we think. At the root of the problem is a failure to take a holistic perspective and recognise the complexity of our environment. This is compounded by the fact that we see ourselves as independent of the world, rather than being an integrated part of it. Our inability to live in harmony with nature and recognise our connectivity with the environment results from a fundamental but erroneous belief in separation. The well-known American biologist, Edward Wilson, points out that we risk losing 'most of the rest of life, and part of what it means to be a human being.' We find it hard to envisage solutions working *with* rather than *against* nature. Those who are connected deeply with the natural world, on the other hand, see beyond this isolation and sense of false superiority. As biologist and best-selling author, Stacey O'Brien, remarks in her book, *Wesley, The Story of a Remarkable Owl*:

> *'Wesley was as playful at age thirteen as he was when he was a year old. Of course, I could say that he learned a certain behaviour in order to experience the infusion of endorphins that play realised, but really, is this necessary? Maybe he just did it for fun. Where did our emotions come from if not from our animal ancestors? Many human emotions are similar to those of animals. We are them and they are us.'*

It is not just our lack of connection that is important. The belief that we are in *control* of our environment is equally destructive. The severity of the economic downturn in 2008, for example, is partly due to government policies determined to minimise the adverse effects of minor downturns in previous economic and business cycles. Behind this thinking lies the mistaken belief that we can micro-control the economy. In fact, loose monetary and fiscal policies have had the direct effect of exacerbating the recession when it finally came. This necessitated massive government intervention on an unprecedented scale, which has served principally to shift the problem of debt from the commercial banks to the state ('sovereign debt'). In simple terms, we were living beyond our means and this issue has not been resolved, regardless of who is currently holding the cheque!

Our failure to recognise the complexity and inter-relatedness of the environment is one of the major reasons why our 'management' of the natural world's resources is, so often, disastrous. Many of us are only connected at the 'head' level. But an intellectual construct does not put fire into our belly. It does not motivate us from the heart or gut, both of which link action to the very core of who we are. Simply put, we just don't care enough to go through the discomfort of changing our behaviours. Instead, we rely heavily on somebody else doing the job for us – governments, international bodies, activist groups and even large corporations. And, guess what, it turns out that these bodies often struggle when they lack deep-seated and committed support from a broad base. We need look no further than the sad tale of the alarming overfishing of bluefin tuna in the Atlantic and Mediterranean seas, to see how this failure plays out.

The mysterious case of the disappearing tuna fish
Bluefin tuna have been fished from the Atlantic Ocean and Mediterranean Sea for over 7,000 years. The Greeks sliced, salted and pickling them and Roman soldiers ate them for lunch. For the last forty years, tuna in these seas have been under the protection of the International Commission for the Conservation of Atlantic Tunas ('ICCAT') and over this period numbers have plummeted by 75%. Current quotas are being set at levels that most scientists and conservation groups regard as far too high for long-term fish

replenishment. Although ICCAT is moving slowly towards reducing quotas to sustainable levels, based on scientific evidence, it is not proposing to do so immediately. Instead, action is contemplated sometime safely in the future, perhaps between 2011 and 2013, when many believe it will be far too late to avoid disaster. The plight of tuna fish in the Atlantic is echoed throughout the world, partly due to the sheer quantum of the increase in fishing. In the 1950s about 600,000 tons of tuna were caught worldwide. By 2008 that figure was close to six million tons. We are quickly reaching the point where the tuna fish will become an endangered species. Taken at face value alone this is very bad news. However, the situation is exacerbated by the fact that tuna fish play a vital role in the ocean's food chain. To put it bluntly, if we take out a major predator from the ocean, the entire balance of the ecosystem is disturbed with unknown consequences.

There are, no doubt, a myriad of reasons why ICCAT is unable to take decisive and radical action to reduce fishing quotas (including the difficult politics of balancing the concerns of different interest groups and nation states). But what should concern us more is that this failure is echoed time and time again in so many areas that are ultimately critical for own survival. Naturally, the pursuit of self-interest (personal, group, nation state, trade block or whatever form it takes) will make international cooperation more difficult on a world stage. However, we are hampered by a failure in our thinking. We suffer from what I call the *three great illusions; the illusions of independence, size and control.* These are an inevitable product of a reductionist mind-set that has lost connection with the essential interrelatedness of our world. We will be looking at the devastating legacy of these illusions in more detail in the next chapter. But, for the moment, we can simply acknowledge that opening up our ability to think strategically, at a deeper and more profound level, allows us to see the whole as opposed to merely the parts. That's a *good* start. It will not magically solve all the world's problems overnight. But it will enable us to look at those problems holistically from a platform of common interest. And that's a *great* start.

Crisis and opportunity

Our world is in crisis. But crisis brings with it opportunity. The Chinese character for change is made up of two characters: danger and opportunity. Crisis and opportunity are always two sides of the same coin. As international author, Susan Jeffers, puts it, 'we can't get rid of the chaos but we can get very creative with the turmoil.' There is another important aspect of the link between crisis and opportunity. The further off balance we become (the greater our hubris) the larger the corresponding opportunity will be. Think about this. The more difficult the issue, the more intractable it appears to be, the greater the gain from a creative solution. This should provide us with a powerful incentive to change because big 'wins' can happen very quickly. Take one very simple example, food waste.

In most developed countries food waste is rife. Reliable estimates of exactly how much waste occurs are hard to come by but it is commonly thought that rich countries throw out about 25-30% of what is bought. In fact, this understates the problem because the estimates include only the food that actually makes it to the cupboard or refrigerator. A US study in 2009, published by the National Institute of Diabetes and Digestive and Kidney Diseases, found that Americans waste, on average, some 1,400 calories a day. Over a year this amounts to staggering 40% of the total food supply in the US (up from 28% in 1974). What is more, this does not take into account food thrown away in the supply chain before anyone has the opportunity to buy it. To put these statistics into perspective, food waste accounts for more than a quarter of America's annual freshwater consumption and some 300 million barrels of oil every year. In addition, rotting food emits methane gas, which is a much more potent greenhouse gas than carbon dioxide. The upside equation is obvious. It also makes abundantly clear that each one of us can make a significant difference by making relatively small behavioural changes, the cumulative effect of which can be enormous.

I sometimes use a collection of plastic milk containers and cardboard juice cartoons in one of my presentations. I ask students to think of alternative ways of packaging these staples and what the overall effect of switching might be. Together, we explore the options, such as changing to frozen juice concentrate (thus avoiding transporting bulky liquids) and even powdered milk (which likewise can be reconstituted in the home). Not surprisingly, students are resistant to the concept of powdered milk. I have yet to make a convert. However, they become more engaged with the idea of switching to plastic bags for milk, which are then used with a plastic pouring container that is bought in advance. This means that the milk can be stored much more efficiently, both in transport and at the retail store. What surprises the students most, is that very large benefits accrue all the way through the distribution and retail chains as a result of a more creative approach to product, packaging and logistics. This includes obvious environmental benefits but it also has a considerable financial upside for all the parties in the supply chain (since it eliminates unnecessary packaging, transportation and retail space). We only have to take a cursory look at the grossly over-packaged goods that sit on our retail shelves to know that significant gains can be made very easily. Inevitably, competitive market dynamics pass on much of the cost saving to the consumer in terms of lower prices. This creates a genuine 'win-win' solution for all. So why don't we act? The answer is partly that it would require coordinated action throughout the entire distribution system and this is difficult to achieve. But it is not impossible. That is the where the creative part of the solution lies. Indeed, as we shall see later on, Waitrose is a very good example of an organisation that is addressing these very issues right now. The momentum for change is already building.

The call to business

'A brand for a company is like a reputation for a person. You earn reputation by trying to do hard things well.'
Jeff Bezos, Chairman and CEO, Amazon

Business is an integral part of our world and it will play a major role in resolving the major challenges that currently face us. Like it or not, commercial organisations are at the sharp end of many of most pressing problems in our world today. To survive and prosper, companies need to be remarkably open and receptive to both challenges and opportunities. These qualities mirror the root of the word, 'business', which is derived from the old English, 'bisignis', meaning to be attentive and show concern and consideration. There is a reflective quality to these words and it is important. Reflection lies at the very heart of strategic thinking; the ability to grasp the whole picture and to act accordingly. This is the broader remit of business today and it is deeply paradoxical. To be able to think strategically means not only recognising our unique contribution (the unique selling proposition in business terms) but also understanding how it relates to what is going on in the wider world. To do this, business needs to be both introspective and also aware of its connection with the bigger picture. As we will see, there are many leaders in the commercial sector who are rising to meet this challenge. They include some of the most admired and successful companies in the world and we be looking at Apple, in particular, throughout in this book. However, *Freedom from Fear* will also draw from a very broad range of examples, covering both large and small companies, profit and non-for-profit organisations and individual leaders who are making a very big difference in their areas of endeavour, sometimes almost single-handedly.

There is nothing new in suggesting that commercial organisations have an important role as major agents for change in our world. We only have to look at the impact of Google, Apple, Amazon and eBay, to see how successful companies can profoundly affect our everyday life. But truly successful companies do more than simply change things. They become a powerful force for good. Sergey Brin, co-founder of Google with Larry Page, observes that, 'everyone wants to be successful, but I want to be looked back on as being very innovative, very trusted and ethical and ultimately making a big difference in the world.' This requires business leaders to think differently and to have the courage to put their ideas into practice. Many of the organisations that feature regularly in *Fortune Magazine*'s list of the world's most admired companies, have the capacity to do precisely this. Companies such as Apple, eBay,

Amazon, Google, Toyota, Honda and Johnson & Johnson, not only demonstrate the capability to think holistically and do things differently as a result. They also have enviable follow through capabilities. Strategic leadership is as much about execution as it is about ideas. Implementation is often the hardest area of all.

Strategic leadership in business is not easy. First and foremost, it means challenging some of the most destructive elements in our current way of thinking, particularly the notion that we are separate from the world around us. It also requires a clear understanding of what the organisation stands for and how it seeks to translate this mission into reality. This is easier said than done. Meg Whitman, former CEO of eBay, comments that keeping an organisation focused on its mission 'can be tremendously challenging in today's competitive and ever-changing world.' Strategic leaders typically have a longer-term orientation and a broader view of responsibilities than traditional business managers. They think holistically, recognising how their organisation fits into the whole. eBay, for example, is acutely aware of the importance of maintaining a healthy trading community and the impact that this community has on the wider world. This is a 'win-win' relationship for all concerned. Meg Whitman talks of the 'multiplier effect' that eBay has had by creating other small businesses, which in turn supply it with intellectual capital. In the United Kingdom, eBay estimates that 178,000 users run a business, or use the site, as their primary or secondary source of income. In 2006, the global marketing research firm, ACNielsen, estimated that the global equivalent was 1.3 million users. The figure is undoubtedly higher today. Commercial businesses, such as eBay, not only recognise their impact on community and society, they also factor it into their strategic decision-making. eBay has explicit values, which continue to guide how it does business, connecting buyers and sellers around the world. They may be simply expressed. But they are also very powerful:

'We create opportunities for people.
We care. Because we know people depend on us.
We make a difference in the world.'

eBay is not alone. Amazon and Apple prize their communities in a similar way. They are acutely conscious of the importance of relationship in their businesses and the part they play in changing society as a whole. Strategic leaders are restless and rarely satisfied with the way things are. Jeff Bezos, CEO of Amazon, expresses this as wanting Amazon to be 'something completely new' and Steve Jobs, as we shall see later on, is on a mission to unleash the potential of technology by humanising it. Sergey Brin, co-founder of Google, talks of continuing 'to use technology to make really big differences in how people live and work.' Few would argue that Google has not succeeded spectacularly on this score to date. Later on in this book, we will also explore how retailers, such as Starbucks and Waitrose, are making a profound difference in their communities, sometimes in extremely trying circumstances. All these companies are good examples of organisations that follow a set of unchanging principles that separate 'who they are' from what they do and how they do it. Constancy and change are strategic bedfellows, not enemies. The secret, as we shall see, is knowing what to change and what not to change.

It is not only commercial organisations that are waking up to the new reality. Some of the best examples of organisations with a genuine long-term orientation are charities. The National Trust is one of the largest conservation bodies in the world and, by its very nature, is guided by its long-term aims and philosophy. One of the most conspicuous examples of its philosophy is the so-called '50 year rule', which applies to any new purchase the Trust makes. In essence, this rule states that before making any acquisition the National Trust must have sufficient funds available to maintain it for 50 years, determined by a conservative formula that includes a significant contingency for potential but unknown costs at the time. Not surprisingly, this long-term approach, combined with an extraordinary capacity for attention to detail, has made the National Trust an invaluable knowledge resource for the effects of climate change and other long-term environmental issues. Naturally, this is useful for its direct application elsewhere but it also has the potential to inspire creative solutions in other contexts entirely, by applying insights gained. This is the beauty of a strategic approach that looks at the whole rather than the parts. Thinking strategically opens up new opportunities and innovative solutions that might otherwise escape us.

There are many who argue that the world of business is somehow different from other aspects of society. Commercial concerns, they argue, must ultimately answer to the 'bottom line' of profitability and this effectively rules them out from being socially responsible citizens. This may have had some logic when problems and challenges were on a small scale and local in nature. But times have changed. Many of the big issues that we now face are global and they can only be addressed effectively by us all working together. In this new world we must *all* rise to the challenges in front of us. It is no longer a question of corporate entities doing 'a little good on the side' through their corporate social responsibility initiatives. To have maximum impact we need to act from the deepest part of ourselves, matching our unique capabilities and skills with an holistic understanding of the world. For commercial concerns, this means having a deep understanding of their unique selling propositions ('USP') and making the connection between this USP and the part that they play within the wider world. Only by connecting the dots between our inside and outside worlds will we transform the nature of our reality. Strategic leadership is a common endeavour as our best business leaders understand. Commercial and not-for-profit organisations both have a critical role to play in determining our future. As Sam Walton, the founder of Wal-Mart, pointed out, 'outstanding leaders go out of their way to boost the self-esteem of their personnel. If people believe in themselves, it's amazing what they can accomplish.' We are in this together.

The unseen enemy

*'In this infinite sea of potentials that exist around us,
how come we keep recreating the same realities?'*
Joe Dispenza

Humility and open mindedness are vitally important in developing new ways of thinking. In *The Age of Stupid* a bewildered Pete Postlethwaite, alone in a world ravaged as a result of climate change, asks, 'why didn't we stop climate change when we had the chance?' Increasingly, primary and high school teachers are hearing their pupils ask the same thing. It's very hard to explain to a nine-year old child why inaction appears to be the order of the day when you have just finished telling them why it is so important for the world to wake up and act. The question, 'what are we thinking of?' is a very good one. It is certainly one to ask before it becomes 'what *were* we thinking of?' Why is it that we cannot seem to mobilise the will and commitment to adjust our lifestyles and work together towards living in harmony with each other and our environment?' The answer is essentially very simple. One word. Fear.

It's hard to maintain our sense of security and balance in this world. We are bombarded daily by the media with new fearful images on everything from climate change to community meltdown in our cities. This may, of course, have little to do with truth but it does wonders to sell media copy. Many of us work under intense pressure in our jobs, sometimes fielding hundreds of emails a day, with uncertain security and even less interest in our work. Although we have obtained a standard of living that would have been almost unimaginable a few generations ago, it has not been accompanied by the anticipated increase in our feelings of wellbeing, security and happiness. In reality, true happiness is an inside job. But in this hectic world, many of us have little or no time to look inside. Time scarcity has become a disease all of its own.

Fear is also deeply embedded within our decision-making processes, both at work and in our private lives. We are frightened of making mistakes, so we choose 'lowest common denominator' solutions that may not work very well but at least are unlikely to get us into trouble. When things *do* go wrong we hope to be safely elsewhere. Someone else can take the blame. Governments act in exactly the same way and who can blame them? As Joan Borysenko, the distinguished pioneer in integrative medicine, remarks, 'fear is poisonous to creativity because when we're in survival mode, the tendency is to regress and hole up in some "safe" haven.' We are far less likely to leave our comfort zones and seek innovative solutions. It immediately puts an end to us thinking 'outside of the box.' We retreat to the known and avoid the unknown. However, fear affects more than the creativity of our responses to issues and challenges. It permeates our entire way of thinking. As a society, our perspective has become increasingly short term and that is *not* a good starting position for addressing many of the systemic challenges that we face. These demand an holistic perspective, a long-term orientation and an incremental approach with consistent application.

Humanity has come a long way by reaching for the stars but this can so easily spill over into hubris, which manifests in our world as a kind of collective insanity (rampant waste, ecological devastation, unthinking consumerism, enduring poverty, racial and religious abuse and huge inequalities in global wealth to name but a few symptoms). The Greeks used the word, 'hubris', not only to mean an overwhelming arrogance or pride, but also to convey a sense of being out of balance. This was normally corrected through 'nemesis', a re-balancing of affairs, often in a particularly unpleasant manner. Traditionally, we have tended to justify our hubris in terms of self-benefit, based on the illusion of separateness. This is not only ethically and morally wrong, it no longer works at any level because we now face common problems that affect us all. Like it or not, we are bound together. Ultimately, for better or for worse, we share a common fate. This point is made rather nicely by Fernand Pareau, an 82-year-old French mountain guide, who likens our situation under threatened climate change to a group of climbers, independent yet bound together, reliant on each other to make it through. This team approach requires collective thinking as well as our independent skills and capabilities. It is an integration of the individual with the whole. And it is our destiny.

Freedom through acceptance

Fear is the central challenge that we face as individuals, as a society and as members of the human race. As the American naturalist, philosopher and poet, Henry David Thoreau, observed, 'nothing is so much to be feared as fear.' We may not like it. We may seek to hide from it. But, if we are to resolve the challenges ahead of us, we need to meet it head on at every level. Fear is 'hardwired' into us for a reason, to keep us safe by alerting us to danger. This is a very useful function for obvious reasons. It serves us well by energising us when necessary. Even in the modern world, how many deadlines are only met when a sense of fear finally takes charge? As fear is biologically conditioned we cannot 'overcome' it through willpower, but we *can* make friends with it. 'Freedom' from fear is attained not by intellectual will, but by acceptance. In acceptance comes non-attachment and this brings the freedom we so crave. Only *then* are we able to concentrate our energies to really address the issues that we face. Until that point fear will continue to colour our thinking, sometimes overtly but more often at the subtle unseen level. We can still make some good decisions but we block our path to that deeper level of wisdom, where we begin to use not only our heads, but the complete human package; mind, heart, body and soul.

In Buddhism, this path to freedom is expressed through the Four Noble Truths. The First Noble Truth is that life means suffering. This recognises life as it is; the essential nature of the human condition. However, the Second and Third Noble Truths recognise that the origin of suffering is attachment and we can end this suffering by withdrawing our attachment to it. Finally, the Fourth Noble Truth describes the path to the cessation of suffering, which is one of *gradual* self-improvement that treads the middle ground between excessive self-indulgence (the hedonism so common in our world) and excessive self-mortification (asceticism). In other words, fear will always be with us. It is necessary and useful in the world in which we live. However, it can become our best friend if we learn to detach from it. As such, it can still energise us and provide an incentive for action, but it will no longer get in the way of our access to the deeper wisdom we hold within. We are able to unlock our ability to think holistically (to see from the whole) and to understand how we might act (or not act) to make the most positive impact on the world around us. As soon as we are in this place we are a strategic leader, no matter what the world around us thinks. And, it makes no difference at all whether we are doing 'big', 'small' or 'no' things. We have donned the mantle of leadership and accepted our call. We are ready to play our part. And that is a truly sacred moment.

I realise to put such a bold statement at the beginning of a business book may be considered a dangerous thing by some people. But this time in our history is not the time to play safe. The challenges in front of us are simply too important and the issues too entrenched to fall back on old solutions and restricted ways of thinking. The world in which we now live is totally dominated by fear. This fear lurks beneath the surface, expressed as anxiety, stress, tiredness, depression, alienation and addictive behaviour. Addictions (such as the use of substances, drink, food, work, excessive use of technology and sex to name but a few) help us cope on the surface, but only at the expense of losing ourselves in the process. We may think, 'I'm not so self-destructive', but the nature of an addiction is that it controls us in some way. I wonder how many of us could get through the day without our caffeine shot? In reality, chronic lack of self-esteem pervades all aspects of our society. Despite our veneer of invulnerability, we know deep down that we have very little real control over the most important areas of our lives; just ask anyone who has discovered that they have a serious or life threatening illness. The most powerful moment in *The Age of Stupid* is where Pete Postlethwaite delivers the final monologue in the movie:

'We wouldn't be the first life form to wipe itself out. But what would be unique about us is that we did it knowingly. What does that say about us? The question I've been asking is: why didn't we save ourselves when we had the chance? Is the answer because on some level we weren't sure if we were worth saving?'

Beginning the leadership journey

'A good head and a good heart are always a formidable combination.'
Nelson Mandela

There is really only one place to begin the leadership journey and it is from a place of humility. This may seem like an odd statement to make in a world that so obviously celebrates charismatic, and often highly egocentric, personalities. But that is in the here and now. With the passage of time many of these 'in your face' celebrities fade away from public memory, leaving those with a more durable and consistent track record to take their place. And, if you know where to look, you will find a great deal of humility in leaders who, at first glance, do not appear to lack full confidence in themselves. No one would accuse Steve Jobs, CEO of Apple, of not knowing his mind. He has a reputation for ruthlessness and of showing little or no tolerance for those who do not share his vision. Apple is Steve Job's vision manifest. If you don't share that vision, you don't work for Apple (or, if you do, it is likely to be a short lived and miserable experience). However, if we take a look at Steve Jobs more closely, a very different person emerges. When we read his commencement address at Stanford University in June 2005, we see someone who is deeply reflective and concerned with 'right action' for the benefit of others:

'Remembering that I'll be dead soon is the most important tool I've ever encountered to help me make the big choices in life. Because almost everything – all external expectations, all pride, all fear of embarrassment or failure – these things just fall away in the face of death, leaving only what is truly important. Remembering that you are going to die is the best way I know to avoid the trap of thinking you have something to lose. You are already naked. There is no reason not to follow your heart.'

Other leaders have similar traits. Richard Branson certainly does not suffer from a lack of vision or self-determination, yet he does not take himself too seriously either. Virgin's businesses are built around redefining the customer experience and this would simply not be possible without an enduring ability to stand back and take on the perspective of the customer. Humility can happily coexist with a strong ego. I have both clients and close friends who run businesses and have *very* forceful personalities – that's how they get things done. But they are also deeply reflective and put themselves firmly in the service of what they are trying to achieve. Strategic leaders are, by nature, not blinded by personal achievement and self-aggrandisement. They tend to be people in service to a cause and they remain open to the wisdom of the world around them (even when it represents bad news or failure). They learn from where things went wrong, dust themselves off and continue. Perseverance and resilience go hand-in-hand with strategic leadership.

It is easy to confuse humility with blandness. Strategic leaders are anything but bland. In fact, the dance between authenticity, personality and creativity can make them very colourful indeed. We only have to look at the lives of people like Walt Disney and Henry Ford to know that. So, whilst best-selling management writer, Jim Collins, argues that the best chief executives are 'humble, self-effacing, diligent and resolute souls', *The Economist* can write that 'the best ambassadors for business are the outsized figures who have changed the world and who feel no need to apologise for themselves or their calling.' Both are right. Strategic leaders dig deep into who they are and take this into the world but, critically, they have a purpose for what they do that lies beyond themselves. This is deeply paradoxical, which is partly what makes leadership such a compelling subject. This combination of self-knowledge, passion and determination is something that we can all cultivate. It's not dependent on positional authority or where we stand within an organisation. In his address on leadership, Sergeant Rogers Trahan, who is attached to the 81st Medical Support Squadron at Keesler Air Force Base in Mississippi, makes this point very clear: 'Leadership has no rank; anyone can be a leader'.

Finding a pathway through the book

Freedom from Fear is intended to be a companion to *The Strategic Mind* and deals explicitly with the translation of strategic thinking into action. It is divided into three sections mirroring the essential components of strategic leadership. The first part looks at strategic thinking. In part two, we examine leadership, particularly the process by which we become a leader. And, in the final part, we bring these topics together to see why strategic leadership has so much to offer the world. It is possible to move between sections without reading the book consecutively and each chapter has been written so that it can be read independently. As a result, each section has a slightly different 'flavour'.

Part 1 – The nature of strategic thinking

We begin with considering the nature of strategic thinking; what it is, why we need it and how we develop the skills to practice it (*chapters 1-2*). We look first at the scale of the challenges confronting our world and why our response to them is often inadequate or incomplete. We examine the *'three illusions'* inherent in the way we currently think and we consider why developing the capacity to think strategically is so important. The second chapter summarises the key concepts that underlie strategic thinking so that this book can be read independently from its predecessor, *The Strategic Mind*. Inevitably, these chapters are more conceptual than the remainder of the book, which has a more story-based approach.

Part 2 – Becoming a strategic leader

The second section of this book (*chapters 3-9*) is concerned with the leadership journey itself, illustrated through a wide variety of stories and case studies, for these are the very best of teachers. This is the point where we apply strategic thinking to leadership in a practical context. Becoming a strategic leader requires the ability to see the whole *and* the capacity to act on this knowledge. It is both reflective and active. We begin at the most basic level by thinking about *what* leadership means to us in the context of *who* we are (*'Taking*

Responsibility'). We then look at *where* we can act (*'Seeing the Whole'*) and *with whom* (*'We not Me'*). The next three chapters (*'Travelling Light'*, *'Going With the Flow'* and *'An Inside Job'*) are concerned with the all-important question of *how* strategic leaders make a difference. And, finally, we examine that very special point when we actually *become* a leader (*'Wake Me Up'*). At the end of this section of the book we have examined the 'what', 'where', 'with whom' and 'how' questions of leadership through a great many case studies and examples. We have an idea of how the process works and what it takes to become a leader. Perhaps, I should issue a 'health warning' up front. The journey to leadership is not easy and it is certainly not for the fainthearted. I believe, however, that it is one that we are *all* capable of making in our own way. We can *all* make a difference and together we can make a *big* difference.

Part 3 – Making a difference

The final section of the book (*chapters 10-11*) is concerned with how we make that difference by the practical application of strategic leadership to the challenges that face us. It is only a 'taster' because the subject area is enormous, one that deserves a separate book in its own right. Nevertheless, it points the way to the future and a better one at that. It may seem strange that the initial chapter (*'Staying the Course'*) is concerned not with the end result of our leadership journey, but with the ability to keep on track and maintain our sense of purpose, vision and drive. This is deliberate. Accepting the mantle of leadership means anticipating that our journey will not always be calm, comfortable and safe. There will be times when we will need to 'ride the tiger' and it is wise to be ready in advance for what may be a very wild ride indeed. If we are in it for the long term, we had better make sure our foundations are solid and secure. The final chapter (*'Creating a New Earth'*) is a foretaste of what our world *could* look like if we take up the mantle of strategic leadership, if we find the courage to answer our call and follow our personal leadership journey.

Strategic leadership through stories

'If you think in terms of a year, plant a seed; if in terms of ten years, plant trees; if in terms of 100 years, teach the people.'
Confucius

The stories and case studies in this book are taken from all areas, including both corporate and not-for-profit sectors. We also follow the stories of five core organisations as the book progresses. Each one is a strategic leader in its field. **Apple**, **Starbucks** and **Waitrose** (part of the John Lewis Partnership) are solidly in the commercial sector, while **National Trust** and the work of the **Prince of Wales** are taken from the not-for-profit sector. Each of these strategic leaders face significant challenges in their work and core activities. None is perfect. And all have something of enormous value to teach us, each in its own unique way. Interestingly, all of them have had their fair share of detractors and that's one of the reasons why I have chosen them. We learn most by observing the practical path of leadership in action, rather than the theory of what could be.

PART 1

THE NATURE OF STRATEGIC THINKING

Our Tree

'It takes so long for a tree to grow
So many years of pushing the sky.

Long branches stretch their arms
Reach out with their wooden fingers.

Years drift by, fall like leaves
From green to yellow then back to green.

Since my Grandad was a boy
And then before his father's father

There's been an elm outside our school
Its shadow long across our playground.

Today three men ripped it down.
Chopped it up. It took ten minutes.'

David Harmer

1
THE CHALLENGE BEFORE US

*'By three methods we may learn wisdom: First, by reflection,
which is noblest; second, by imitation, which is easiest; and third
by experience, which is the bitterest.'*
Confucius

The task ahead

In 1950 Detroit was a thriving urban centre of two million people.
Nicknamed 'Motor City' because it was the acknowledged hub of
the world's automotive industry, it was the fourth largest city in the
United States after New York, Los Angeles and Chicago. It had a
thriving culture and boasted a vibrant downtown music scene with
its famous live jazz venues. Music exploded in the 1960's after Berry
Gordy Jr. set up Motown Records and the label became virtually
synonymous with the city. Motown became a powerhouse for
popular recording acts as well as playing an important role in racial
integration within the music industry. Its unique blend of soul, pop
and R&B produced some of the most celebrated artists of all time
including Marvin Gaye, Stevie Wonder, Michael Jackson and Diana
Ross to name but a few. Unfortunately, not much else has gone
right for the city since. Ask a resident in 1950 to predict what
Detroit would look like in 2010 and it is very unlikely that any would
have forecast the scale of devastation that would ensue. The city
has literally imploded.

Today the population of Detroit is just over 800,000 and this is
spread over 140 square miles making the existing municipal
infrastructure unsustainable (the current budget deficit is estimated

at $300 million). The city continues to suffer from a sinking tax base and now has little viable industry. General Motors was the largest car company in the world until it was surpassed by Toyota in 2009. It succumbed to bankruptcy in that year and is now fighting for its survival. Unemployment rates at 28% are some of the highest in the United States. Nearly one third of Detroit's housing stock is currently vacant (some 100,000 homes) and much of the city is gradually returning to prairie, the pre-industrial landscape of the region. Derelict and abandoned homes are ubiquitous (the municipal administration lacks the funds to pull them down) and the average price of a home has declined from $98,000 in 2003 to $15,000 in October 2009. There are seeds of hope in some areas but Detroit faces a gargantuan task in urban renewal. It may be that the only viable solution is to shrink the city to something more sustainable and clear the remaining area for wholesale redevelopment or return to nature. Perhaps only something this radical will successfully reintegrate Detroit with the sprawling suburbs of the metropolis around it. Interestingly, however, adversity brings out the better side of people. Aretha Franklin, 'the Queen of Soul', is proud of her city and speaks on behalf of many who live there when she says, 'I was brought up in Detroit, and most of my family's here. I like the mentality. It's a very supportive city. Detroiters will come all out if they really feel like what you are standing behind has merit.'

Detroit is an example of what can happen when the world changes and we do not adapt quickly enough. Today, we face change on a much greater scale than Detroit faced in the 1950s and it is useful to frame our thinking by considering some of the more important issues and challenges that we face. This is the only place in this book where we focus on problems rather than resolution. Observing the scale of the challenges that confront us focuses the mind and make it abundantly clear why the call for strategic leadership is so important in all aspects of our life; in our work, our communities and around our interests. We do not need to dwell on our past mistakes. It is, however, important to know *why* we made them, so we will also consider the limitations in our current way of thinking, in particular the three great illusions of our time; the illusions of independence, size and control. This will help us to acknowledge our responsibility for the devastating consequences of our actions and provide the wake up call that we so desperately need. We can then move on to look at resolving these problems by developing the capability to think strategically and building the courage to answer the call of leadership. With our eyes open once more, we will be able to see the opportunities that lie before us at this pivotal point in human history. For there are many of them. They are simply hidden in the shadows, slightly beyond our view.

Sadly, it seems that we are quickly becoming desensitised to the state we are in, perhaps because the media coverage is so intense that we need to tune it out to maintain our sanity. According to the Pew Research Centre the number of American voters who believe that there is 'solid evidence' that the earth is warming fell from 77% in 2007 to 57% in November 2009. This may reflect a more informed public (since there are a number of natural cycles affecting the earth's temperature and these may either exacerbate or counterbalance our effect on the climate) or a scepticism born of hearing too much hyperbole. As it becomes increasingly clear that climate change theories are 'works in progress' (and therefore inevitably flawed in some respects) we run the risk of disregarding the very serious damage that we are inflicting on our environment. When we do so, we are also taking our eye off the ball in terms of the potentially disastrous consequences of our actions on our future world. For the moment, current climate change predictions are our 'best guess' of what may happen in the future so we should take them seriously.

The world is shrinking and not in a good way

We are becoming used to chilling environmental forecasts. Too used to them perhaps. It is generally believed that hunting and habitat loss threaten more than 20% of the world's mammals with extinction. This is likely to be a significant understatement. A recent report by the International Union for Conservation of Nature

('IUCN'), using data gathered over five years by more than 1,700 scientists, concluded that the number of mammals in peril is likely to be much greater, perhaps as high as 36%. Other animals fare little better. Common birds are in decline across the world and if current trends continue, fisheries will be exhausted by 2050. Potential climate change makes the future even less certain. A report by IUCN in October 2008 concluded that 31% of amphibians are at risk and the status of a further 25% is uncertain. Nearly a quarter of reptiles and a third of all crabs are also threatened, as well as a third of the world's birds and nearly three quarters of its warm water corals. This critical loss of biodiversity matters and it is not just a case of losing the inestimable beauty of a large proportion of the natural life on Earth.

Nature thrives on diversity and the natural world provides vital processes (now sometimes called 'ecosystem services') that are critical to human survival. These include the sequestration of carbon in soil and forests, the pollination of crops and the purification of water in wetlands. It is biodiversity that underpins these natural services. To put it bluntly, bees can't pollinate if they have all died and trees can't store carbon if they have all been cut down. Indeed, scientists believe that ecosystems need to contain more than a limited number of species to thrive, so the drastic reduction in biodiversity undoubtedly spells big trouble for us in the future. Even in the short-term, changes in complex environmental systems such as weather patterns (which determine how much rain falls and where) can spell disaster for communities, countries and even very large parts of the earth's surface. If we add the potential rise in sea levels and other climate-related changes the scale of the challenge quickly becomes apparent. We don't need to look at the effect of shifting monsoon rainfall patterns or a change in the Gulf Stream (or any number of other alarming scenarios) to know that it is advisable to pay attention to changes in the world around us. What we really don't know is how these factors will play out.

It is wise to pay attention to 'small' things. They tell us a lot. If we want to know what is happening to the 'big picture' one of the very best ways to find out is to pay attention to what is happening at the smallest level. In the case of changes to the Earth's climate this is particularly true and it is in the 'small' things that we see the most alarming signs that matters are seriously out of balance. Take the precipitous drop in the numbers of invertebrates that underpin life. Buglife (a charity in the United Kingdom that seeks to save rare species and wildlife sites under threat) refers to these creatures as 'the small things that run the world' and with good cause. Without invertebrates 'the food we eat, the fish we catch, the birds we see and the hum of life that we hear simply would not exist.' Gerald Durrell, the renowned naturalist and author, was an early champion of what he called the 'little brown jobs', whose roles in their ecosystems cannot be underestimated. In essence, these small bugs underpin life on Earth as we know it and many are now under great threat, suffering steep declines or facing extinction.

Even more worrying is the 'small' but highly disturbing increase in the acidity of the oceans, which threatens life at the very foundation of the Earth's food chain. My younger son, Jamie, has a succinct way of putting things. 'It's all about the phytoplankton Dad,' he told me the other day, 'when the acidity gets to them it's game over'. He's right. Phytoplankton live in the oceans and other large bodies of water and obtain energy through photosynthesis. They account for half of all photosynthesis on earth and are responsible for much of the oxygen in the earth's atmosphere, half of the total amount produced by plant life. They are an essential part of the oceanic and freshwater food webs. According to the Institute of Science in Society, 'when phytoplankton are in jeopardy, all life is in jeopardy, on land and at sea. Marine life will literally starve to death.' It continues:

> 'Imagine vast expanses of oceans devoid of life as far and wide as you can project your senses, no whales, no fish, no seabirds and no corals beneath ... That's not a scene from a science-fiction film, but a likely future scenario unless we take appropriate action now.'

In short, we are at a critical point in Earth's history and our past ways of doing things are not necessarily a good guide for the future.

Nowhere is this more evident than with the fundamental necessities of life: water, food and energy.

Water, food and energy

Today one billion people go to bed hungry. Moreover, between now and 2050 the world's population is likely to rise by a third and demand for agricultural food will increase by 70%, making it even harder to feed the earth's population. More critical still is water scarcity. Today, 1.2 billion people, about one fifth of the world's population, live in places that are short of water and this is likely to get much worse as water usage rises with population and income growth. As *The Economist* points out, water abstraction in many areas of the world is already moving perilously close to safety levels and often beyond them. Indeed, the International Water Management Institute ('IWMI') estimates the farmers will use 2,000 cubic metres more water each year by 2030 if people are to be fed. That equates to an increase of a quarter on today's levels. A report by McKinsey & Co. estimates that the world will have 40% less water than it needs by 2030 and some regions will fare even worse. India, for example, will only be able to satisfy 50% of its water needs if nothing changes. Already, many of the world's great rivers no longer reach the sea including the Indus, Rio Grande, Colorado, Murray-Darling and Yellow Rivers, and these also serve as the arteries of the world's main grain-growing areas.

As water becomes increasingly scarce in many parts of the world, the risk of ecological disaster intensifies, together with the inevitable human conflicts that occur when resources are scarce. And no resource is as important as water. Climate change threatens to make matters worse by increasing the vulnerability of plant ecosystems and intensifying water management problems. Plants suffer when too much rain stimulates rapid growth followed by shortage or drought. It is also more difficult to capture and store water if rainfall is more erratic and intense. Much is then lost to flooding. On top of this, the misguided subsidies of bio-fuels by governments could prove to be as disastrous for water as they have been for food. Bio-fuels require more water use than normal crops as well as diverting land from productive agricultural uses. Indeed, the history of the twenty first century is likely to be defined more by water and food shortages than it is by the energy depletion issues that are extensively covered in the media today. A disturbing portrait of our potential future may be playing out in the Himalayas right now.

In the heart of the greater Himalayas sits the vast Tibetan Plateau. It contains the largest area of land ice outside the Polar Regions, some 100,000 square kilometres of frozen water, in glaciers that stretch across parts of India, Pakistan, Nepal, Bhutan and China. Scientists sometimes call this plateau the third pole and it plays a vital role in the distribution of water throughout India and Central Asia. *Time Magazine* christened it the 'water tower of Asia' and describes its fundamental importance to nearly half the world's population:

'When the ice thaws and the snow melts every spring, the glaciers birth the great rivers of the region, the mightiest river system in the world: the Ganges, the Indus, the Brahmaputra, the Mekong, the Yellow (and) the Yangtze. Together, these rivers give material and spiritual sustenance to 3 billion people ... Monsoons come and go, filling the rivers at times and then leaving them lethargic, but the ice melt has always been regular and dependable in a region where water – or lack of it – defines civilization.'

Given that most of South Asia, much of China and parts of India already suffer from water scarcity, any threat to the annual glacial melt is very serious indeed. Yet, evidence is mounting that warmer temperatures are now reducing precipitation and scientists believe that the third pole is retreating noticeably, despite its high altitude (over 6,000 metres). Some scientists claim that ice coverage in the Indian Himalayas has decreased by a fifth since 1960, although the full extent of the glacial retreat is currently unknown because politics and logistics make comprehensive studies difficult. The situation has not been helped by the well-publicised error in the

Intergovernmental Panel on Climate Change ('IPCC') Fourth Assessment report that the Himalayan glaciers would disappear by 2035. The likely timescale is actually far longer and the error was later blamed on lack of adequate peer review. Some sceptics have seized upon this as evidence of an over-reaction to climate change. Unfortunately, compounding one error with another does not bring us closer to the truth. The fact is that any persistent loss is alarming. The consequences for the huge population downstream that depends on the reliability and consistency of the ice melt for water are immense. The effect of reduced ice melt from the Tibetan Plateau would come on top of massive groundwater depletion and potential changes to monsoon rainfall patterns. Taken together, these factors could be devastating, making water scarcer as well as changing the pattern of its availability.

Scientists are still scrambling for hard evidence of the scale of the problem but they increasingly speak out on the urgency of action. The well-known climatologist, Veerabhadran Ramanathan, who is a Director for the Centre for Atmospheric Sciences at the Scripps Institution of Oceanography, is working on establishing just how quickly some of the critical glaciers are melting. He doesn't mince his words. 'To me', he says, 'continuing down our path is akin to committing suicide ... but for my granddaughter, I'm optimistic that we're going to solve these problems.' John Cook, an Australian Scientist who runs a website called 'Skeptical Science', which aims to explain what peer reviewed science has to say about global warming, reaches a balanced conclusion. 'The Himalayan glaciers are of vital importance to half a billion people. Most of this crucial resource is disappearing at an accelerating rate.' This should cause us serious concern regardless of any errors made in the IPCC report.

We know that even under the most optimistic scenarios energy resources are likely to lag behind consumption as fossil fuels decline at the same time as emerging nations rapidly industrialise and acquire first world consumption habits. Although energy use by OECD nations is expected to fall slightly by 2015, the annual growth rate of energy use of non-members is predicted to be ten times that of members between 2007 and 2030. Indeed, China's energy demand is expected to overtake the US by 2015 and China and India combined are likely to account for over a third of global energy use by 2030. It is also quite possible that the predicted decrease in OECD nation energy use may not materialise after all. These 'big picture' numbers, however, do not do justice to the challenges faced by some nations. The United Kingdom, for example, faces a looming energy shortage over the next fifteen years, with potential blackouts across the country and a dangerous reliance on imported gas. A similar position faces Europe as a whole, particularly Germany, which has committed itself to building no more nuclear power stations and closing down those it already has.

Take nothing for granted

If almost all the news appears to be bleak it is worth remembering that many of the models that predict the future are relatively simplistic and rely rather too much on linear extrapolation. This suits governments very well. Politicians sell certainty after all. In reality, current models rarely map more than the surface relationships of complex natural systems. At the end of the day we really don't know what is going to happen. While many people fear that population growth will create 'Malthusian' famine and war (named after Thomas Malthus, the nineteenth century economist who predicted that population would ultimately outstrip the world's food supply) demographic models show a more complex picture. The Earth's population is expected to peak at just over nine billion in 2050 and begin to fall quickly thereafter. The world's fertility rate is already in decline and is likely to fall below the global replacement rate at some point between 2020 and 2050. In fact, the current fall in fertility rates is both very large and very fast. Poor countries are mirroring developed nation population transition cycles at much faster rates, and this includes countries long associated with high birth rates such as those in Africa. This will have enormous repercussions for future generations, which is why declining fertility has been called one of the most dramatic changes in social history. It is entirely possible that our grandchildren will be worrying about a global fertility problem rather than a population explosion. Nevertheless, an increase in global population from 6.8 billion today to 9 billion in 2050 means a rise of one third within 40 years. The resource implications of an additional 2.2 billion people on this earth are immense.

As with demography, there is plenty of debate on exactly what is happening on climate change, just as there is on economic policy and every other major issue of our time. Scientific knowledge progresses by challenging and sometimes overturning accepted orthodoxies. Unlike politicians, good scientists thrive on doubt so we can expect accepted wisdom to change over time. There is no such thing as certainty in science. Moreover, most climate models explicitly assume that our current lifestyle will continue more or less as it is now, albeit modified by the need to reduce carbon emissions and develop alternative green technologies and energy sources. In other words, developing nations will simply emulate developed nations in a taste for consumerism and the good life. It would be wise to question this assumption. If everyone on the planet lived the same lifestyle as people in the Western world do today we would need at least two extra planets to sustain ourselves. It is time to be thinking in the reverse direction with the so-called developed nations learning a few lessons from those countries that have not yet acquired such self-destructive lifestyle habits.

It is also wise to remember the corrosive inequalities that exist in our world. 842 million people are currently underfed and half of humanity, 3 billion people, lives on less than $2.50 a day. In addition, 20% of the world's population does not have access to safe drinking water, 40% lacks access to improved sanitation and 25% does not have access to electricity. We need a new way of doing things rather than simply an extension of the existing system to one and all. Vaclav Havel, formerly President of the Czech Republic, wrote as early as the 1970's that 'a better system will not automatically ensure a better life. In fact, the opposite is now true: only by creating a better life can a better system be developed'. In other words, we begin first by developing a strategic approach that recognises the big picture and incorporates the need to move forward in a sustainable way, getting more from less. Only after that has been achieved do we develop practical policies to tackle specific issues.

The crisis in thinking

Most of us accept the need for action to resolve the serious issues and challenges that we face. It is not lack of intent that holds us back. What we share in common is not simply a failure to act but rather of acting ill advisably. We have a failure of thinking. We are hampered by belief patterns that are embedded deeply but invisibly into the way we think. I call these the three great illusions; *the illusions of independence, size and control*. They are so pervasive that we accept them without question, often failing to recognise their existence at all. The first step on our leadership journey is to challenge these ingrained patterns of belief. By doing so we open up to new insights into the world around us and uncover hidden opportunities that lie hidden in the shadows. Only then is the time right for us to act.

To the more practical and action oriented among us this may be a little frustrating. Perhaps, it sounds a little too philosophical and insubstantial. We might want to have an impact right *now*! I sympathise, but we must be patient. We will be looking at lots of practical examples of the power of new thinking, in every conceivable arena of human endeavour, as we progress through this book. For now, let's look at just one. In 2009, a group of Irish peacemakers (from both sides of the fence) worked with Arab and Kurdish Iraqis to help settle their differences and avoid further bloodshed. The Irish peacemakers had unique skills and experience in this area but it would have been very difficult beforehand to predict the context in which they could be so fruitfully applied. The situation itself, combined with the willingness and openness of the Irish envoys, enabled their skills to be put to good use.

The three illusions

Taking an external perspective of the challenges that face us is critical but it is equally important to look inside as well. The three illusions, as I call them, are deeply ingrained patterns in our way of thinking, and they colour our perception of what we can and cannot do. They are:

1. **The illusion of independence** – the idea that we, as human beings, are independent from the world around us, that the observer and the observed are separate. In reality, we are all deeply connected within the web of life and our notion of separateness is an illusion – the observer and the observed are in relationship!
2. **The illusion of size** – the idea that big is important and success can be measured in terms of size. This idea permeates all aspects of contemporary society, not only in terms of individual and organisational achievement but also in our ideas of economic growth and general well being. In fact, there is little correlation between what is truly important and size.
3. **The illusion of control** – the idea that we can control the environment around us, based partly on the first illusion of independence. In fact, our relationship with the world around us is far more complex than we currently acknowledge and we would be wise to recognise the natural limitations in our ability to control it. Instead, we should attune ourselves to the wealth of opportunity that flows from learning to live in relationship with it.

Illusion of independence

When we think of physics, most of us think of Newtonian physics. It's a pretty good guess that this formed quite a large part of our high school physics curriculum. This is the world composed of separate atoms that relate to each other by way of action and reaction. We can observe this world without changing it. Of course, there is much more to physics than that. The world of quantum physics tells us that everything in the universe is interwoven with everything else. The world does not consist of separate interacting parts but sets of systems that are so interwoven that they take their identity from the nature of the relationship itself. In this world we are interconnected with the 'external' reality we observe as part of a broader system. This goes beyond the cause and effect of Newtonian physics and the idea of separateness that lies beneath it. We are one with the universe because that separateness is an illusion; we cannot eliminate ourselves from the bigger picture. In *The Dancing Wu Li Masters*, an overview of the 'new' physics, Gary Zukav writes:

> 'Common sense contradictions ... are at the heart of the new physics. They tell us again and again that the world may not be what we think it is. It may be much, much more... We are part of nature, and when we study nature there is no way around the fact that nature is studying itself. Physics has become a branch of psychology, or perhaps the other way round... (it) is the study of the structure of consciousness.'

Nothing exists in isolation; all things are in relationship, both with each other and with the whole. We need look no further than the surprising history of the potato. The potato was first domesticated in the uplands of Peru over 8,000 years ago. Today, it is the fourth most important food crop in the world (after maize, wheat and rice). It is responsible for much more than you might think. It not only underpinned the industrial revolution in England in the nineteenth century but it also disrupted the entire social fabric of pre-industrialised society. Friedrich Engels equated its importance to iron for its 'historically revolutionary role'. The key to the disruptive power of this humble tuber is its high yield, ease of cultivation and its remarkable balance of nutrients, so much so that it is possible to survive almost entirely on a diet of potatoes. This had a profound impact on the Old World when the Spanish first brought the vegetable into Europe in the sixteenth century. Initially, it proved useful to feed to conscripted miners to dig up silver to be shipped back home. It also brought more than the Spanish had bargained for by debasing the metal and disrupting the entire monetary system through inflation. Since then the potato has played a much wider and unanticipated role in history. It came at just the right time to fuel the emerging industrialisation in Europe.

Not only did the potato liberate workers off the land but it also allowed the new industrial workforce to be fed. John Reader, author of *Potato: A History of the Propitious Esculent*, explains that the arrival of the vegetable was one of those remarkable synergies, 'it arrived in Europe and established itself as a staple food … precisely when Europe's burgeoning industries were beginning to cry out for workers'. This led not only to Europe's rise but also to the Irish potato famine that contributed so significantly to emigration to the United States and its emergence as a great industrial power. Indeed, the influence of the potato goes much further. The great tragedy of the Irish potato famine in 1845, when a million people perished, forced the repeal of the Corn Laws in England and paved the way to the adoption of free trade. As the Duke of Wellington complained, 'rotten potatoes have done it all.' Over time, however, this became one of the central planks in the rise of Britain as a global economic power.

If we take more than a cursory look at the world around us we will find evidence of the interconnectedness of life in all areas. We are all one. That is the truth. But that is *not* the way we live. Quite the opposite, we live in a world that celebrates our independence from each other. Successful people are those who stand out, who have made their mark upon the world, not those who blend into the community. We live in a society that is defiantly 'me' centred rather than 'we' centred; the individual has become paramount and the community secondary. We may call the world a village but, in reality, our sense of relatedness with those around us has receded, resulting in a sense of isolation and alienation from others. This actually makes us *more* fearful of life, especially of differences in others. We might be told to embrace and celebrate our differences but there are few of us who follow this creed. This is the backdrop to attempts to tackle some of the biggest challenges that the human race has ever faced, so many of which require us to work together. It's not a good starting point. But it *is* where we are now. And it *can* be done, as we shall see later in the book.

The importance of relationship is not merely a philosophical or metaphysical concept. Great cities and entire industries are built around relationships. Firms from the same industry have long gathered together in close proximity, a phenomenon known as clustering. This is evident in industries as diverse as finance and banking, the automotive sector and creative sectors such as entertainment. This not only pools creative talent (just think of Hollywood) and makes deal making easier (the City of London) but also leads to more effective supply chains, logistics and distribution systems. Toyota's suppliers, for example, tend to group around its main factories, part of the famous 'just in time' lean production systems that the company pioneered in the automotive industry. In fact, if we look historically at almost any industry we can see the same phenomenon, whether it was lace makers based in Nottingham in the nineteenth century or information technology and internet-based companies clustered in Silicon Valley today. Often high tech clusters are based around prestigious universities that specialise in research in relevant areas (such as Cambridge, MIT and Stanford). It is somewhat of an irony that in an age where communication technology is capable of allowing us to conduct activities from almost anywhere, location has become far more important not less. As *The Economist* concluded in an article on cities and commercial life, 'physical proximity appears to have virtues in commercial life that no amount of technological gimmickry can replace'. People matter. Relationships matter. We forget the importance of our connection with each other at our peril.

We live in an age of paradox. We are more connected than ever before by technology and shared media, yet we are increasingly isolated from those around us, even those who live right next to us. Our relationships are becoming increasingly broad and shallow, allowing us to have hundreds of 'friends', many of whom we barely know. Our most important community of all, our immediate family, is fraying. Many of us no longer have stable nuclear families, let alone the extended families that were once the norm in previous generations. We relate broadly but we lack depth. Ironically, even though technology allows us to participate in an almost unlimited variety of shared interest groups and causes, we are much less connected with the communities in which we actually live. We are technologically connected without feeling connected at all. Many of us feel isolated from other people and the world around us despite the '24/7' media coverage that tells us exactly what is happening on the other side of the world. We are missing relationship. We crave for our part in the whole, our part in the process of life itself.

Salami strategy

It is not always easy to 'see' the complex web of connectivity in life. I sometimes illustrate this using a story of a supermarket setting up a delicatessen counter. Seeing an independent deli store doing well in the neighbourhood the supermarket replicates the operation by increasing its range of salami meats from four to thirty five. The operation is a great success, plenty of choice for customers and at a price below that of the independent deli. However, several years down the line the store manager receives a report from internal operations questioning the profitability of the deli. The report begins by explaining the '80:20 rule'. Seven types of salami account for 80% of the sales and the other twenty-eight salamis account for 20%. Using metrics contributed by the finance department, it can also be seen that these 'long tail' products are making a loss after 'appropriate' cost allocation. The implications are obvious and the supermarket cuts back to twelve salamis (the counter supervisor held her position well). Most customers are happy, but a few of the more discerning ones drift back to the independent deli, which has now added an excellent Italian-style café to its proposition. Life never stays still!

At first, it appears that profitability has increased without any serious tradeoffs. Additional cost cutting efficiencies (substituting cheaper suppliers for a marginal reduction in quality) boost margins and sales in the short term. Several years later, however, the same '80:20' exercise is repeated. The logic is exactly the same this time around. After the exercise, ironically, the supermarket is back to its original offering of four salamis, although it improves the selection of packaged meats elsewhere in the store. The packaged products (which offer better margins and less wastage) improve profitability overall so the exercise is justified in financial terms. However, the supermarket deli counter no longer has a critical mass. It is not unique in any way and doesn't attract customers in its own right. Customers who are passionate about their meat products stop buying from the supermarket. They return to either the original deli or to a new one that has been set up to take advantage of a new generation of customers who have been educated by the supermarket to enjoy a more diverse range of meat products! These independents are small and flexible enough to be responsive to market conditions at street level. They also realise that that each type of meat product within their range is related to the whole proposition. They move slowly to change the mix and add or drop products, testing extensively with customers (many of whom they know by name) and respecting the fact that even apparent loss makers may have a role to play if customers want them available for occasional purchase.

Illusion of size

'Too big to fail is one of the biggest problems we face in this country.'
Ben Bernanke, Chairman of the United States Federal Reserve

We remain besotted with size, with the concept that 'big is beautiful', that bigger is better. In 2004, China introduced a measure of 'green GDP', which adjusted conventional economic metrics to reflect the cost of pollution. Unfortunately, when the figures were computed, the cost of destructive environmental practices (hardly unique to China) meant that growth slowed dramatically. As a result, the proposal was initially dropped and then abandoned altogether. The concept of gross domestic product ('GDP') was originally invented as a way of measuring economic activity in the 1930's at the end of the Great Depression and it's certainly showing its age. GDP simply aggregates things that are valued in monetary terms. It therefore includes dysfunctional activities such as oil spills, car crashes and the development of weapons of mass destruction, while excluding any activity that does not have a market-based value placed upon it. If we pay somebody else to look after our children we boost GDP, whereas if we do it ourselves we do not. In fact, our choice to spend time at home with our children actually decreases GDP if we forego doing something else as a result. This is, of course, serious nonsense.

For a measure that is so ubiquitous, GDP is also surprisingly problematic. In 1987 there were celebrations in the streets of Rome when the Italian economy overtook the United Kingdom in an event nicknamed 'Il Sorpasso'. The reason was the inclusion of Italy's infamous black market activities in national measures for the first time (valued somewhere between 25% and 30% of the economy). By 2000 the UK was back on top, with a GDP value 35% higher than Italy. But that's not the end of the story. In October 2009, Italy once more took the lead (dubbed, not surprisingly, 'Il Secondo Sorpasso'). Although the severity of the recession in the UK was a contributing factor, the primary cause was the decline of Sterling relative to the Euro. This time there was little celebration in Italy. If the economy had to stand alone, its currency and ranking would quickly fall. Yet, despite all the problems with GDP as a measure it still stands paramount in our world (partly because it is consistent even if it is flawed). Only the tiny Himalayan kingdom of Bhutan has bucked the system. It has introduced the concept of gross national happiness ('GNH') in an attempt to define the quality of life in more holistic terms, reflecting Bhutan's unique culture based on Buddhist spiritual values. GNH is founded on the promotion of 'four pillars' of wellbeing and happiness: sustainable development, the preservation and promotion of cultural values, conservation of the natural environment and good governance. Naturally, GNH is somewhat easier to talk about than to define in practical terms but it is remarkably successful as a unifying vision for Bhutan's economic development planning process.

The illusion of size permeates all aspects of our society. In reality, there is little correlation between what is truly important and size. Many restructuring and cost cutting measures taken by companies, for example, fail because they simply do not understand this point. They remove 'small' but vital elements of what makes a company successful. Efficiency drives undertaken to improve financial performance often eliminate key elements within the product and marketing mix for exactly the same reason. In reality, it is not easy to pinpoint the key parts of an organisation's unique selling proposition ('USP'). USP is *always* a complex bundle of product/service attributes that relate to each other in a unique way. Underestimating the complexity of the relationship between the different elements of USP (and chopping out some indiscriminately) can be very deadly indeed. But, most often, mistakes are made because there is an erroneous correlation between importance and size, combined with a need to 'evidence' measures taken in financial terms. 'Small' things cannot necessarily be evidenced easily but that does *not* make them any the less important.

It is not only in the commercial sector that the illusion of size plays out. At the same time as we are witnessing the failure of very large commercial organisations (we need only think of implosion of Lehman Brothers in 2008 and the bankruptcy of General Motors and Chrysler in 2009) governments are touting increased size as the answer for the provision of public services. The language is often the same as in the commercial sector in the past ('consolidation', 'greater efficiencies', 'economies of scale', 'greater purchasing power' and so on). Nowhere is this more prevalent than with the undertaking of huge information technology projects, which often promise the world but, in practice, deliver very little at enormous cost. Sadly, the need to maintain services at a human scale is all but lost in this wholesale destruction of public wealth. In reality, there are cost effective small-scale human solutions but they are largely hidden from us by our belief that 'bigger is best'. One simple example is the potential to make more use of distributed intelligence systems in the public sector. Highly successful organisations such as Amazon and eBay use distributed intelligence to organise complex market activities and they do so very well. Self-organising principles (and the associated use of open source software) open up more opportunities. There is plenty of scope for creative solutions providing we open our mind and let go of outdated belief systems.

Big is not always beautiful. Joe Baker, a professor in Kinesiology and Health Science at York University in Toronto, published a study in 2009 that found that smaller cities are more likely to produce elite athletes than larger ones. This appears counterintuitive but his working hypothesis is that cities with populations over 500,000 pose problems for young athletes, preventing them from gaining access to essential resources. 'Ever try to organise a game of pickup hockey in Toronto?' he observes. He concludes that the 'optimal community size for the development of a professional athlete is greater than 1,000 but less than 500,000. Sports scouts that limit their searches to larger areas are potentially missing large pools of talent. Thinking counter-intuitively is important.

Toyota's great challenge

There are plenty of large dysfunctional organisations. But to learn most about the dangers of equating success with size, it is best to turn to a highly successful one. There is no better example than Toyota, which, by any measure, is one of the most successful corporations in the world. Traditionally, Toyota has set the pace in the automotive industry (even being dubbed the 'machine that changed the world' as a result of its pioneering lean production systems). It was no surprise to see it overtake GM to become the largest car company in the world in 2009. It had long been the most admired company in its industry, and it was the organisation that all the other automotive companies benchmarked. What *was* far more surprising was to see Akio Toyoda, President of Toyota and the grandson of the founder, wringing his hands in public about the state of the company. Large product recalls, declining quality control and an admission that the 'pace at which we have grown may have been too fast' has made public what has been known within Toyota for some time, that traditional values have given way in the race for market domination. The situation is serious enough for *The Economist* to write in February 2010 that 'until recently, Toyota was the peerless exemplar. For now, at least, it is seen as an awful warning.'

Toyota had been aiming to achieve 15% of the global automotive market by 2010. Mr Toyoda believes that this focus on gaining market share (increasing in size) is having unfortunate and potentially devastating side effects, in particular damaging the company's stellar reputation for build quality and reliability. He has vowed to return to the fundamentals of dependability and affordability, combined with creating new models with greater design flair and personality. This heralds a return to the patient, incremental approach that has made Toyota famous in the past, even if this sacrifices market share and slows down the all-important new model development cycle. The focus is again on 'thinking small' within a huge corporation, with painstaking attention to detail at all levels. By doing so, he hopes to avoid the five-stage fate that befalls many corporate behemoths that is deftly described by Jim Collins, an American management writer, in his book, *How the Mighty Fall*. Jim Collins describes the first stage of decline as hubris born of success. This is followed in the second stage by the undisciplined pursuit of more of the same; the company continues to do what has worked before only more so. By the third stage, there is a general, and dangerous, denial of risk and peril (most aptly seen in large financial organisations and banks prior to the credit crunch) that results in a desperate search for some form of salvation (the fourth stage). This is where Mr Toyoda believes that Toyota may be today, just before entering a potentially fatal spiral of decline (the fifth stage). This fourth stage is marked by 'silver bullet' solutions such as big acquisitions, leaps into new technologies and constant restructuring, all of which often simply hasten the decline of once great organisations that have lost their way.

There is nothing inevitable about this spiral of decline. IBM is classic example of a very large organisation that once appeared to be locked in permanent decline but has successfully managed to reinvent itself as a service-based company. Apple and Hewlett Packard are two other well-publicised examples of successful turnarounds. In Toyota's case, Mr Toyoda is advocating building on the historical strengths of the company, combined with meticulous attention to customer needs. He has no intention of allowing Toyota to experience the fifth stage of the process described by Jim Collins as the 'acceptance of irrelevance or death'. Known in the industry as a keen 'car guy' with a love of racing, Mr Toyoda is seeking to put that passion back into the heart of the company. Using his favourite metaphor, that Toyota's engineers should be like chefs, seasoning their cars with tantalising 'flavours', he talks about cars that 'inspire dreams and admiration in everyone from children to adults'. Maintaining the traditional strengths of Toyota in durability, affordability and build-quality with exciting and innovative new models is a tough balancing act. But Toyota's engineers are some of the best in the world and engineers love nothing better than a challenge. Blogging under his alter ego, 'Morizo', he sums it up succinctly, saying, 'I have simply loved cars since I was little.'

Toyota provides a wonderful example of a large company that is open and adaptive enough to recognise problems that result directly or indirectly from its size and take action to resolve them. It also has a strong culture that can help it restore the attention to detail that marked it out as different in the early days (alongside other Japanese companies such as Honda). Most importantly, its culture is one of humility, which allows it to keep its organisational ears and eyes open. Mr Toyoda has promised to 'work vigorously and unceasingly to restore the trust of our customers.' Not all large companies are so fortunate.

Illusion of control

Accurate risk assessment is the single most important critical success factor in the financial services industry. So, until recently, mathematical modelling techniques that allowed financial risk to be quantified, 'captured', packaged and sold on, were a boon. The process of 'redistributing' risk was certainly very profitable for those in the industry. The only problem was that it didn't work. As it turned out, risk was not being passed on to those who could handle it more safely, or somehow eliminated by being packaged into smaller parcels. It was simply being passed around in circles. The unfortunate result is history. Risk remained (often back with those who had originally sold it on) and the resulting losses were so large that society as a whole has had to pick up the cheque. The process of sorting out the financial mess (and writing down bad debt at all levels in the economy) will take decades, the amount of time directly reflecting the degree of irrational exuberance and poor decision-making that preceded the crash. The bottom line is that we placed far too much reliance on quantitative models with relatively simplistic assumptions and we failed to see the inherent weaknesses of these models (such as a tendency to overestimate recent data, a phenomenon known as 'recency bias'). It is a great lesson in our tendency to overestimate our degree of control.

The desire to eliminate risk is not restricted to the commercial sector. Governments often try to eliminate small risks in the most trivial of areas, often with perverse consequences. Playground equipment outdoors is removed because there is a small chance of a child being hurt, so children spend more time inside getting fat. Evidence suggests that cigarette warning labels designed as a deterrent to smoking actually encourage it by stimulating the area in the brain known as the nucleus accumbens (the 'craving spot'). Attempts to levy additional taxes on junk food and unhealthy eating ('fat taxes') may have similar counter-intuitive results. At the very least, heavy users of junk food are likely to be the most resilient to price increases, thus reducing the impact of measures. Since eating is only part of the equation for healthy living any tax deterrent should really take account of other factors too. If, for example, food becomes dearer and people spend more time cooking with fresh ingredients at home, they may do less exercise, thereby offsetting the health effects. Moreover, it is not simple to decide what to tax.

Butter may be high in animal fats but it may be a healthier choice overall than margarine for other health-related reasons. The same argument may be made for the choice between sugar and artificial sweeteners. In all these cases the control 'input' underestimates the complexity in the system with perverse and undesirable, unanticipated consequences. The most bizarre example of all is probably the health and safety requirement that leaning gravestones should be levelled to minimise the possibility of someone being hurt in the event that the tombstone falls. This causes havoc if the grass in churchyards is not regularly cut, both to visitors and to maintenance staff alike.

At the root of all these unanticipated consequences is a belief in our ability to control the world. When combined with a search for short term 'cost-effective' solutions this can be particularly deadly. It leads us to rely on limited and simplistic assumptions and then extrapolate these to the whole system. We ignore trade-offs and other external costs and make decisions that are damaging to the system as a whole, particularly in the long-term. In mid 2009 the Welsh Assembly put forward plans to cull badgers to prevent the further spread of Bovine TB. This was to be carried out in conjunction with other cattle based measures, making the measurement of the effectiveness of different elements within the plan very difficult, if not impossible. Moreover, links between Bovine TB and badgers have not been proved scientifically so it is far from certain whether the measures would have been successful in the first place. The highly complex nature of the disease is minimised so that action can be taken in the short term. At the very least, this may prove ineffective but it may actually make matters worse. We will never know. As happens so often, our preoccupation with 'doing' prevents the reflective process that would allow us to make much better decisions in the long term.

The more that we see ourselves as independent of the world the more we fall into the trap of thinking we can micro control the environment around us. In fact, we are in relationship with the world around us and it is a far more complex relationship than we currently acknowledge. Economist and writer, Steven Levitt, argues that the problems of the macro economy, for example, are so hard, and the levels of complexity so immense, that 'it's almost hopeless to think that we would have really good models of those systems'. It is a core understanding of quantum physics that it is not possible, even in principle, to make a complete prediction about the future. It makes no difference if we have the best measuring devices, the best models and all the time and determination in the world. It is simply not possible. We are limited to possibilities, the odds that something is going to happen or not going to happen. In the words of Gary Zukav, in his overview of the 'new' physics, 'we never can know with certainty what will happen to (what) we are 'observing'. The singer, Barbra Streisand, learned a similar lesson about complexity and interrelationships to her cost when she tried to block the publication of an embarrassing photograph. Her very efforts caused the offending photo to spread like wildfire on the Internet in what bloggers now refer to as the 'Streisand effect'.

When we learn to recognise the inherent complexity of the world around us, and the natural limitations in our ability to control it, we move towards working in harmony *with* the world around us, rather than *against* it. We learn to accept what John Maynard Keynes called the 'inescapable uncertainty about the future' and we cease to try to manage it in detail. As a result, boundaries and tradeoffs become much more visible to us, as do the opportunities that so often lie hidden within the nature of the relationship itself. This is not defeatist. It is sensible. It prepares us to deal with the real events that occur rather than those we think *should* occur. We live in the awareness of the moment. So when a 'black ṣwan' occurs (the least expected catastrophe that often does the most damage) we are fully prepared to accept it and deal with it.

Observing the limitations in our thinking

Unanticipated consequences are a blessing as well as a curse. It is hard to see the limitations in our thinking in advance. There is, however, one very good practical way to 'test' the assumptions that underlie our thinking. Observe the results and look for unanticipated consequences or anomalies. By doing so, we need only be an observer. Practical examples abound of thinking gone awry. A study by Raffaella Sadun, of the London School of Economics, found that supermarket chains denied an out-of-town site in the United Kingdom tend to set up in town centres instead. This brings intense competition to local high street stores, some of which prosper (the clustering effect attracts more shoppers), some adapt (becoming specialists for example) and others perish. So planning permission rules designed to protect the high street from change may have the reverse effect.

Observing unanticipated consequences also allows us to see the opportunities that exist if we change our way of thinking and our approach. Road safety rules provide a wonderful example of this process. Road safety and other 'traffic calming' paraphernalia often have counter-intuitive results, transferring a sense of responsibility from the driver to the planner. Research into shared space road schemes (which remove visual distractions and urban clutter including signage, lights and segregated pavements) indicate that drivers act less recklessly and safety improves. This is also true when the lines designating the middle of the highway are removed in smaller roads. Ian Walker, a traffic and transport psychologist, specialising in vulnerable road user safety and transport choices at Bath University, conducted his own field research by simply getting on his bike and monitoring the behaviour of those who passed him. He found that drivers allowed him more room when he was not wearing a helmet (or wearing a female wig!) but rushed past him leaving little room to manoeuvre as soon as he put the helmet on. An experiment in Munich found that fitting anti-lock braking systems in taxicabs made no difference to the number of accidents as those drivers with the superior brakes merely drove more aggressively.

Shared space schemes in small towns in Belgium and the Netherlands have been enormously successful and are currently in place in over 400 towns and cities across Europe. A similar scheme has been introduced into Kensington High Street, which has led to a 44% cut in accidents (much to the chagrin of some of the opponents of the scheme). Shared (or 'naked') streets not only make roads safer and reintroduce a shared sense of community, they also, counter-intuitively, ease traffic flow and shorten journey times. Average speed increases, as drivers no longer have to stop at lights. The success of shared space schemes lies in the transfer of responsibility from planners to users and the recognition that the vast array of traffic control mechanisms that clutter our streets often do more damage than good. When the Evening Standard reviewed the scheme in Kensington it concluded, somewhat uncharitably, that 'the most dangerous people in London are the road engineers'.

It is always good to maintain a sense of humour about some of the crazier aspects of our control-oriented world. The idea put forward by a member of the Danish parliament to put down all mongrels 'to eliminate aggressive traits from the doggy gene pool' springs immediately to mind. Laughing at some of the madness around us helps us not to take ourselves too seriously. *Time Magazine* recently covered an idea put forward to create mini-machines that are capable of taking in carbon dioxide and releasing oxygen. Build enough of these, the theory goes, and humans will be able to mitigate some of the effects of their carbon emitting activities. The editorial finished off with the revelation that such things already exist. They are called trees. Thankfully, in many cases, common sense does finally prevail. In Denmark the mongrel pups appear to have won the day. Another member of the Danish parliament summed up the nation's views when he said that he would 'reach for his shotgun' if the initiator of the scheme ever came calling.

Challenging accepted wisdom

There are many courageous souls in the world who are willing to question conventional wisdom and then act on their beliefs. Some are very well known. Most are not. It would be nice to end this chapter by looking at one of the latter examples. In 2001 Portugal introduced legislation to decriminalise the use and possession of all drugs. At the time, many believed that this policy would lead to dire consequences, even leading to Portugal becoming the drug tourist destination of choice. So, it is a little surprising to see how successful the policy has been. The Portuguese Government has sponsored local bodies to encourage addicts to undergo treatment and to stop recreational users sliding into addiction. This has worked well. Now that addicts do not fear criminal prosecution (although drugs still remain illegal) more are prepared to treat their habit. As a result, the Cato Institute, an American think-tank based in Lisbon, claims that drug usage in many categories 'are now among the lowest in the European Union'. There is little evidence of drug tourism. Numbers convicted of drug trafficking have fallen and the incidence of other drug related problems (including sexually transmitted diseases and deaths from overdoses) has also declined dramatically. By looking at the system as a whole the new approach has had surprisingly positive consequences. The secret of success according to Manuel Cardoso, Deputy Director for the Institute of Drugs and Drugs Addiction in Portugal, is:

> *'Before decriminalisation, addicts were afraid to seek treatment because they feared they would be denounced to the police and arrested … now they know they will be treated as patients with a problem and not stigmatised as criminals.'*

We too can question accepted ways of doing things and the beliefs that stand behind them. Sometimes we can even have our cake and eat it too. Most books on reducing our carbon footprint advise us to eat local food and reduce the average journey of food to farm, which is currently between 1,500 and 2,000 miles. This makes sense, but there are other ways of reducing the carbon footprint associated with the food we eat. The biggest one is to move down the food chain, substituting white meat for red and fruit and vegetables for meat and dairy products. This also happens to be much healthier for us as the very foods that have a high carbon cost (red meat, pork, dairy products and processed snacks) also have high fat and calorie content. A 'green diet' consisting of fruit and vegetables, whole grains, lean meats and fish turns out to be best for us. It also has a much more dramatic effect on our carbon footprint then we might at first imagine. The higher up the food chain we go the more energy is devoted to producing the food. So while most food takes about two calories of fossil-fuel energy to produce one calorie of food energy, raising beef can take up to eighty. The mix of our diet actually matters much more than where the food originates (the journey from source to supermarket typically accounts for only 4% of a food's carbon footprint). That's why Kate Geagan, author and dietician, advises us to 'focus on eating lower on the food chain, with more plants and fruits and less meat and dairy … It's that simple'. So, perhaps the old English proverb is right. We will be eating less cake after all.

2

FOUNDATIONS IN STRATEGIC THINKING

'Any fool can make things complicated, it requires a genius to make things simple.'
E. F. Schumacher

Turning the corner

When Harry Patch and Henry Allingham died in 2009, at 111 and 113 respectively, they were the last two remaining British veterans to have fought on the front during the First World War. Both men fought at Passchendaele, a town close to Ypres in West Flanders. The battle in which they took part is synonymous with the horrors of trench warfare in thick oozing mud. It was part of the bloody conflagration that engulfed Ypres, in which 800,000 soldiers died, were wounded or reported missing. Harry Patch was a 'Tommy', or foot soldier, while Henry Allingham was a spotter and retriever of crashed planes. Both saw and endured almost too much and neither spoke of their experiences until they were well over 100. They had experienced enough horror for one lifetime to want to open the wound once more. Eventually, however, after gentle encouragement from others, Harry and Henry did tell their story because it 'seemed more disrespectful to ignore what had gone on than to talk about it'. Their message was simple but urgent. 'T'isn't worth it', said Harry Patch, 'War isn't worth one life.' 'War's stupid ... nobody wins', agreed Henry Allingham, 'You might as well talk first, you have to talk last anyway'. 'We were all victims' was Harry Patch's conclusion.

They spoke of what they experienced and endured so that the world would not forget the brutal reality of war and the debt that we owe to the millions who perished. They relived their experiences to give us a second opportunity to learn from the horrors of that 'Great War', the conflict that was billed as the 'war to end wars' but, inevitably, simply led to so many more. And they travelled. Henry Allingham went to Germany and met Robert Meier who had served as an infantryman on the Western Front. They laid a wreath together at a local war memorial and gently shook hands. Harry Patch travelled to see Mr Kuentz who had also fought at Passchendaele but on the other side. They went to the German cemetery at Langemarck where, on impulse, Mr Patch picked up an acorn and gave it to the man who had once been his 'enemy'. 'Now we are friends,' said Mr Kuentz.

Upside down thinking

It took a lot for Harry Patch and Henry Allingham to finally open up about their experiences in the First World War. Probably more than we will ever know. My father, who fought with the Polish artillery when Germany invaded Poland in 1939, never spoke to anyone about the five years he spent in the war camps after he was captured, not even to my mother. After he died I asked his best friend, who had shared some of his experiences in the camps, to tell me what had happened. He refused to talk about it. 'There are some things you do not want to know' was all he would say. The memories and experiences of the war camps were too painful even then for discussion. So Harry Patch's simple gesture with the acorn is no small thing. It was a gesture made on impulse perhaps, but one made from heart, body, mind and soul, from the very core of his being. 'Now we are friends' was the simple response from Mr Kuentz but one that turned the world of Passchendaele upside down. And it is the very same thing that we are seeking to do with strategic thinking today – to turn our world upside down.

Sue Palmer is Head Teacher of Farley Nursery School, near Salisbury, in the heart of the beautiful Wiltshire countryside. This school is different from other schools for the very young, where children spend most of their time in their classrooms. At Farley, the opposite is true. Youngsters spend as much of their time as possible outdoors, 'planting, growing, investigating' and this helps them gain awareness and respect for their environment. In practice, this 'outdoor learning ethos' translates into huge benefits for the children. They learn better through play, their level of confidence and independence is enhanced and, most important of all, they have lots of fun. Being in the fresh air also brings better health and resistance to germs. And the children's language ability advances more quickly as it has more meaning to them in the context of their everyday world. Sue Palmer talks of being on a voyage of discovery with her children. When she previously taught in a primary school she noticed how much the children wanted to be outside and how playtimes were the highlight of their day. So when she started her own nursery school she decided to give the children free access to the garden:

> 'What followed was that the children have chosen to be outside most of the time: the doors are never closed. Their minds are open to the wonders of nature. They experience the changing seasons first hand and the learning opportunities just follow: our children really are able to learn through their play. Our prime aim and ethos has remained unchanged, and that is simply that happy children learn.'

Thinking differently is not easy. It is hard to stand out from the crowd. How easy it would be for Farley Nursery School to follow the classroom intensive experience of other schools, particularly with the intense pressure that is put on schools to perform against standard national criteria (that fail to account for many of the intangible benefits that Farley offers). At a personal level, none of us wants to be ridiculed or thought a fool. Yet, in literature, it is so often the fool who possesses the real wisdom. If only King Lear had listened more intently to the Fool, think how much suffering he could have saved. But then, of course, there would have been no story. And in many parts of the world the consequences for thinking out of turn are far worse. It can take great courage to risk challenging the status quo and we need a healthy sense of self-belief to do so. Developing this self-acceptance and certainty of purpose is a core part of our leadership journey, as we shall see later on in this book. But first, we must define what we mean by strategic thinking more fully.

Moving beyond accepted wisdom

Accepted wisdom is not always the best foundation for tackling problems. In the sixteenth century, bathing, especially in hot water, was frowned upon as a health risk. Physicians believed that water aided the spread of disease by cleaning out the pores in the skin, thus making it easier for disease to enter. The young Louis XIII of France did not take a bath until he was seven years old. Elizabeth I bathed only once a month and her successor, James I, apparently only washed his fingers. When Henri IV of France learned that the Duc de Sully had taken a bath he warned him not to endanger his health further by going out. Instead, the King visited him in Paris 'so that you come to no harm as a result of your recent bath'. It was commonly believed that dirt was a protection against disease and good hygiene was better maintained by wearing materials such as linen, which would absorb sweat from the body. What was not 'drawn out' from the body was masked by heavy perfumes and oils. As a result, when King Louis XIV of France died his feet had significantly corroded away. Of course, our knowledge of microbiology and the advance of modern medicine have changed our view. It is now dirt that is the common enemy and we have learned not only to clean ourselves all over but also to clean our surrounding environment to limit the spread of disease. After all, who knows how many germs may lurk on kitchen cloths and work surfaces? To our parents' generation this comes across as faintly ridiculous as they have always known that a 'little bit of dirt is good for you' in building resistance to disease. There is a delicate point of balance in any way of thinking or acting.

Strategic thinking is the very opposite to relying on accepted wisdom. Its foundation is the ability to see the whole and extract significant patterns from it. I define it as *'the intuitive ability to see the whole'*. Thinking strategically means building the capacity to probe more deeply, which involves putting aside the space for reflection *before* action. It doesn't necessarily imply rejecting common beliefs but it does require questioning and evaluating them from a wider, more holistic perspective. It is not only the beliefs of others that we need to question. Far more critical is to take a good look at our *own* beliefs and assumptions. These significantly colour the way in which we see the world around us in ways that are often hidden to us. The key is becoming more conscious of our habitual response mechanisms so that we can open up to the possibility of new thinking and new outcomes. Becoming aware of deeply engrained ways of thinking (and challenging the assumptions that underlie these belief patterns) is one of the most powerful ways of developing the ability to think more deeply and effectively. It also means that we begin to take full responsibility, an essential prerequisite for becoming a leader.

Paradox at the heart of strategy and leadership

'Take away paradox from the thinker and you have a professor.'
Soren Kierkegaard

There is an essential paradox operating at the heart of strategic thinking. The larger the problems, the greater the urgency and the more difficult they appear to be, the more important it is for us to move slowly, reflecting deeply before we commit to action. How frustrating! And there's more to come because the bigger the challenges and issues, the more important it is for us to take small incremental steps rather than great leaps into the dark. This may seem unadventurous, perhaps even dull, but it is often in the summation of small acts that the greatest changes are made. This is, after all, the not-so-secret recipe for success for many of the most admired Japanese corporations, such as Honda and Toyota. This is no way negates the importance of having a clear vision for the future or pragmatic opportunism. When we are open to the wider world, with a clear view of what we are seeking to achieve, we can act quickly and decisively, seizing opportunities and grasping possibilities that others simply cannot see. The irony is that to be able to act decisively and effectively we must first master the lesson of slowing down and thinking reflectively.

Leadership and strategy are full of paradoxes; the recognition that apparently self-contradictory statements can exist simultaneously. Not 'either/or' but both. Indeed, paradoxes (and anomalies that do not appear to conform to existing ways of thinking) are useful because they alert us to deeper relationships that lie beneath the surface of our existing knowledge. We can only learn from this, however, if we take notice of those peculiarities and irritants that rise to the surface level of our lives. It is very easy to dismiss these as nothing more than a nuisance. Nothing could be further from the truth. They are, in fact, life's biggest learning opportunities. The exception proves the rule is an old English idiom. It means that the exception *tests* the rule. We are wise to take the original meaning because it keeps our minds open to new interpretations, insights and possibilities. In the last chapter I mentioned that one recommended way of reducing our carbon footprint was to shift our food consumption down the food chain, switching to a more plant based diet and reducing the amount of meat we eat. Intuitively this makes sense. But is it right? Statistically, raising cattle requires more energy than growing the equivalent amount of grains, fruits and vegetables. So whilst most produce requires two calories of fossil-energy fuel to cultivate one calorie of food energy, the ratio for beef can be as high as 80:1. So, case proven? Well, not quite. We might begin by recognising that this is simply an indication of how things *are*, not how things *could* be.

There is a wider system at work in raising cattle and we can make changes to it. We could, for example, switch from feeding cows grain to using grass instead and also eliminate the use of fertiliser (using local manure as an alternative). We might consider moving from large industrial farms (which guzzle fossil fuels and have lengthy distribution systems) to smaller, more localised, lots. We could also take greater account of the characteristics of the local environment and habitat, since some agricultural land is not suitable for other crops and there is no direct opportunity cost to raising animals on it. It might also be worth remembering that cows trample decaying matter into the soil, which helps keep carbon dioxide out of the air. All these factors would reduce the associated carbon emissions from raising cattle. In practice, this is only the beginning of the thinking process and it is not important here what the 'right' answer is. New approaches will directly affect the cost of producing beef, which might double under some of these scenarios. At the end of the day, 'one size fits all' solutions will not work. Instead, we can learn to observe and respect natural systems and learn from them. Barbara Damrosch and Eliot Coleman, organic gardeners in Maine, are doing just this and are planning to raise grass-fed beef to help *slow* climate change. 'The idea that giving up meat is the solution for the world's ills is ridiculous', says Coleman, 'we'll be able to use (natural) manure to feed the plants, and the plant waste to feed the animals … and even though we can't eat the grass, we'll be turning it into something we can.'

It is not the amount of stuff we process in a day that truly matters. It is the underlying *quality* of the decisions we make. This means giving our work the gift of our time. Time spent in reflection. Time to dig more deeply. Time to sit up and take notice of those things that don't quite 'square up'. For if we do, we often find nuggets of gold that would normally be swept under the carpet or be explained away. Hopefully, by doing so, we will be able to move away from Bart Simpson's definition of paradox, 'you're damned if you do and damned if you don't'!

Focusing on the long term

We live in a world that is preoccupied with the short term. Indeed, we are biologically wired to focus on short-term problem resolution. After all, this is what has been critical for our survival in the past. Unfortunately, something important has happened over the course of the last two millennia. Our ability to affect the whole as a result of our individual actions has been steadily increasing. The cumulative effect of our short-term actions is now affecting our long-term survival. Climate change is one very topical example. Theories suggest that there is a 25 to 30 year lag between our current behaviour and its effect on the environment. Our survival as a species depends on us building the capacity to develop long-term solutions, which may not play out in our own lifetimes. Our focus needs to move into the future while our attention remains squarely in the present (which is the 'secret' behind successfully manifesting our dreams and visions rather than simply daydreaming). This is a very difficult balance to maintain and we all need plenty of practice at it. But it is important. It will enable us to create a better world (or perhaps prevent disaster), not only for ourselves but also for our children and our grandchildren. We are ready to become stewards of our world.

In practical terms, this means taking responsibility for the negative consequences of our actions as well as the positive ones, both for ourselves and for others affected by our behaviour. This requires space for reflection, freeing up our time from day-to-day clutter to look more closely at how our actions affect the whole. Naturally, this is something that is easier to write about than to practice! When we are stuck in traffic, desperately late for a meeting, the last thing we feel like doing is to give way to drivers merging from the side. Yet this is the best course of action to ensure that the system as a whole continues to flow effectively. And, guess what. If a sufficient number of us behave more courteously on the road we will, over time, change the rules of the game for the benefit of all. The next time we are horribly late there will be a greater chance that somebody will let us in when we most need it. We are effectively trading off short-term advantage for long-term gain (which is exactly what we need to do for many of the most pressing problems that face our world). Ironically, this trade-off has other, less obvious, advantages. We are able, for example, to incorporate feedback *as* we make decisions (allowing us to seize unforeseen opportunities along the way) rather than long afterwards (when we are reduced to rectifying matters that have gone awry). Sadly, this approach goes against the grain for many of us who prefer to follow the old adage that 'a bird in the hand is worth two in the bush'. Our thinking is conditioned to prioritise a small actual advantage over the chance of a greater one. This worked reasonably well for most of our history when short-term survival was the critical issue. It does not work well for us today. It is, in fact, the path to our destruction.

Taking valuable time to develop a long-term orientation may be a leap of faith in a world where we are constantly told that we need to act quickly (or more truthfully, *re*act) to get to grips with the sheer scale and urgency of the big issues before us. Slowing down certainly appears to be counter-intuitive in this context. But acknowledging our relationship with the whole and making decisions accordingly is the only sustainable approach over the long term. The evidence is all around us. Highly successful and industry 'busting' organisations such as Apple, eBay, Honda and Toyota, have all thrived by having clear long term visions *and* paying meticulous attention to detail in the here and now (in other words, focus in the future but attention squarely in the present). These organisations are often radical in their thinking (they can sometimes be very radical indeed) but they place enormous importance on getting things right and building incrementally for the long term. Step by step. On the other hand, organisations that are marked by the search for 'silver bullet' solutions, extensive re-engineering and cost cutting exercises (GM and Chrysler spring to mind) are often those in terminal decline. Preoccupation with the short term is frequently characterised by lack of consistency in core purpose and objectives, frequent 'U' turns in strategy and lack of follow-through disciplines in execution. It rarely results in reinvention, which is what is really required.

Digging deeper

To develop our capabilities in strategic thinking we must be prepared to go deeper. We will be entering a world that is often paradoxical and reflects more fully the complex nature of the universe, the interconnectedness of all things and the nature of our relationship within it. This world will seem strange to us because we are not used to thinking or living like this. For most of us, it is a huge leap forward because it requires nothing less than a change in our consciousness. We move from a universe with 'me' placed firmly in the centre to one in which we participate as part of the whole. A funny thing then happens. Once we make this transition we are inevitably hit with the realization that we are incredibly fortunate to be here. We begin to see the world as an unbelievably beautiful place, one that nurtures us but also needs our protection. We stop seeing others as 'they' and begin to see them as 'us'. For maybe the first time in our lives we begin to accept real responsibility for the whole, and this opens us up to all kinds of previously invisible opportunities. It is a magical process that is hard to describe but we know it when we experience it. Rusty Schweickart, Apollo 9 astronaut, describes how walking in space was the event that changed his perspective of life. He not only saw the 'big picture' but also had a deep sense of his interconnectedness with it. He was able to see the Earth as a whole, recognising the paradox of this holistic viewpoint: there are no boundaries because we are all part of that whole:

> 'You recall staring out there at the spectacle that went before your eyes. Because now you're no longer inside something with a window looking out at the picture, but you're out there and what you've got around your head is a goldfish bowl and there are no boundaries. There are no frames, no boundaries.'

Sometimes, like Rusty Schweickart, this realization comes as a 'big bang', resulting from some life changing or highly traumatic experience. For Gerald Durrell, it was the despair that came from seeing the devastating impact of human activities on animals and their habitats. It led him directly to his life's work as a naturalist. In addition to setting up Jersey Zoo in 1959 (now called the Durrell Conservation Wildlife Trust), his many books, TV and radio broadcasts have helped millions of people to reconnect with animals and share his delight in discovering the natural world. Lee Durrell, Gerald's wife, summarises his achievement as compelling people to reconnect with animals and 'rediscover the link that binds us together as living beings.' Naturalist and broadcaster, David Attenborough, who shares the same passion, has picked up the baton. He has been presenting natural history programmes on the BBC for over 50 years and is best known for writing and presenting the 'Life' series, a monumental achievement that surveys all life on our planet. His wildlife filmmaking has become the benchmark for all those working in natural history and it has brought a deep appreciation of the beauty and sanctity of the natural world to millions of people. Such achievements are only possible when we think and act from our entire being.

The same process is often true for people who become seriously ill. When my children were much younger we used to visit a traditional toyshop run by Andrew Farrow in the market town of Devizes in Wiltshire. In late 2006, he fell out of a tree while pruning some branches and consequently spent 14 months in hospital, coming out with no sensation, movement or function below his armpits. His spinal cord injury is 'complete', which means he will not recover and will never walk again. For most of us this would be our worst nightmare. But when you meet Andrew he is not only upbeat and optimistic but he also radiates a deep love of life. I bumped into him recently having coffee and I made the mistake of tempering a comment with a qualifying remark, such as 'under the circumstances'. He corrected me immediately, telling me that he was incredibly lucky and loved life just as it is. He writes a very informative and moving blog (*liveyourpotential.co.uk*) and is currently retraining to be a primary school teacher. His page on the Prince's Charities website simply says, 'Life is good and full of excitements!'

For most of us, the transition in perspective from 'me' to 'we' is likely to take a little more time. It may, and often does, take a lifetime. Sometimes it happens so slowly that we don't even realize how much we've changed. If you don't believe me, try simply chatting with some folks in their 80's and 90's. You will be amazed at how much wisdom and humility can be packed into a single human being! This is, of course, one of the many reasons why elders are revered in traditional societies, something that we have, sadly, largely forgotten. Now would be a very good time for us to 'remember' our elders by giving them the respect that they deserve and integrating their wisdom back into the community.

Seeing the whole – mind, body, heart and soul

'The ability to understand is in every one of us.
We all understand more than we believe we do.
*The most important thing is to learn to **really** look.'*
Graeme Sims, The Dog Whisperer

Learning to think strategically requires us to use our full set of human abilities, our heads (mind/intellect), hearts (feelings), bodies (senses and experience) and soul or spirit (our connection with the whole). This may not be easy to understand at first because most of us rely heavily on just one part of that equation. As our society is strongly head-based we tend to favour intellectual decisions based on a rational scientific paradigm that sees us as separate from the world around us. This certainly dominates our work arena (at least on the surface), where we rely on external measures of success rather than internal ones. This has a distinct downside because, as Albert Einstein observed, 'not everything that can be counted counts, and not everything that counts can be counted.' Thinking strategically requires us to become more aware of all our human abilities, the broad summation of who we are. We can then bring the full package into our working lives and unlock the potential that lies within. And the best place to begin this journey is by observing how we currently think. It is easy to recognise that we invariably favour some parts of our nature over others. It may be the heart ('people are the most important thing after all'), the body ('I go on my gut feeling if the decision is important'), the soul ('we have a moral responsibility to the Earth') or the mind ('this is an ideal situation in which to use this model'). Although we are all different, we do share enough common characteristics to be able to be grouped into core personality types that share common ways of interpreting the world and acting in it. These can be a very useful first base for developing our thinking process.

Psychological profiling techniques (such as Myers-Briggs, the Enneagram system, the Birkman Personality Test or Colour Profiling) are widely used in management and career development, recruitment, coaching and team building exercises to enable us to understand others and ourselves more fully. They provide a very practical foundation for assessing our individual preferences and also open up a valuable window into the way others think and behave. This helps us to understand more fully how we choose to see the world and how this limits our thinking. We can then recognise and acknowledge our strengths as well as identifying areas and perspectives where we are less comfortable. More importantly, these tools can also jump start a process that allows us, over time, to move towards a more holistic thinking approach, drawing from both conventional 'left brain' analytical methodologies and more creative 'right brain' modalities. Although the 'left' and 'right' brain typologies are simplistic (current research indicates that both hemispheres of the brain are used in almost all tasks) there does appear to be a difference in the way in which they operate. The 'left' brain specialises in narrowly focused attention, while the 'right' brain is used for broader tasks. Thinking strategically requires the use of both aspects: attention to detail (analytical and structural aspects associated with the left brain) and an ability to see the wood from the trees (a relational aspect associated with the right brain). This takes practice and patience.

Tools and techniques are useful but only part of the process of getting to know our whole selves better. Reflection and observation are also critical, as is feedback from others whom we trust. All these approaches help us recognise and honour our intuitive abilities, our 'gut feel'. We might call this 'instinct', 'intuition', business 'savvy', a finely tuned sense of opportunity or countless other things. It is nothing new to the many entrepreneurs and senior business leaders who rely heavily on gut feeling to make critical decisions. Most immerse themselves in the facts and figures first but then use their intuition to make the ultimate decision. Some leaders are more outspoken about this process than others, none more so than Steve

Jobs, CEO of Apple. Intuition plays a key role in strategic decision-making across the company. In an interview with *Fortune Magazine* in March 2008 he talked about the role of intuition in recruitment at senior level:

> *'Recruiting is hard. It's just finding the needles in the haystack. We do it ourselves and we spend a lot of time at it. I've participated in the hiring of maybe 5,000-plus people in my life. So I take it very seriously. You can't know enough in a one-hour interview. So, in the end, it's ultimately based on your gut. How do I feel about this person? What are they like when they're challenged? Why are they here? I ask everybody that: Why are they here? The answers themselves are not what you're looking for. It's the meta data.'*

My entrepreneurial clients would agree with Steve Jobs. 'Gut feel' plays a similarly important role in their endeavours. Many other business leaders concur. Carly Fiorina, formerly CEO of Hewlett Packard, talks of the importance of 'a strong internal compass' at the core of leadership and the need to 'engage your heart, your gut, and your mind in every decision you make'. Apparently, Masaru Ikuba, founder and Chairman of Sony, had a personal ritual for making important decisions. He would drink herbal tea and ask himself, 'should I make this deal or not?' If the tea gave him indigestion, he wouldn't make it. 'I trust my gut,' he said, 'and I know how it works. My mind is not that smart, but my body is.' Simon Woodroffe, founder and Chairman of YO! Sushi restaurants, talks of researching a project thoroughly for three months in order to gather the knowledge base needed to make a decision and then 'the rest is intuition – does it feel right?' And it is not just senior business executives who recognise the importance of drawing from a deeper well. We *all* do so on occasions and for many people it is part of their day-to-day job.

The key to thinking strategically is to dig deeper and to become much more conscious of the assumptions that lie behind our thinking. When we learn to do so, we open up into a new world, one that is full of potential and opportunity. We begin to develop the ability to see the whole and understand our relationship with it more fully. At first, we may have only glimpses of this world, but over time, and with practice, our perspective becomes both wider and broader. We learn to see more clearly with effort. Making the transition into this state is not done through the mind alone. It is done through our entire being, all the essential characteristics that make us human: mind, body, heart and soul. It is part of our journey to becoming fully integrated human beings.

Working at our full potential

There are many people who work with their whole selves. They are not necessarily leaders in any conventional sense, or in positions of power and wealth. Sometimes we have to look a little harder to find them because their abilities are 'common sense' in the context within which they work. They include health care professionals, teachers, police officers and driving instructors, all of whom work with people in areas where quick decision-making is vital at critical moments. We recognise this most often in crisis. The New York firefighters who ran up the stairwells of the World Trade Tower as the building was crumbling on that fateful day in September 2001 are rightly acknowledged as heroes. But firefighter, Louie Cacchioli, who was buried in the collapsing rubble of Tower Two that day, rejects the term. 'I was just doing my job,' he says, 'I don't consider myself doing anything out of the ordinary in going to a fire … If there's a chance of saving lives, that's your first priority.' That priority led to 343 firefighters dying that day as they rushed up the stairs of the burning towers and helped countless people to escape by guiding them down. We don't have to look at dramatic events, however, to see what happens when people draw on their entire being in everyday life. It is literally all around us. Those who work with animals provide a good example.

Graeme Sims has earned his living training dogs. He has demonstrated dog skills to millions of people in over 7,000 dog shows. His book, *The Dog Whisperer*, is dedicated to closing the communication gap between dogs and their owners. 'Dog whispering starts and finishes with understanding', he writes 'and, however good the dog might be, if you don't try to understand what it is thinking you stand no chance at all of succeeding.' Understanding your dog requires communicating through body language and expression (the dog's normal communication channels), something humans rarely do consciously. As a result, we need to draw upon a set of skills that we are not accustomed to using. In essence, what Graeme is advocating is raising our awareness, both of how our dogs communicate and of ourselves. If we are ready to accept this we can begin to learn to speak dog. It works. Our small terrier, 'Buddha', is very self-willed and loves to chase animals. As we live in a rural area we need to be constantly alert. But every so often fate gets the better of us. On several occasions we have been climbing to the top of a hill on a fine summer's day and we realise too late that a flock of sheep is lazily chewing away at the grass on the other side. Buddha is off, rounding up the sheep (although he has had no formal training to do so) and we are left to whistle for his return. He always comes back swiftly, overriding his natural instinct as a result of the bond that we have built between us. It's never more than a minute or two. As Graeme concludes:

'If you walked along our valley road and looked up at the hills you would see a man working fifteen dogs precisely, to the inch. Then you might say, 'I can do that because I only have to manage it with one!''

Interestingly, Grahame Sims' first basic rule with a puppy is to build a strong bond of trust. That becomes the foundation for working with your dog and learning to communicate with him or her at a deeper level. This is true not only of dogs. Establishing a bond of trust is critical for all those who work with animals. Dr Lynn Rogers has become known as the 'Jane Goodall of the bears' by earning the trust of wild bears and then observing them at close quarters in their natural environment. By doing so he has been able to conduct research that brings into serious question many of the current beliefs we have about bear behaviour. His findings indicate that black bears are the most timid and 'safe' large mammals in North America, in stark contrast to mainstream belief and media hype. In reality, just three people have been killed by black bears in the Eastern United States in the past 100 years. In comparison more people have been killed by lightning strikes or vending machines than by bears. Ted Oakes, writing in *BBC Wildlife Magazine*, sums up as follows:

> *'One memory that will stay with me forever is the sight of Lynn coaxing a huge male bear out of the forest onto a weighing scale on a dark night. The bear weighed nearly 226kg and had been blinded in one eye years ago by a poacher with a shotgun. Yet this wild bear, "One-eyed Jack", who had no reason to be friendly to humans, silently allowed Lynn to stroke his fur and touch his claws while investigating his wounds. That moment spoke volumes about both Lynn and the true nature of black bears.'*

Maybe this all seems far removed from finding solutions to our pressing day-to-day problems. Not at all. By becoming more fully human and embracing all the facets of our being we open up possibilities that we could never previously have imagined. Jane Goodall, the primatologist renowned for her research on great apes, talks of being inspired by the 'extraordinary people who have rescued species from the brink of extinction when everybody else laughed at them.' One example she gives is the Californian Condor. At one time there were just twelve birds remaining in the wild, whereas there are now some 300. 'This bird would have gone,' she comments, 'but for a small group of people who would not give up. As long as we have people like that, there's hope for the future.' We too can achieve the 'impossible'. But I must issue a word of caution. It is best to start from a position of humility. As Graeme Sims remarks, 'one difference between dogs and people is that dogs don't deceive themselves.' So, it is wise to start at the beginning and then gradually open up to our full potential. It is not a process that can be rushed. It will take the time it takes. Our job is simply to be with the process. As Graeme remarks:

'In this book the "simple" is profound. Each step is like a staircase. If you attempt to jump a step, the top will never be reached and even the very simple will understand that there Is only one place to start.'

So it is with each one of us. We don't have to change the world in one fell swoop. We certainly don't have to solve complex problems all on our own. We begin by one simple step, looking at the way we think and learning to dig a little deeper.

Beginning the journey

Developing our capabilities in strategic thinking opens up enormous opportunities. But it can also be very frustrating. As the old saying goes, 'we don't know what we don't know'. Often, in the early stages, we find ourselves moving from a position of *unconscious* incompetence to *conscious* incompetence. This doesn't always feel like progress! The path before us to *conscious* competence is full of practical difficulties and pitfalls. Although we begin to recognise the limitations in our existing approach and sense the potential of 'joining up the dots', the practical application may continue to evade us. I could, of course, cast a positive light on this or minimise the practical difficulties in the hope of selling more copies of this book. It wouldn't alter the facts. Time and performance pressures often force us back into the 'here and now' of short-term solutions and tactical strategies. The 'real world' kicks back and it can really hurt. We vacillate when we suggest more radical solutions with a longer-term perspective. Those around us sense our lack of commitment and we falter. We fear being seen as too idealist, too naïve, too impractical or even too caring. We don't have a response to the battle cry, 'we need strong action *now* to turn this situation around.' So we fall back on the known, the 'tried and true' approach that has worked (or not worked) so well in the past. We regroup to fight our position another day. Welcome to the world of strategic thinking. This is how it is.

For much of the time we may feel that we lack the organisational support, commitment, patience and often the resources, to take a longer-term strategic view. Similarly, while we may have a clear vision of what we want to achieve, we may find it difficult to communicate and execute our vision in the face of numerous, practical, financial, resource and political pressures. It is for these reasons that I wrote *The Strategic Mind* around seven key disciplines that form the basis for developing our ability to think at a deeper and more profound level. The book also demonstrates the practical application of each key principle in case studies that cover corporate, voluntary and public sector organisations. There are clear benefits in breaking down a subject as complex as strategic thinking into 'bite sized chunks', so that key principles can be practiced and applied in specific contexts to help gain support and commitment from others. It is worth revisiting these seven key disciplines briefly in this book before we move on to the practical application of these principles within the context of strategic leadership.

The seven disciplines of strategic thinking

At first sight some of the seven disciplines may appear counter intuitive ('act slowly'), while others will be more familiar ('dream') but they are all vitally important and work as an integrated whole. They are:

- Know your own story
- Think small
- Go slowly
- Serve others
- Reflect
- Be simple
- Dream

Know your own story

The foundation for success for both individuals and organisations alike is to know who we are and what we stand for, both in terms of where we come from (our background, family and history) and where we are going (our purpose and vision). Authenticity and originality are intimately connected with success. In *The Strategic Mind* I looked at the achievements of Virgin and Apple, amongst other organisations, to see how this works in practice.

Think small

We understand intuitively that vision is critical to strategic leadership but we often overlook that so is attention to detail. Successful organisations tend to obsess over the 'small' stuff because they appreciate how important detail is in the successful execution of strategy. They don't forget that 'big' things are always built from small beginnings using an iterative step-by-step process. Moreover, what may appear on the surface to be an insignificant detail often turns out to be far more important than it seems! Entrepreneurs willingly embrace this paradox. They have a strong sense of vision combined with a tendency to 'meddle' with day-to-day operations. They know intuitively that the 'small' things need to be right to make the 'big' vision possible. At a practical level, some of the largest and most successful organisations today are also built on an almost obsessive attention to detail. In *The Strategic Mind* I explored this principle through a variety of case studies including Amazon, Wikipedia, Fish Records and the Prince's Trust.

Go slowly

Things that are built on solid foundations tend to last. The ability to be flexible and adaptable (and make decisions quickly when necessary) comes, paradoxically, from the time spent knowing who we are and what we stand for. It is interesting to reflect upon the fact that the seeds of the largest plants and trees spend their early life entirely underground in the darkness, getting ready for the right time and conditions to shoot for the sun. Honda, Toyota, The National Trust and the Wildlife Trusts in the United Kingdom were some of the organisations that I used in *The Strategic Mind* to illustrate this principle.

Serve others

No one and no thing exists in isolation; we are all in relationship with everything else. Serving others moves us from a position of pushing our 'stuff' out towards others to aligning ourselves to meeting the needs of the greater whole, thus acknowledging the web of life and tapping into the synchronicity that lies within. This fundamental principle lies at the heart of holistic thinking; if we cannot see ourselves in relationship but fall prey to the 'illusion of independence' we will always be limited to a partial understanding of the whole. I explored Starbucks, Care for the Family, Cafédirect and two successful schools in *The Strategic Mind* to see how this principle works in practice.

Reflect

Reflection is the lynch pin of strategic thinking. We cannot access a deeper part of ourselves and the inherent wisdom contained therein unless we put some time aside to do so, time spent away from the constant demands of our hectic day-to-day schedules. This time can be spent in a formal practice, such as meditation or yoga, but it can equally be centred on walking, exercise, sport or being in nature. It is not so much *what* we do as becoming conscious of the importance of slowing down, observing and reflecting before acting. Reflection is the foundation of strategic thinking and it is the most difficult discipline to put into practice. I looked extensively at BP in *The Strategic Mind* and examined how John Browne, its former CEO, built an enduring legacy at the company, leaving BP as a highly successful commercial organisation and a strategic leader in green energy.

Be simple

Simplicity plays a critical, and largely unrecognised, role in defining strategic and competitive advantage. The ability to focus on our task in hand is one of the key determinants of successfully meeting our key goals and objectives. It allows us to direct our energy in a purposeful manner, avoiding fragmentation and distraction. Simplicity in life allows us to reduce the baggage that we carry around with us and makes us far more flexible and adaptable in our personal and working lives. It works even better within organisations where 'complexity creep' can reduce innovation, creativity and sometimes even the will to live of the people who work there! In *The Strategic Mind* I looked at organisations such as eBay, Pret a Manger, Innocent Drinks and Waitrose, where a 'less is more' philosophy is a key element of their success.

Dream

There is nothing as powerful as a dream. We instinctively recognise the truth in this statement but the process by which our dreams become a reality is far less obvious. Some dreams come from a positive vision of a better place or a sense of opportunity of what *could* be. Many, however, reflect some area of our lives where we have either experienced pain or where things simply aren't working as well as we would like. Dreams often lurk in the shadows, occasionally arising directly from the most painful experiences of our lives. It is our desire to mitigate this pain for ourselves and for others that often drives us to change the circumstances that led to it. The process of revealing and energising these dreams – at the simplest level a better way of doing things than we have experienced – provides the commitment and passion to make them a reality. We often look at people who are regarded as great leaders and comment that they have made the impossible happen. So can we all! I explored the power of dreams in *The Strategic Mind* through the stories of Apple, the International Centre for Families in Business, Tilley Endurables and Garth Brooks.

Holistic discipline

Naturally, in practice, the disciplines of strategic thinking overlap and form an integrated whole. In addition, learning to think strategically is not a solitary pursuit. The act of sharing our insights with our colleagues and friends brings another deeper dimension to the process. We often find ourselves in the frustrating position of *almost* knowing something. It's as if we are two-thirds of the way there but we just can't put those final parts of the jigsaw together. Then a work colleague or friend mentions something (perhaps not even directly relevant to the issue at hand) and we know we finally have it. The feeling when this happens is almost always the same, '*how* did I manage to miss this?' There is great synergy in working together with others. We can do this through formalised processes such as workshops, techniques such as story-telling and scenario analysis, or numerous other routine work-based practices. Alternatively we can do it informally by simply 'hanging out' and spending time together. It is easy to dismiss the profundity of this process because it is so normal. Strange as it may seem, I find that the 'simple' act of bringing people together around an agenda of walking in nature, followed by some form of structured debate can yield astounding insights and unblock all manner of seemingly intractable problems. This process combines the power of creating a reflective space, in a particularly positive environment, with the synergistic effects of working together in groups.

Bringing it all together

There are two clear dimensions to strategic leadership. The first is developing the ability to think at a deeper and more profound level. The second is to use this knowledge in practice as a leader. *The Strategic Mind* was written primarily as a resource for doing the former. This book has the leadership dimension clearly at its core. As a result, the two books can be read together profitably to gain greater insight into how both dimensions work together. This is not necessary, however, and I have structured each book so that it can be read independently without serious loss of meaning or content. We will now shift emphasis and begin looking at the practical application of strategic thinking to leadership and move away from the process of strategic thinking itself. But before we do, there remains one very important thing that needs to be said. What happens if, despite all our commitment and intentions, we find that we are not very good at developing an holistic perspective? Does this mean that we cannot be strategic leaders? Absolutely not!

Both my sons are mildly autistic with a condition known as 'Asperger's Syndrome'. This makes their thinking *less* flexible and adaptable than their peers. My youngest son, Jamie, finds it difficult to see the 'big picture' when it comes to homework assignments or practical matters such as what the teacher's expectations are likely to be for a particular piece of work. However, in his areas of interest (the sciences, particularly environmental science) he has his own intuitive way of connecting the dots. When I studied mathematics at school I slavishly learned all the formulas and methodologies because without them I was lost. I do maths by rote, or I don't do it at all. Jamie, on the other hand, seems to have developed mathematical shortcuts that leave me far behind. Even in the early years of high school, when I would sometimes castigate him for not following due process (his school books were often utterly unintelligible!), he inevitably had the right answer. When I ask him now how he does something he simply replies, 'it's obvious dad', and I am none the wiser. Recognising our unique abilities and learning to accept rather than fear differences is at the heart of strategic thinking. This is, of course, another paradox. Generally, we are seeking to broaden and deepen our thinking, yet at the same time we need to encourage different types of thinking, some of which will have the opposite characteristics. The reason is simple. Taken as a whole, our world needs access to the broadest and deepest ways of thinking to solve some of the challenges that we now face. Autism provides a perfect example.

The shift from seeing autism as a disease caused by early emotional trauma to a condition based on genetics is quite recent. This has very powerful practical implications as the following letter from Professor Michael Fitzgerald of Trinity College, Dublin, published by the National Autistic Society in Winter 2009, demonstrates. It is entitled *The Age of Autism*:

'We have entered the age of autism. The 20th century was the age of psychoanalysis, with its catastrophic and inaccurate view of autism ... The great developments in the 21st century will be driven by persons with high-functioning autism, although this has been true since the industrial revolution and the Age of Enlightenment. These were peak times for persons with high-functioning autism. Indeed, the Second World War was shortened by almost two years by a person with high-functioning autism, Alan Turing, who was involved in breaking the Enigma code. Global warming in the 21st century will, in all likelihood, be best dealt with by people with high-functioning autism. Indeed, if homo-sapiens are to survive in the very long term, after the sun burns out, it will be up to persons with high-functioning autism to find alternative means of survival for the human race.'

We are all born with different characteristics, personalities and abilities. We are absolutely unique. None of us is completely balanced or 'normal' in this respect. Some of us will find strategic thinking easier than others. This has nothing to do with whether we are successful or talented or not. In *The Strategic Mind* I explored how Sir Richard Branson has forged a business empire partly because, and not despite, being dyslexic. Other examples of people who have suffered with dyslexia include Winston Churchill, Walt Disney, Pablo Picasso and Albert Einstein (one of the truly great thinkers of all time!). We can all learn to think more deeply and profoundly but there will be some natural boundaries and limitations, depending on our personal make-up. Our objective is to find that natural place of balance and consciousness, where we can combine our new thinking skills with our own unique natural talents and gifts. Whether we work alone, or more likely with others, we are then in a position to help move our workplace, community or even our whole society forwards towards a more balanced, healthy and sustainable world. That requires working together, each of us coming from the place where we can contribute most (our 'x' factor if you will) to the efforts of the whole.

Becoming leaders – the courage to commit to action

In a world full of people, only some want to fly.
Isn't that crazy?
Seal

We think that we are a great deal cleverer than we really are. We also believe that we are in control and that bigger is best. Worst of all, we see ourselves as independent of the natural world. These are all unhelpful belief systems and one of our tasks is to question these assumptions and to discover the deeper truths that lie within. If we don't, our hubris (lack of balance) will be met quickly with nemesis (a return to balance, often in a distinctly unpleasant way). We are hampered in this task by reliance on over simplistic models and frameworks that do not reflect the complexity, diversity and interrelationships that underlie the natural order. As a result, we tend to adopt policies that offer only short-term partial solutions (often with unforeseen effects for the system as a whole) and some that can only be described as insane (the mistaken use of bio-fuels is a prime example). Ironically, our action orientation and our desire to move quickly may benefit us personally, but they rarely produce sustainable results over the long term. Sadly, when our existing ideas, models and action plans are questioned (or even debunked) we often resort to the path of least resistance, taking no action at all. We put our head in the sand, depressed by the enormity of it all and our own seeming inability to make a difference. We are wrong of course. Each one of us can make an enormous difference and that is what this book is about.

We all have critical roles to play. We can all become leaders in our own way. We fool ourselves, however, if we believe that we can change the world solely by the clarity of our thinking or by the creativity of our new ideas. There will always be healthy resistance to new ways of thinking before they are integrated into the mainstream and become accepted practice. The path of leadership is inevitably messy. As nineteenth century philosopher, Arthur Schopenhauer, wisely observed, 'all truth passes through three stages. First, it is ridiculed. Second, it is violently opposed. Third, it is accepted as being self-evident.' Walter Bagehot put the same point more humorously, 'The greatest pleasure in life is doing what people say you cannot do.' The questioning of accepted truth is an essential prerequisite of the role of any leader. The very foundation of leadership is the capacity to think differently and to have the courage to commit that insight into action. Part 2 of this book looks at the process of developing the courage and commitment to become a leader. It covers seven key elements of that process: taking responsibility, developing the ability to see the big picture, acting on behalf of others, achieving simplicity and clarity of purpose, going with the flow, accessing our full power and developing the courage to act. We begin in the next chapter with the importance of knowing ourselves and taking full responsibility for our actions. In the words of the Lao-Tse (the 'Old Master'), the Chinese sage in the six century BC who is associated with writing the Tao Te Ching and the founder of Taoism:

'A tree as big around as you can reach starts with a small seed: a thousand mile journey starts with one step.'

PART 2

BECOMING A STRATEGIC LEADER

... and by-and-by Pooh and Piglet went on again.
The wind was behind them now so they didn't have to shout.
Rabbit's clever,' said Pooh thoughtfully.
'Yes,' said Piglet, 'Rabbit's clever.'
'And he has Brain.'
'Yes,' said Piglet, 'Rabbit has Brain.'
'I suppose,' said Pooh, 'that's why he never understands
anything.'

A. A. Milne, The House at Pooh Corner

3
TAKING RESPONSIBILITY

'Our remedies oft in ourselves do lie,
Which we ascribe to heaven.'
William Shakespeare, All's Well That Ends Well

Leaders in action

In the shadow of Auschwitz, a flamboyant German industrialist became a living legend to the Jews of Krakow, the ancient capital of Poland. During the course of the war, Oskar Schindler, a member of the Nazi party, renowned womaniser and war profiteer, saved the lives of more than 1,000 Jewish people from certain death. The magnitude of this achievement can scarcely be imagined. In Poland today there are less than 5,000 Jews, compared with the three million who called Poland their home before the Second World War. The descendents of 'Schindler's Jews' number more than 6,000. Throughout the worst horrors of the Holocaust, Schindler achieved the unimaginable.

It is often easier, and a good deal more interesting, to witness leadership in action than to read about it in theory. We know it when we see it. That Oskar Schindler was an exceptional man is not in doubt even though there are many things we do not know. Did Schindler have a vision of what he sought to achieve? Did he dare anticipate a future that, in the eyes of all those around him, was simply impossible? Or did he react to events as best he could, driven by a sense of inevitability in what he had chosen to do. We simply don't know. What the Jewish prisoners under him remember is that there was an almost God-like certainty in the promises that he made to them, one that defied all logic. It seems that Schindler himself was deeply influenced by the Talmudic verse that states, 'Whoever saves one life, saves the world entire.' What is very clear is that Schindler was a man who knew himself deeply and had an unshakeable certainty in his quest. Many other recognised leaders from widely different backgrounds and contexts share these same characteristics.

Mikhail Gorbachev, former leader of the Soviet Union, was a man of the Soviet system. If it had been otherwise he would never have risen to the ultimate position of power, General Secretary of the Communist Party. Although he didn't set out to be a revolutionary he *was* a man rooted in his own truth and it was this that enabled him to act so decisively when he came to power. Zdenek Mlynar, a young Czech communist, who later played a pivotal role in the ill-fated Prague Spring liberalisation in 1968, was Gorbachev's best friend at Moscow State University. 'We are talking about a man,' he recalls, 'who attributes more importance to his own experience, lived and felt, than to what is decreed on paper.' These experiences included Gorbachev's pre-war childhood in a peasant family in Southern Russia, two grandfathers caught in Stalin's repression and family stories of the famine caused by forced collectivisation in one of Russia's most fertile regions.

Gorbachev was a man who believed foremost in what his ears and eyes told him at a time when the Soviet Union was in deep denial about the everyday reality of life under the communist system. This deeply held belief in personal experience led directly to his policies of political and economic restructuring ('perestroika') and his determination to introduce greater openness and transparency ('glasnost'). In an extraordinary chain of events this resulted, in quick order, in the freeing of Eastern Europe, the ending of the Cold War and political supremacy of the Communist Party and, finally, to the dissolution of the Soviet Union itself. It was the absolute sense of certainty about who and what he was that allowed the Soviet Leader to take on the impossible, to assume total responsibility for changing the system, however insurmountable that challenge may have appeared. As he said at the time, 'if not me, who? And if not now, when?' These are strong impactful words, which is why Barack Obama has since taken up this rallying call.

Other leaders show the same ability to see things differently and then take action, regardless of the size of the issue or problem they confront. Ex-President Jimmy Carter has played a very significant role in reducing the scourge of guinea worm disease. Fewer than 10,000 people in five African countries are still afflicted today compared with 3.5 million people when he started his work with the Carter Center in 1988. His passion for fighting the disease was born when he saw its horrifying and devastating effects, both on individual sufferers and on their villages. Whole communities would go hungry because the farmers were too sick to work in the fields. What made the difference, however, was his ability to see the issue in the light of his childhood memories in rural Georgia:

> *'I know that when farmers are ill, their families and communities suffer as well. I'm also aware that proper health care is a basic human right, thanks to the superb treatment I received at a clinic in my hometown of Plains and the abiding example of my mother Lillian. A registered nurse, she taught me that lesson every time she ministered, free of charge when necessary, to any person, black or white, in the segregated South of my youth.'*

It is this unique insight into the devastation of the disease combined with his deep-seated compassion for fellow human beings that has allowed Jimmy Carter to act so decisively over the last twenty years and make such a dramatic difference. In short, leaders take responsibility for acting in the here and now, based on a firm commitment to their purpose and a deep certainty in who they are and their place in history. In doing so they often bring a different perspective to the problems that they face, one that is born both from personal experience and from the uniqueness of their life stories.

Responsibility lies with me

*'Nobody made a greater mistake than he who did nothing
because he could only do a little.'*
Edmund Burke

It is easy to persuade ourselves that leaders are special people who
possess unique talents and gifts, which, sadly, we do not. If we are
feeling uncharitable we may even point out some of the favourable
circumstances enjoyed by others (positional power and authority,
resources, connections, 'right timing' and so on) and contrast this
with our own, more meagre, circumstances. We may also believe
that we are too small to matter. 'What can *I* do,' we ask ourselves
'that would *really* make a difference? Our next sentence may begin
with the words, 'if only' but is more likely to be a general
pronouncement that somebody *else* should take responsibility for
the problem (management, the company and government are but
three of the normal candidates for blame in this exercise). We are
effectively passing responsibility to somebody else and, more
subtly; we are moving it into the future. Strategic leaders rarely use
the words 'if only' and they *do* accept responsibility in the here and
now, at this very moment. It's as simple as that. Taking
responsibility is the keystone for strategic leadership. As Edmund
Burke, the Irish philosopher, said so memorably, 'all that is
necessary for the triumph of evil is that good men do nothing.'

It is a natural human tendency to underestimate the difficulties
of others and overestimate our own. We are normally very happy to
judge our colleagues (what clarity hindsight brings!) but hide behind
the inherent uncertainty of the future when we make our own
decisions. The first step towards leadership is to take full
responsibility for our actions *no matter what*. We are then free to
move away from criticising others and take more notice of what
stops us from moving ahead with those things that are truly
important to us. It is for this reason that I define strategic leadership
as the capacity to think strategically *and* the capacity to act upon it.
Whether or not Oskar Schindler had a grand strategy, he acted on
his belief in the sanctity of life. Regardless of the risk involved,

Mikhail Gorbachev set about reforming the moribund system of the Soviet Union. And Jimmy Carter took practical action to eradicate the scourge of Guinea worm, regardless of the enormous difficulties that confronted him at the time. 'Some people see things and ask why,' remarked Robert Kennedy, 'I see things and ask, why not?' But before we take action we do need to be very clear about who we are and what we stand for. As Winston Churchill observed of history, 'the longer you look back, the farther you can see forward.' We sometimes have to be prepared to make that journey back into our own personal history and background to gain the sense of clarity and certainty that underpins our ability to make a lasting impact on the external world.

The better we know ourselves, the deeper our self-understanding, the more effective we will be. For some of us this deeper knowledge may mean that we stop the whirlwind of activity for a while. If we are acting out of a sense of responsibility that is external, one that is thrust upon us rather than coming directly from our own internal conviction, we will always lack effectiveness. We may move ahead, but it will only be through expending great effort. In short, this is an exhausting way of doing things, somewhat akin to a salmon swimming upstream but without the obvious inducement. It can be physically and emotionally draining, often debilitating and frequently ends up being counter-productive. For some of us, however, it is a habit that has been acquired early in our lives and we are not fully conscious of it. Our parents or carers encouraged us to take on too much responsibility too early. We were pushed to become decision makers when, in reality, we still needed the support and care of others. So, the journey will be different for each of us depending on our nature, upbringing and experiences. Some of us will need to develop the courage to act on our deeply held convictions, whereas others would gain most by slowing down first and searching inwards to find that place of deep conviction and self-knowledge. But for all of us, the rule is *intention comes before attention*. Intention is an inside job. Attention provides the focus in the outside world. Both are important but so is the order in which we do them. *As within so without*. That is the rule. As stories are often our best teachers, it's time to see these principles in action in leaders who are making a very significant difference in their work.

The Prince of Wales

The Prince of Wales was born into responsibility. There were no other options available. It's a tough and demanding path to inherit, one few of us would choose voluntarily. What is remarkable, however, is how the Prince of Wales has transformed that external responsibility into a powerful and passionate internal commitment based on a deep-seated belief in justice, fairness, equity, balance and stewardship of the natural world. He has been a 'thought leader' in our society long before that term was invented (and suffered the consequences in the early days as his contrarian views were belittled or dismissed by the mainstream). What a difference a couple of decade makes. Many of his ideas are now seen as very prescient and well ahead of their time. He is currently engaged in a huge variety of projects that range from environmental causes and education through to providing opportunities for those on the sidelines of our society. There is a common theme that lies at the core of all these projects. It is the acknowledgement that we are one. This simple spiritual truth binds together the environmental charities, organic food ventures and business/social endeavours that the Prince of Wales has launched, nurtured and supported over the years. It is his sense of the sacred that underlies his passionate commitment for supporting causes that protect our shared humanity and release the untapped potential of those who are cast adrift by society by rebuilding a sense of community and common endeavour.

The Prince's Trust was founded in 1976, almost 35 years ago, with the help of £7,500 in Royal Naval severance pay. It exists to support and encourage those who are disadvantaged or excluded in some way. It provides small loans to those seeking to start a business, as well as offering courses for additional training, personal development and support in getting a job. The Trust helps some of the most disadvantaged groups in Britain and has been an outstanding success. Since 1976 it has helped nearly 600,000 young people, 70,000 of whom have set up their own business with loans from the organisation. Indeed, after four years, half the businesses funded are still trading profitably, a very successful outcome in the current business environment. In 2008 alone the Trust spent nearly £35 million on charitable activities and supported over 40,000 young people. By keeping grants and loans small (and the latter repayable) businesses are encouraged to take personal responsibility and it works. The development programmes offer invaluable business skills and also a sense of social inclusion, providing broad benefits to our communities. It is this mix between the caring ethos and the practical training skills that The Prince's Trust provides, which makes it a uniquely successful organisation. One that can make a dramatic difference in the lives of so many young people.

The Prince of Wales also has a transformational role to play in many other areas. The Prince's Rainforests Project, for example, is a direct appeal for us to come together to adopt innovative policies to slow down the rate of deforestation and, eventually, to halt it completely. It is a widely based global organisation, set up in 2007, which includes public, private and NGO partnerships, with the goal of 'making the forests worth more alive than dead.' The Prince of Wales is in no doubt about the importance of the venture, 'success would literally transform the situation,' he says, 'for our children and grandchildren and for every species on the planet.' In common with many of the endeavours of the Prince of Wales, it has resulted from his willingness to think differently, his courage to adopt new ways of doing things and his capability and commitment to act upon his belief.

Starbucks

Like all highly successful global companies that have fallen on hard times Starbucks has its fair share of detractors. When the company started to struggle visibly in 2007-2008, it coincided with my choice to feature it as a prominent case study in *The Strategic Mind* (as an exemplar for 'serve others', one of the seven disciplines of strategic thinking). Briefly, I am slightly ashamed to admit, I debated substituting something less controversial but I'm pleased that I quickly came to my senses. We don't live in a perfect world populated with magical organizations with 20:20 visions. We live in a very real world where even successful companies stumble, often as a result of their own arrogance or other self inflicted wounds. We learn more by looking at companies that are in the thick of it than producing an ever-changing merry-go-round of contemporary successes. Starbucks has stayed.

We will be looking at different aspects of Starbucks during this book but I would like to concentrate here on one of the key drivers of its business proposition: creating a sense of community and following through with making the world a better place within that context. This will lead us back to the idea of responsibility that is embedded within Starbucks' culture, and its origins in the beliefs of its CEO and founder, Howard Schultz. Along the way we will discuss the tension that inevitably results from the conflict between a business model founded on a boutique Italian coffee shop and the realities of running a global enterprise. But it's best to start at the beginning. The defining moment for Howard Schultz came when he was Director of Marketing and Operations for Starbucks, then a very young concern. He visited Italy and was bowled over by the coffee bars on every street corner, which served excellent espresso and acted as the social glue for Italian society, a meeting place for the community. It was these two elements that he has since tried to reproduce and replicate. The essential proposition of Starbucks was always to 'serve a great cup of coffee' but this was not all. The defining principle of the endeavour was 'to build a company with soul'. Arguably, Starbucks has succeeded remarkably well with these two core elements. It is with replication, an essential element of building a global business, that things began to go seriously awry, resulting over time in over-expansion and a 'watering down' of the core customer experience.

The timing of Starbucks' ill-advised race for growth couldn't have been worse. Just as the company was beginning to face up to the self-inflicted problems caused by overexpansion, the global credit crunch hit, followed by deep recession. The 'feel-good' lifestyle product of the 1990's quickly became an over-priced luxury in the new economic reality. To make matters worse, two well-armed competitors, McDonald's and Dunkin' Donuts, took aim at Starbucks with cheaper versions of its upscale coffee product. Since then Starbucks has had a savage time of it, with steep declines in profitability and share price. Large numbers of stores have been closed, significant cost cutting has been put in place and more effective management practices have been introduced. Many conventional business practices that were out of the question in the boom period (noticeably advertising and consumer research) have been introduced. Starbucks has come of age and it is looking, well, rather more like a traditional corporate entity. As I write this, the severe medicine seems to be working and fourth quarter sales in 2009 point towards stabilization and a potential turnaround. A deal signed with Subway to serve Starbucks' 'Seattle's Best' coffee in half its outlets in the US (and a further 800 stores in Canada) may mark the beginning of a resurgence for the company and the beginning of a new, more modest, era of growth. No point emphasizes this more than the highly controversial introduction of a new instant coffee, 'Via', aimed primarily at the $17 billion retail market in the United States.

Riding the tiger

Being the CEO of a major corporation engaged in a tough turnaround project is not a place for the fainthearted. When you are in charge of a brand as familiar as Starbucks, which is under attack from all sides, it would be easy to feel unloved. This is especially true when the company is well placed to serve as 'whipping boy' for everything from the fear of American cultural domination to anti-globalization protestors. For some people, Howard Schultz can do nothing right. In their eyes, Starbucks has come to symbolize everything that is wrong with the capitalist corporate model; faceless uniformity combined with the maximization of profits at the expense of the community. This is, of course, grossly unfair and inaccurate. However, it is well worth remembering, because it indicates just how difficult Howard Schultz's task really is. That task is not just about returning Starbucks to profitability and growth. It is far more than that. Schultz wants to remain true to the original vision for the company, one that treated its staff and partners exceptionally well and worked towards making the world a better place. A company with soul. One thing is abundantly clear when you read through the interviews that Howard Schultz has given over the past few years. He's ready to acknowledge that mistakes have been made. He knows that the company now has to do the conventional business 'stuff' (it's hard to argue with introducing effective supply chain logistics). But it's not what truly motivates him. He's committed because he knows he has to be. But that's not why he's there. What 'lights his fire' is ensuring that Starbucks does not betray its community aspirations. He is a serial entrepreneur who will not give up the vision. He wants Starbucks to be both a successful well-run business and a unique force for good in society. He's riding the tiger and that's one hell of a place to be.

Working with entrepreneurs has taught me to pay special attention to their background and early years. When Starbucks began to expand rapidly in the 1990's Schultz insisted on a full range of employee benefits that were unprecedented in the retail industry at that time because they covered part time workers. All employees working at least 20 hours a week were given comprehensive health coverage, including cover for unmarried spouses. He also introduced a generous employee stock option plan at the same time, resulting in high staff loyalty and low turnover. This was part of the 'soul' of the company and it has its roots in Schultz's own humble beginnings. He was born and raised in New York in a housing project in Brooklyn. His father, Fred, had numerous low paying jobs including taxi driver, factory worker and truck driver, but he didn't stay long enough in any of them to gain significant benefits. When he suffered injury at work he had neither health insurance nor workers' compensation to help the family through the difficult times. 'He was beaten down, he wasn't respected,' Schultz recalls, 'He was an uneducated man, a war veteran, and unfortunately he never quite got his piece of the American dream. I've always wanted to build the kind of company my father never got the chance to work for, in which people were respected.' Is this a dream worth building a company for? In the case of Schultz the answer is 'absolutely' and he is not about to let that dream go.

There are many who contest whether it is possible to manage the tensions inherent in such an enterprise but Howard Schultz is a classic entrepreneur: 'optimistic, relentless, mercurial, and eager to prove people wrong'. In an interview with *Business Week* in August 2009 he consistently remarks that 'I love to be the underdog', a reference back to the early days when success at the Starbucks venture was far from assured. This is an extraordinary statement from the boss of one of the best-known brands on the planet, and the most followed company on Facebook. He's not about to give up on his mission anytime soon! Taking responsibility for others, whether employees, partners or local community, is in the DNA of Starbucks and it will remain so as long as Howard Schultz is at the top. If the day arrives when he departs for pastures new, we can be sure that any new venture he founds will be based on the same fundamental principles. Schultz is not averse to enjoying his wealth and, at one time, was a billionaire. That is no longer the case, but it doesn't worry him. 'I never wanted to be on any billionaire list,' he says, 'I never define myself by net worth. I always try to define myself by my values.' He goes on to define this further and it is interesting that he does so in relational terms, his role within the community. 'My mother taught me something at a young age – she said "you are the company you keep". To define yourself by some label or some level of resources – that's pretty shallow.'

Welcome to the Apple family

Taking responsibility is an inside job. It is most self-evident when we take the initiative to reach out to the external world, to improve the lives of those immediately around us, to the broader community, or even to the world as a whole. At its roots, it is the unique expression of who we are at our deepest level writ large in the world. It may have little to do with the expression of external compassion or making the world better. It is simply what really makes us tick made manifest. In January 2010, Steve Jobs, CEO of Apple, introduced the company's new, heavily anticipated, touch screen tablet, suitably called the iPad. He was greeted with a massive media blitz of the kind that is normally reserved for media celebrities. Apple's boss hailed the device, which had jokingly been called the 'Jesus Tablet', a 'truly magical and revolutionary product'. Few commentators disagreed with him, given Apple's record on innovation and its proven track record of transforming the computing, music and telecom industries. *Time Magazine* referred to Steve Jobs as a 'veritable Innovator Bunny' and *The Economist* dubbed him as 'mercurial and visionary', adding that his record suggests that when he blesses a market it takes off. 'Tablet computing promises to transform not just one industry,' it declared, 'but three; computing, telecoms and media'. To prove a point, it blessed Apple's boss by including a picture of him on its front cover wearing suitably beatific robes and wearing a golden halo under the title, 'The Book of Jobs'. Competitors have learned to fear Apple when it moves into their territory, and with good reason.

No other contemporary business leader is as lionized as Steve Jobs in today's world and Apple is one of the very few global companies that can claim to be phenomenally successful yet counter-cultural at the same time. It is also fearsomely competitive and is regularly voted the most innovative company in the world. For those of us who have switched to Apple products the old adage still remains true, once an Apple user always an Apple user. I remember the experience of buying my first iMac very well. As I left the shopping mall, the silver Apple logo prominently displayed on the side of my box, a German couple remarked, 'you will never regret this – we bought our first Apple two years ago and it has changed our lives.' This is customer advocacy to die for and most Apple users still feel part of the 'Apple family'. In fact, a good friend of mine chastised me for not taking a picture of myself with the box. This is, apparently, an established custom among Apple users to celebrate and remember their first purchase. We will be looking at Apple several times throughout this book but I want to concentrate here on the relationship between Apple's fearsome record of innovation and the man who steers it.

Taking responsibility for Steve Jobs means not accepting anything that is not perfectly aligned with his vision of what *could* be. It is stretching the limits of what is possible beyond the definition of the word. It is achieving the impossible. Why? Because Apple's boss expresses the deepest part of himself through that innovative process and because, no matter what the rest of the world has to say, he *knows* what is 'right'. This sense of being right does not come from the head. It comes directly from the gut, so Steve Jobs knows when not to compromise. No amount of head based analysis will convince him if it runs counter to his intuition. Apple is not in the business of releasing half-baked 'beta' products. It is in the business of producing beautifully stylish consumer products and services that work seamlessly. Nothing else will do. Compromise is not an option. This allows Apple to take the high ground. It adopts product categories that don't work properly, or fulfil their full potential, and then moves them into that place. And, it does so seamlessly, with such apparent (although undoubtedly deceptive) ease. Apple does not invent new product categories. It excels at showing the world how to making existing half-baked ideas actually work. If something doesn't function properly, it bugs Steve Jobs and he sets about the process of making it do so. The Macintosh computer, the iPod and the iPhone are all classic examples of this restless and relentless need for product technology to reach its potential. This undoubtedly makes him a very demanding person to work for, particularly when he insists on full commitment and won't accept anything less than 'perfection'. As a result, however, Apple has already transformed the computer, music and telecoms markets. It is now adding media to that list. No wonder the iPad has been so widely anticipated.

The dance of personality, authenticity and creativity

'Accidents and inspiration lead you to your destination.'
Mary Chapin Carpenter

Few of us can hope to emulate the success of Steve Jobs, Howard Schultz or the Prince of Wales in our lives. Looking at (some of) the key factors that underlie Steve Jobs' ability to create an endless flow of innovative products, for example, may help us improve our own follow through capabilities, but there is a natural limit to how effective this 'benchmarking' process can be. At the end of the day, we are who we are, not somebody else. The real lesson on offer is not how to be more like the strategic leaders we have looked at. It is how to be true to ourselves and tap into the power that comes from aligning our path with our unique abilities and talents. The entrepreneurs that I work with are often difficult people. They can be self-centred and demanding, lack a sense of balance and obsess about what they do. They rarely describe themselves as well-rounded human beings. Most are engaged '24/7' in their work, if not physically then certainly mentally and emotionally. And, they expect others to share that commitment. Howard Schultz, CEO of Starbucks, talks of having to learn the positive effects of a balanced working life. 'I've gotten much better about this,' he says, 'I try to be home for dinner with my family most nights. I've learned a balanced personal life makes for a more productive business life.' But it doesn't come easily to many of our most dynamic business leaders. The most important thing we gain by looking at their stories is that they are aligned and *this* is the root of their ability to make a difference, whatever their endeavour may be and however they choose to express it.

Self-expression is a dance between our personality, our creative approach to life, and our ability to remain resolutely authentic in a world where compromising our values often seems to offer the best reward. We begin by getting to know both our story and ourselves. In *The Strategic Mind*, I looked briefly at Sir Richard Branson's story and how his dyslexia has heavily influenced his journey. This is not fluff. It gets to the very heart of what Sir Richard Branson is all about and why he has made the choices he has. Most importantly, it explains many of the seemingly paradoxical aspects of his character and helps us see him as a real person rather than as a caricature based on the superficial 'hero or villain' mythology that so pervades our society. Something important then happens. We begin to glimpse the real person. We lose our ability to demonize them by unconsciously transferring the less desirable aspects of our own personality onto them or, alternatively, making them an unrealistic fantasy figure by imbuing them with our unrealized dreams and aspirations. Having worked extensively with Virgin for several years I have no doubt that Sir Richard Branson is a wholly genuine person with a deep desire to make the world a better place. I can hold the contradictory aspects of his nature without judging them and concentrate on his achievements. The key lies in understanding that Sir Richard is exactly who he appears to be, neither sinner nor saint, but a man who has forged a hugely successful career out of his early traumatic experience. He is a man who knows his story and lives it.

The journey to knowing ourselves fully and learning to express ourselves from this deep place is normally one that takes a lifetime. It is the making of us as leaders but it is not easy. It is often punctuated with unpleasant surprises and, sometimes, painful experiences. These forge us into who we are and what we can become. We develop the courage to step out into the world and act upon what matters to us most. This is always deeply intertwined with our most authentic self-expression. This provides us with the focus, courage, knowledge and inner strength (based on our natural gifts, talents and abilities) to become a strategic leader. Nicholas Lore, founder of the Rockport Institute, an international career counselling network, talks of the power of the 'wholehearted acceptance of one's own individual nature' being a much more profound form of personal growth than change. 'Most of the people we most admire,' he says, 'reached their level of achievement not by changing into somebody else but by embracing their natures fully and using their personalities as instruments of self expression.' The object is not to change but to become who we are. In that journey experience is often our best teacher. And, sadly, I don't know of any shortcuts, not ones that work in any case. I have come to see the wisdom in H. L. Mencken's dictum, 'every complex problem has a simple solution that doesn't work.' Real work takes time and effort. And lots of it. Period.

The Enneagram system

> 'The Enneagram is probably the most open ended and dynamic of typologies ... (it) indicates with startling clarity certain constellations of meaning about something that is essentially beyond definition: the mystery that we are.'
> **The Enneagram Institute**

I don't believe in 'quick fixes'. I am suspicious of anything that promises enlightenment or mastery in any field in 'ten easy steps' or as a result of following some simple set of practices. Let alone something as complex as leadership. Growing as a leader takes time, commitment and plenty of hard work. Studies suggest that the key to success in almost any field is practice and lots of it. As a rough rule of thumb we need to practice for 10,000 hours (roughly ten years at 20 hours each week) to build sufficient skills to master something ('the 10,000 hour rule' as Malcolm Gladwell calls it). But that doesn't mean that we can't access useful tools and techniques along the way. Psychometric models, such as the Myers Briggs Personality Indicator, are useful reflective exercises, which can help us learn more about who we are, how we function and what steps we can take to work more effectively with others. After all, developing leadership ability requires not only a high degree of self-awareness but also an understanding of how those around us think and act. In my own case, I have found that the Enneagram system, which dates back to the ancient Greeks and Pythagoras in the sixth century BC, has provided the most profound transformative insights.

The Enneagram is primarily a system for self-understanding but I have also found it extremely useful for working with clients on developing their leadership skills. This is not, unfortunately, the place to extol all the virtues of the Enneagram. It is too subtle and complex a system for that. For our purposes here, I am using it principally as an illustration of a particularly powerful tool that can help us on our journey to becoming a strategic leader by providing insight into who we are. It is based on nine core personality types and the spiritual concept that identifying and transforming the negative characteristics of our personality type brings us into our own true power. Unlike many other common psychometric tests, however, recognizing our basic type is only the beginning of the journey. Each core personality type is influenced by a number of factors and by looking at these we gain a practical understanding of the intricacies of who we are, one which is far more profound than is immediately apparent from the overall descriptions of the core personality types. The power of the Enneagram is in its ability to open us up to our potential by becoming more conscious and less identified with our ego. It also allows us to respond to others with compassion and understanding, to begin to see the real 'whole' person rather than responding mechanistically through habit to their surface personality structure. For this reason, it is particularly insightful for developing a strategic perspective, one that is, by nature, holistic. Finally, whilst the Enneagram is not intended to be a cheap party trick to categorise others (whom we don't really know) it does offer profound insight into many of our greatest leaders because it is possible to recognize key patterns and behaviours in their stories. This is especially true with entrepreneurs who have founded organizations that vividly contain the imprint of their personalities. Interestingly, most of the leaders discussed in this chapter appear to share the same Enneagram type, a point worth contemplating in its own right.

The Enneagram is principally an oral tradition and this is how I first studied it, by listening to the stories of others and finding the personality type that fitted me best. That is, I believe, still the best way of approaching the system. However, given the time constraints that many of us face, it may be more practical to begin with an introductory book. I would recommend *The Enneagram, A Private Session with the World's Greatest Psychologist* by Simon

Parke as an excellent starting place. It has two distinct selling points. It is good and it is short. As Simon says in the introduction, 'it is my belief that we do not know ourselves; that we organize most of our suffering ourselves, and we abort most of our happiness before it can be born. This is an unfortunate way to live. For as Socrates once said, "Once we know ourselves, we may learn to care for ourselves – but otherwise, we never shall."'

Following our star

> *'Knowing is not enough; we must apply. Willing is not enough; we must do.'*
> **Goethe**

In many cases the most heroic and impactful acts of personal leadership are between individuals and remain largely invisible to the rest of the world. Almost anyone who has made their mark in the world will tell of members of their families, friends, formal and informal mentors and other 'silent' supporters who stood behind them and made their journey possible. We can never be sure how our input plays out in the wider world. It is unlikely that the name, Miep Gies, will mean much to you. In 1933, on the strength of her jam-making skills, she joined Otto Frank's pectin factory in Amsterdam as a secretary. When, in 1941, Otto asked Mrs Gies, 'Are you willing to take on the responsibility of taking care of us when we are in hiding?', her response was 'of course.' For 25 months between 1942 and 1944 Mrs Gies hid eight Jews in four rooms above Otto's office; four members of the Frank family, three from the van Pels family and a dentist whose name was Dr Pfeffer. There was no question of saying 'no', she only wished she could do more.

Miep Gies was a refugee herself. She was born in Vienna in 1909 but, with little food in a country traumatized by the aftermath of the Great War, her mother sent her away to the Netherlands at the age of 11. She always remembered her first drink of frothy milk with her new Dutch family, her warm bed and how 'so many hands had reached out to guide me' on her first day of school. Although she was helped in looking after her charges by her friends and husband, Jan, it was Miep Gies who automatically took charge. She delivered food and supplies each day for over two years, bringing in news and doing her best to keep up the spirits of the Jewish families. When they were finally arrested in 1944 she gathered up and hid the pages of a diary written by Otto's daughter in blank account books smuggled from her office. She never read it but gave it to Otto, the only one of her charges to survive, after the war ended. The name of Otto's daughter was, of course, Anne.

Knowing our story and what really matters to us enables us to build the courage to act. To become strategic leaders, however, we also need to know *where* to act. This requires us to see the big picture, to be able to see the whole, which is the subject of the next chapter.

4
SEEING THE WHOLE

*'I've looked at life from both sides now
From up and down, and still somehow
It's life's illusions I recall
I really don't know life at all.'*
Joni Mitchell, Both Sides Now

Starting with the big picture

John Law was a Scottish lawyer who had a weakness for women and gambling, so it is no surprise that he ended his days in poverty. He was also a brilliant mathematician with a keen interest in probability. He was born in 1671 but was forced to flee to France after he killed a rival in a duel in 1714. There, he renewed his acquaintance with the Duke of Orleans who was Regent for the young Louis XV, then only five years old. France was reeling in debt after years of reckless spending under Louis XIV. The Duke, remembering Law's financial and mathematical prowess, sought his advice to sort out the State finances. Law was highly innovative in his approach. He persuaded the French to set up a paper currency backed by the new Bank Générale rather than silver and gold. The world's first 'fiat currency' had been born. Law hoped that the significant increase in money supply would boost commercial activity, which would fill the government's coffers with additional tax revenues. This was, however, just the beginning of his financial inventiveness. He was nothing if not a man of vision.

In 1717, Law set up the Compagnie d'Occident (later more commonly known as the 'Mississippi Company'), a vehicle to finance trading opportunities between France and its North American colonies. This convenient combination of running a bank and operating a major trading company was, at first, a marriage made in heaven. Law was effectively financing new trading opportunities through an increase in the paper-based money supply, backed by the absolute authority of the monarchy. Handily, the money that was raised through share issues was available to pay back government debt. Everybody won! Indeed, the scheme appeared to be a perfect virtuous cycle, especially as people could only guess at what riches lay waiting in the New World. In today's language, Law had engineered a massive increase in the money supply and organised a stimulus package simultaneously. Not bad thinking for the beginning of the eighteenth century. For a while, things went splendidly well, so much so that Law began to acquire trading rights in Africa, China and the East Indies to expand his business empire. Share prices in the Mississippi Company rocketed as a classic asset bubble set in. Then, as in so many cases since, things began to go seriously awry. Inflated asset prices fuelled future expectations and the system began to feed upon itself.

The Louisiana colony, as French territory in North America was then called, stretched for 3,000 miles from the mouth of the Mississippi into Canada. Unfortunately, the main focus of Law's plans, the Mississippi Delta, turned out to be a mosquito-infested swamp and up to 80% of the early colonists died. It quickly became apparent that revenues would not be sufficient to pay the promised dividends to shareholders. For a while Law was able to stave off disaster by financing dividends from new share capital, which could be issued at highly inflated values as a result of hyperbolic expectations. Ultimately, of course, the system crashed, with disastrous consequences for both the investors and for France. It would be a further 80 years before France again introduced a paper currency and, in historical terms, this marked the high-water mark for the nation's territorial ambitions in North America. By 1803 it was all over. France signed over its remaining colonies to the United States in what is known as the 'The Louisiana Purchase'. In addition, the nation's finances remained weak throughout the eighteenth century, one of the key factors that helped trigger the French revolution in 1789.

It pays to look at the big picture. Sometimes it is essential to do so. One of the lessons that we can take away from John Law's venture is that attempts to maintain asset prices above their real value are doomed to fail. Economic fundamentals are important. In 2010 many developed economies may be tempted to try to avoid the painful restructuring that is now clearly necessary as a result of the loose financial policies and cheap credit that led to the global recession of 2008. No matter what policies are adopted (and many that we currently employ would be strangely familiar to John Law) we can learn from the debacle of the Mississippi Company bubble nearly two hundred years ago. Economic wellbeing is grounded in fundamentals and it is these that need to be addressed as our first priority for the future. In reality, it will take several decades for the United Kingdom to unwind its massive debt problem, which will be significantly exacerbated by demographic change. The cost of adjusting to an older population in the UK (sometimes called the 'demographic time bomb') is estimated to be six times the level of the measures taken to stabilise the economy after the credit crunch in 2008. Yet, the retirement age has not changed significantly for more than half a century, despite significant increases in life expectancy. It is time to tackle this issue. And, the sooner the better.

Broadening our vision

Given a rapidly ageing population in most developed countries (with a consequent reduction in the ratio of the working to non-working population) few things make more sense than pushing back the retirement age, probably by ten to fifteen years. This is not, however, merely an evil necessity. Looking at the big picture allows us to significantly reframe the way we look at retirement. If we dispense with the idea that gainful employment necessarily means full time work, we can begin to build a much more natural and healthy transition from full time employment to retirement. This might include part time working, portfolio work, voluntary and community work and family care (grandparents taking an active role in looking after grandchildren). It would also encompass leisure activities that could potentially include as many active elements (sport, walking, education and community events) as passive ones.

This does not mean that we need to remove the safety net for those who are ill or incapacitated. In fact, quite the opposite is true. We are simply recognising that we live, on average, a great deal longer than in previous generations, and we are tapping into the potential that those years bring. By doing so, we could strengthen our families, communities, welfare systems (reallocating resources to more critical areas) and the economy as a whole (utilising key skills and experience and increasing the tax base). It is a 'win win' for both ourselves and for society because it enables us to give something back to future generations during our latter years at the same time as potentially enriching our lives. The tribal councils of many native peoples explicitly take into account the effect of their current decisions on future generations. We may have lost this wisdom for the moment, but setting a more realistic retirement age would be a very good starting point for the process of remembering.

Realistic foundations

None of us is privileged to know the big picture fully or to see the whole. We only sense it. We have flashes of insight, which we can choose to act upon if we wish. To do this, of course, we must first *trust* our instincts. In our daily experience we see only reflections of the whole and it can look very different from alternative viewpoints. Like the well-known Hindu fable of the blind men and the Elephant (later retold by the nineteenth century American poet, John Godfrey Saxe) it all depends on perspective. In the tale, six blind men from Indostan go to see an Elephant hoping to understand the nature of the creature by touching it. They surround the animal and each man feels it from the place where he is. Not surprisingly, each comes to a very different conclusion about what an Elephant is. The first, who is by the Elephant's side, concludes that it must be like a wall. The second grabs a tusk and imagines the beast as a sharp spear. The third takes the squirming trunk in his hands and observes that the

Elephant is very like a snake. The fourth man concludes that the Elephant is like a tree, a reasonable response given that he is feeling the animal's knee. The fifth is holding on to its ear and so imagines a fan. And the sixth, on the basis of groping the Elephant's tail, thinks that it is like a rope. Needless to say, the six blind men cannot agree upon a common definition and all are equally convinced that they are right. They do, however, have something in common. They are all also equally wrong because none of them has seen the whole animal. This is one reason why the most knowledgeable people are often the humblest in their area of expertise. They know what they don't know and that is a great strength. Only politicians claim to know everything and that's hardly a recommendation!

There is a simple exercise that we can do that is very salutary in this respect. Scour the news media and select articles that discuss new knowledge on familiar topics and notice how much traditional 'wisdom' is being questioned every day. In 2009, for example, Gary Packard and his colleagues at Colorado State University published a paper questioning the size of many of the more common dinosaurs. By substituting more complex non-linear models for linear algorithms (to extrapolate overall size from bone size and weight) he concluded that creatures such as the Diplodocus and Brachiosaurus were only half the size that we previously thought. In a similar case, a team led by Bridget Stutchbury, a biologist at York University in Toronto, attached high-tech miniaturised tracking devices to the backs of migrating songbirds to see if they could discover how far the birds travel every day. It turns out that songbirds cover distances up to 500 kilometres a day, more than three times as far as scientists previously thought. They can also travel faster. One purple martin took only 15 days to return from Brazil to its breeding ground in North America. On top of this, the team found considerable differences in the birds' behaviour in the fall and spring migrations. The songbirds' migration rate was two to six times more rapid in the spring. Knowledge rarely stands still. But, sadly, our perspective often does.

Looking at the big picture requires us to bring together our knowledge into some meaningful whole. This is not easy as natural systems are complex and adaptive (and it is not necessarily easy to see the patterns from within the system). There are many reasons, for example, why Britain was the first country to industrialise but there is still room for plenty of debate on their relative importance. Robert Allen, in his book, *The British Industrial Revolution in Global Perspective*, argues that too much emphasis has traditionally been placed on supply-based arguments (scientific advancement, laws, property rights and an adaptive social system) and not enough on demand. He argues that Britain was unique in *one* respect, its combination of high wages and cheap energy in the form of coal. Wages were kept high as a result of the devastating effect of the Black Death followed by trade increasing at a rate that kept pace with the growing population. Other countries didn't fall behind because they were less advantaged in terms of supply factors, but because they lacked the incentive to substitute expensive labour with machinery to exploit an abundant resource. Ironically, Britain lost its competitive edge when it made machines that were more efficient by reducing their consumption of energy, making them cost-effective in countries with more expensive energy. 'The genius of British engineering', Mr Allen concludes, 'undid Britain's comparative advantage.' Observing that a topic that is concerned with events that happened several hundred years ago can still be the subject of healthy debate puts us on notice that we need to be open and humble about the completeness of our knowledge and understanding.

Certainty of purpose

Strategic leaders do not possess 20:20 vision. Nor do they necessarily have special abilities to look beyond day-to-day events and see long-term trends and patterns that are invisible to the rest of us. They do, however, share some common characteristics. They have a clearly defined sense of purpose and remain focused on it even when times are hard. They don't easily accept 'no' for an answer and they are persistent to the point that others may regard as imbalanced. The leaders that I have worked with often imbue a sense of certainty to others, even as they question themselves remorselessly. And, interestingly, they are open to possibilities. They may not know any more about the big picture than we do but they often sense instinctively that the whole is more than the sum of the parts. In short, they see a wealth of opportunity in the world around them and readily seize upon those possibilities that relate most directly to what they are seeking to achieve. They find ways of doing things that those of us who are less persistent, or perhaps more balanced in our lifestyles, do not. When combined with their willingness to take full responsibility, and their ability to act decisively, they not only know *how* to act but *where*. Ironically, entrepreneurs and leaders regularly achieve the 'impossible' because, whilst they often *do* have a unique perspective on the big picture, they refuse to be bound by the 'rules of the game', those assumptions and belief systems that underlie the existing mindset of what is possible and what is not.

When singer-songwriter, Janis Ian, went to meet George 'Shadow' Morton, the man who would be instrumental in signing her to Atlantic Records in the late 1960's, the audition did not go well. Morton barely listened to her first song, hiding instead behind a newspaper that he was, in fact, not reading (something he later described as an 'ugly Brooklyn move'). He waived to her to continue but instead of another song he found himself jumping up and down with his newspaper on fire. Only then did he take the young singer songwriter seriously, eventually not only signing her but also producing some of her early albums. Few of us would act as Janis did on that day. It was the combination of her passion, her certainty around what she wanted to do, and her ability to seize opportunities as and when they arose, that marks her out as a leader. She went on to become one of the premier singer songwriters of her generation, selling millions of records and influencing many others through her confessional song writing style. We can take these leadership characteristics and apply them to virtually any area in life.

Alison Des Forges, a human rights monitor, did more to document the genocide in Rwanda in the mid 1990's than any other person. She also did her best to stop the tragedy by explaining to anybody who was prepared to listen to her exactly what was happening. After the genocide ended (with the Tutsi-led rebel group, the Rwandan Patriotic Front, seizing power from the Hutu government) she meticulously documented the slaughter so that future generations would know what had really gone on. In order to gain evidence she took extraordinary risks. She went to the scenes of massacres and questioned the killers, carefully documenting everything that she heard and witnessed. Mrs Des Forges was steeped in Rwandan history (the subject of her doctoral thesis in 1972) and had plenty of experience on the ground, having spent years in the country investigating political violence for Human Rights Watch. Her deep appreciation of the big picture was vital. She had a much better idea than most people of what might happen when the presidents of Rwanda and Burundi were assassinated in 1994, shot out of the sky when travelling in their luxury jet. This alone, however, does not mark her out as a strategic leader. That distinction results from her single-minded doggedness and persistence to stop at nothing to get to the truth and document it. Few of us have that degree of commitment. In 1993 tens of thousands of civilians were slaughtered in Burundi but it had not attracted the attention of the Western media. Alison believed that this had emboldened the Hutu officers in Rwanda to do the same thing. She told the story of the Rwandan tragedy in all its bloody detail to prevent it happening again, either in Africa or elsewhere. She was able to think strategically, developing a unique perspective into events, and also had the courage to act on that insight. This is the very definition of strategic leadership.

Building our capacity to see the whole

'Learning to draw is really a matter of learning to see – to see correctly – and that means a good deal more than merely looking with the eye.'
Kimon Nicolaides, American painter and teacher

I've been around long enough to know that some people are more adept at seeing the big picture than others. Some of us automatically think in terms of patterns, and are able to draw together seemingly diverse information into a meaningful whole. We don't have to work very hard at it. For others, it is a skill that must be learned more formally, one that requires a discipline of sustained practice. Thankfully, there are some useful frameworks and tools that can help us to make sense of the whole. A useful starting place is the insights from the 'new' sciences, particularly complexity theory. These not only help us to understand the nature of the relationships that make up the whole (and to begin to recognise patterns within these relationships) but also allow us to appreciate the sensitivity of natural systems to small changes within. This, in turn, enables us to move away from the illusions of control and independence that have wreaked such havoc in our world. The scientists who were at the forefront of complexity theory shared an explicit belief that they were looking for the whole and turning back the tide of scientific reductionism. They were establishing scientific principles for a discipline that was to be based on understanding the 'global nature of systems', according to James Gleick, author of the best-selling book, *Chaos, Making of a New Science*:

> *'Watch two bits of foam flowing side by side at the bottom of a waterfall. What can you guess about how close they were at the top? Nothing. As far as standard physics was concerned, God might just as well have taken all those water molecules under the table and shuffled them personally... Tiny differences in input (can) quickly become overwhelming differences in output – a phenomenon given the name "sensitive dependence on initial condition". In weather, for example, this translates into what is only half jokingly known as the Butterfly Effect – the notion that a butterfly stirring the air today in Peking can transform storm systems next month in New York.'*

It is time for the insights from the new sciences to make their way into our everyday world, not least the sensitivity of natural systems to small changes. We are, after all, prone to equate importance with big developments and liable to dismiss minor changes as too insignificant to matter. For many of us, the significance of small changes can be hard to grasp at a practical level, one that relates easily to our personal experience. We are so trained to think in terms of categories and labels that we tend to lose sight of how things relate together within the system as a whole. But it is something that we would be very wise to learn. The over reliance on mathematical and financial modelling by the financial industry is one very pertinent example of the potential cost of not doing so. It is not that relying on models is wrong. Indeed, models play an important role in building a more accurate picture of the world around us by testing theories and mapping relationships to make sense of complex phenomena. The rise of Google as a result of its powerful search algorithms is a startling case of the power of applied mathematics. What is required, however, is the humility to appreciate the assumptions that underlie our models and the limitations that these impose on their decision-making utility. Simply put, we need to remember the vulnerability of any model or framework. As James Gleick concludes, 'In practice, econometric models proved dismally blind to what the future would bring, but many people who should have known better acted as though they believed the results.'

The role of intuition and judgement

So how do we build up a capacity to see the big picture? Firstly, we recognize the complexity of the environment and supplement formal models and analysis with intuition and judgment. Is this not dangerous? I don't believe so. Economists, Michael Goldberg and Roman Frydman, looked at why the financial rating agencies performed better at assessing corporate bonds than collateralized-debt obligations before the financial crisis. One reason was that the agencies used both mathematical models and the expertise of in-house specialists when forecasting the default probabilities of corporate bonds but used only mathematical models for the collateralized debt (partly because the instruments were so new at the time). 'The forecaster is like an entrepreneur,' says Mr. Frydman. 'He uses quantitative methods but also studies history and relies on intuition and judgment.' The problem for the financial agencies was that 'they had no experience, no intuition, no entrepreneur' when it came to many of the new financial instruments that the industry was creating at the time. For a couple of years in the 1990's I worked for an international engineering conglomerate in a financial 'trouble shooting' capacity. This sounds a good deal more glamorous then it actually was. Before commencing any project, I was normally presented with the relevant management accounting information for the subsidiary that I was to going to be working with. Sheer size and density of the information meant that there was no question of taking it anywhere in those days. Over time I learned to completely ignore this official reporting information and begin my assignments with a clean sheet of paper and some meetings booked in my diary with the key people. That simple process kept my mind open to whatever was really going on.

We cannot fully define intuition. It is knowledge that is gained neither by reason nor by perception. Yet it does draw on our lifetime experiences, whether we remember these consciously or not. Many argue that intuition is also based on tapping into the 'collective unconscious', which is often revealed through archetypal imagery and insights (think of the richness in traditional stories and myths). In reality, we simply don't know how the intuitive process works so it is normally a good deal easier to learn to trust our gut feeling and hunches than it is to explain exactly where they comes from. We can certainly learn to be more aware of the value of our experiences (which represent the more conscious level of the intuitive process). These include insights gained from the past, both from our own personal history and those relating to the environment in which we are engaged. Many practical insights are based, for example, on applying experience gained in one area to another. The way that the Great Depression played out has, in an obvious way, critically influenced political decision-making in the recent financial crisis. 'History is bunk', said Henry Ford and he is both right and wrong. He is right in that history never replays itself exactly, so we must be careful of extrapolating too simplistically. He is wrong, however, in believing that history does not have something profound to teach us. It is not in the particular events, but in the repeating patterns and threads of history that we have most to learn. Leaders challenge accepted wisdom and find new approaches and linkages that are overlooked by the mainstream. In doing so they often rely heavily on personal life experiences and intuition.

I remember expressing my worry to the Director of Marketing of a large UK building society in 2006 that bank-lending rates had reached reckless levels by historical standards. He responded with an argument that was based partly on 'special factors' and partly evidenced by how well his organisation was doing in financial terms. I have learned to be very cautious about 'special factors'. In my experience, their appearance tends to go hand in hand with a severe case of over exuberance and they turn out to be 'not-so-special' after all. But financials are more difficult to argue with because we place so much faith in them (often ignoring the assumptions that underlie their preparation). It would be nice to leave this example with the knowledge that my intuition about impending disaster was sound. The truth is, however, that when the conversation took place in 2006 I would have appeared to others to be anything but wise. A much more likely assessment would have been that I was out of touch, overcautious and, no doubt, commercially naïve. Yet, that is the price that we sometimes have to pay for challenging apparently successful dynamics in the short-term because we believe that they are unsustainable in the longer term. It is not easy to challenge conventional wisdom without being made to look a fool. Leaders are, by in large, those who are not frightened by the prospect of looking foolish. Some even relish it.

Celebrating the marginal and the peculiar

One good way of tapping into what is really going on at the bigger level is to look at what doesn't stack up in our everyday world. This is counter-intuitive and we are trained to dismiss the unusual as just that – unusual. By implication, it is not necessarily important to everyday life. We miss a great deal by doing so. There is profound insight to be gained in observing anomalies, exceptions and irregularities that do not square with accepted wisdom. In the language of complexity science we may be able to identify 'emerging phenomena' in the early stages of development before the system as a whole is impacted dramatically. In business jargon, we would be more likely to talk in terms of improving our capability to forecast market changes and trends, foresee the growth of new market sectors or the rise and fall of whole industries. Let's look at a practical example. Steve Jobs, CEO of Apple, and Howard Schultz, CEO of Starbucks, have both talked publicly about why they do not actively seek out customer feedback. Both organisations have traditionally avoided detailed customer research and Starbucks began to consider advertising seriously only in late 2009, as part of its business restructuring. For two highly iconic consumer businesses this appears to be slightly odd to say the least. So, it is worth investigating. One explanation (certainly not the only one) is that the culture of these two organisations is heavily influenced by their leaders. And, both these leaders share similar personality characteristics. There is nothing very startling in that. However, if we apply the lens of the Enneagram personality system to this observation, some potentially very interesting insights arise. Many of our best-known leaders appear to be clustered around specific Enneagram personality types and this enables us to draw some conclusions about why companies such as Apple and Starbucks have been successful and what the more obvious pitfalls are likely to be. The same exercise can be performed in other areas. Artists and media celebrities, for example, show similar clustering effects. As the Enneagram is primarily a self-reflective framework to learn more about who *we* really are, I don't believe it is appropriate to use it out of context here, particularly with people whom I have never met. However, I often work at this level with entrepreneurial and business clients and the insights have been profound. With entrepreneurial clients I find that this thread to my work links me very quickly into the bigger picture and the impact of that can be very significant indeed.

Anomalies and peculiarities often exist at the boundaries of systems so this is a good place to begin to look for what doesn't appear to stack up. When we do, we find something else, something that may surprise us at first. The boundaries of systems are very fertile places. For this reason, Maddy Harland, editor of *Permaculture Magazine,* talks about 'celebrating the marginal' and the importance of edges in the natural world. The edge in nature is a place where different systems interrelate. This often results in a profusion of fertility and diversity. Maddy gives us lots of wonderful natural examples of such places including:

> *'where woodland meets clearing inviting in air and sunshine and a profusion of flowers; where sea and river meet land in the fertile interface of estuaries, full of invertebrates, fish and bird life; where the banks of streams meet the water's edge and fertility is built with deposited mud and sand in flood time, giving life to a riot of plant life... (and) where plains and water meet, flooding and capturing alluvial soils.'*

The rich texture of this language gives us a sense of the power of the edge in natural systems but the same applies equally in human terms. The edge is found where cultural diversity thrives, such as the many meeting points between cultures that exist within global corporations. These are often difficult and challenging places but, paradoxically, those where the greatest learning can take place. Cultural diversity can bring insights born of 'alternative' thinking, particularly if they become places that attract nonconformists or 'outliers', those who think genuinely differently. Such ideas not only bring potential competitive advantage in business terms, they are actually essential for safeguarding the system as a whole in the longer term. Similar innovation and creativity appears at the boundaries between different national and economic systems.

Finland played such as role in the days of the former Soviet Union. If we are looking for inspiration there is no better place to head for than the edge.

Another obvious, but often overlooked, place to build up a view of the whole is to listen to those who speak out against conventional wisdom. In a bull financial market, for example, it is the bears that allow us to challenge accepted behaviour before it becomes too destructive. This is, of course, more difficult than it seems. Outliers and others who hold contrarian views are often arguing in the face of evidence that supports mainstream opinion (such as future expectations at the peak of a bubble). But it is important. Potentially, it allows us to have a foretaste of emerging trends that may dramatically affect the whole system. Even stable environments can be disrupted by unlikely and unpredictable events (that may, in fact, be part of a larger unseen system at work). Such rare, high-impact, occurrences are now generally known as 'black swans' after Nassim Nicholas Taleb's book of the same name in 2007. The term was originally used in sixteenth century London to describe something known to be impossible, since all known swans were white. However, after the discovery of black swans in Western Australia, it came to denote something that was perceived to be impossible at the time but then came to pass.

The interesting thing about 'black swan' events is not that they come out of the blue (for most people) or have a major impact, but that they are quickly rationalised by hindsight and have little impact on the way we think (which is predominantly linear and short term). The challenge of strategic thinking is not to explain things *after* the event. It is to become aware of the deeper long-term cycles and patterns that exist below the surface, and to be open to events *as* they occur. Naturally, no matter how much we understand about the whole, the timing of events will remain unpredictable and some will genuinely hit us out of the blue. But that does not mean that observing anomalies and peculiarities is not a useful process for alerting us to what is happening at a deeper level. The National Trust, for example, monitors lichen on its sites because they are particularly sensitive to climate change. 'Lichens are like canaries down a mine shaft,' says Lichenologist, Bryan Edwards, 'so sensitive to changes in environmental conditions that they are superb bio-monitors and potential indicators of climate change.' As it happens, Britain is particularly conducive for lichen, due to its damp oceanic climate and relatively low levels of atmospheric pollution in the North and West. This ongoing research is part of the vital process of understanding more fully the implications of climate change at a global level. Likewise, the role of the earth's oceans as heat reservoirs is currently getting considerable attention from climate scientists because there are discrepancies in existing models between energy received by the earth from the sun and what is happening to that energy. The oceans' role in storing energy (and then releasing it) may help to explain some of the short term peculiarities in recorded temperatures by deepening our knowledge of climate change systems.

These are both practical examples of research that has resulted from things that are strange in some sense. Being open enough to notice such peculiarities is critical, which makes strategic thinking a challenging and yet creative practice. At the end of the day there is no 'one' way to build a better appreciation of the whole. By far the most important aspect is to remain open; open to possibility, open to things beyond our immediate sensory perception and open to beliefs beyond mainstream opinion. Sometimes, leaders express this in terms of a dogmatic, even inflexible, belief in a better way of doing things. In my work with entrepreneurs and other business leaders I often feel that there is something deeply subjective about the whole process. It is as if the person is continually seeking evidence and opportunity to put into effect what he or she already knows is 'right'. The 'environmental scanning' process that entrepreneurs use is not objective in this sense, it comes from a deep instinct, already honed into what they are seeking to achieve. That is partly why entrepreneurs, such as Sir Richard Branson, are able to fail so many times without giving up. Each failure, to paraphrase Henry Ford, is simply an opportunity for them to begin again more intelligently. That is also why the most important term to describe an entrepreneur is not 'risk taking', 'visionary' or even 'charismatic'. It is 'persistent'. Persistence is not a very exciting word, not at all 'sexy'. But it is arguably *the* most important human characteristic for changing the world for the better. Simply put, without persistence we can never truly be a leader.

The whole business environment

> *'If you put a frog in water and slowly boil it,*
> *the frog will eventually let itself be boiled to death.'*
> **Charles Handy**

Naturally, seeing the bigger picture in business is as difficult as in any other arena in life. Conventional strategic wisdom preaches the importance of establishing a market position that is based on a unique selling proposition ('USP'), one that captures the essence of what makes a company different and allows it to add value to its products and services in a way that is unique in its chosen marketplace. There's nothing new in that. However, to do this successfully, requires a conscious awareness of what is happening to the marketplace as a whole and how it is changing. This is much easier said than done. One of the most common dangers of strategic positioning is that companies find themselves 'stuck in the middle', with no clearly defined value-added proposition. Sainsbury's, a mid-sized British supermarket, has suffered for years with this dilemma. It has found it increasingly hard to compete head-to-head with Tesco, the clear market leader in the UK, in both market share and profitability. For over two decades, it has struggled to respond effectively to Tesco's challenge, unable to decide whether it is a premium food retailer (a territory increasingly dominated by Waitrose and Marks & Spencer) or whether it is value driven, echoing the strategies of Tesco and ADSA. Sainsbury's advertising campaigns have vacillated between the two, causing something of an identity crisis with consumers. While it has lurched from one position to another, it has consistently lost out in the marketplace. As a result, Tesco's market share (some 31%) is now almost double that of Sainsbury's and ASDA (owned by Wal-Mart) overtook the chain in 2003 with Morrisons not far behind. Although management has brought some stability to the chain in recent years (with sales growth if not increased profitability) the chain still lacks a convincing strategy around its core identity and remains vulnerable in the long term.

Companies are often caught out by big changes in the business environment, which they either do not foresee or are not equipped to deal with. Initially changes may be small but the cumulative effect can quickly become deadly, as Charles Handy's frog finds out to its cost when the water heats up. The shift to online sales, and the increasing dominance of Amazon, has caught out a series of UK retailers including HMV, Waterstones, Borders UK, Virgin Megastores and Wesley Owen. These businesses (all of which were 'category killers' with distinctive retail propositions) were forced into middle market positions by technological change. Those that remain are often struggling with 'last man standing' scenarios. This may be good to the extent that weaker physical competitors have exited the market but it leaves the survivors with significant issues in developing clear value-added propositions for the future. Responding to such a significant technological shift is certainly not simple, but knowing what is happening at the bigger level is a critical first step. Only by knowing more about the changing nature of the whole can businesses formulate robust commercial propositions for future success (and sometimes for their very survival).

Many smaller businesses struggle with their propositions because they are not attuned to the deeper trends in their marketplace. Pubs, for example, are particularly vulnerable to being stuck in the middle strategically, not least because of the proliferation of eateries of all sorts. Just think of the number of coffee shops and cafes that have appeared in our towns over the last couple of decades. Pubs with premium propositions (such as gastro pubs, restaurants and those that possess either genuine charm and personality or are simply very well run) often thrive. So do value driven chains such as J D Weatherspoon. Those that are in neither category invariably have a tough time and many fail. The same is increasingly true for shopping centres as a whole. Every business development has a natural life span but many are shortened prematurely by a failure to see how the whole is changing. In good strategy, of course, the devil is often in the detail, particularly in implementation and it is certainly wise not to underestimate the difficulty of this essential part of the strategic process. It is knowledge of the whole, however, that provides the context around core strategic identity. It is *that* important.

National Trust

There is no organisation that better embodies the concept of valuing an understanding of the whole than the National Trust. The Trust is an independent charitable body that protects coastline, countryside and buildings in the UK on a permanent basis. In 2009, it had 3.8 million members (making it the largest membership organisation in Britain), income of over £420 million and total funds of some £750 million. It is not size alone, however, that makes it an impressive organisation. It is the sheer diversity of its activities. In addition to its primary conservation work, the Trust is engaged in a wide variety of educational work, runs multiple businesses, entertains visitors by offering them a special day out and acts as a vital hub in local communities. Freed from the politicisation that arises when an organisation is critically dependent on public funding, the Trust is one of the very few organisations that makes decisions for the long term, those that benefit not only our generation but also the world inherited by our children and grandchildren. Indeed, the Trust cares passionately about its role in conserving the quality of life for future generations. In its annual report in 2009 it states:

> 'We promise to look after things which matter deeply to us as human beings, "for ever, for everyone". Those words "for ever" mean that we must always think and act for the long term. That's why sustainability is at the heart of everything we do, whether conserving a Renaissance tapestry, restoring a mountain valley, or protecting water supplies for future generations.'

In the minds of many people the National Trust is still primarily associated with maintaining large heritage properties. In reality, its remit goes far beyond this traditional role and covers many of the most important issues that face our society today. The list is a heady one including sustainable living, climate change, education, energy conservation, living in harmony with the natural environment, maintaining our quality of life, food nutrition and availability and a great deal more besides. The Trust is increasingly reaching out through partnerships to take a pivotal role in matters of global concern. The Millennium Seed Bank Project, for example, is an international conservation project launched in 2000 and coordinated by the Royal Botanic Gardens in Kew. The endeavour is based at Wakehurst Place, the National Trust's most visited property, and the Trust's support for the conservation of biodiversity has been crucial in turning the project from an idea into reality. The project has already conserved seeds from ten per cent of the word's plant species, including virtually all the UK's native flowering plants. It aims to safeguard 24,000 plant species from around the world against extinction, one reason that the Prince of Wales has described it as 'The Bank of England of the botanical world'. Sir David Attenborough concurs, calling it 'perhaps the most significant conservation initiative ever.' This is vitally important work. Seeds, the 'time capsules of life', enable flowering plants to survive unfavourable environmental conditions between one generation and another. If current estimates are correct and global temperatures rise by 2% during this century, between 20-30% of species will be at risk. The value of such a global network for seed conservation and research is immeasurable.

The National Trust is involved in many other areas of equal importance, both at national and local level. Nationally, this includes studying the effects of climate change on our environment and working with all aspects of sustainability, putting theory into practice on its properties and land. At local level, the Trust undertakes community and educational initiatives, provides volunteering opportunities for young people and showcases healthy food practices, not to mention all the activities that are involved with running the day-to-day operations. While no organisation is perfect (the Trust is, for example, trying to speed up its famously slow decision making process) it offers genuine insight into the kind of organisational mindset that will enable us to meet many of the challenges that will come to epitomise the twenty first century. The National Trust demonstrates a genuine capacity to think strategically for the long term, and expressly recognises the importance of balancing financial, people and conservation benefits in budgeting decisions in the so-called 'triple bottom line' methodology. Its use of partnerships (including government) points to the power of working together, and its increasing educational and volunteering projects provide an experiential depth to learning that is, sadly, often missing from the classroom in formal education. In addition, it is adept at looking at the full benefits and costs of policy decisions, which specifically includes externalities (the economic effects of decisions and choices not reflected in prices). Many commercial organisations are only just beginning to get to grips with the importance of this broader financial perspective.

There is also much to be learned from the way the National Trust funds itself, how it makes the best use of its resources and how it works with and through its people (including volunteers). But most important of all, it works. Imagine for a moment that the UK Government had been handed stewardship of the National Trust's land and properties 25 years ago. What state would they be in now? Speaking personally, I shudder to think. Thankfully, the Trust has been able to continue its work, not just in conserving what is, but also in recognising the importance of understanding our impact on the whole, not only for our future wellbeing and survival but also for that of our children and their children. In doing so, it continues the sacred work of the naturalist, poet and philosopher, Henry David Thoreau who wrote in his journal on January 30th 1861:

'What are the natural features which make a township handsome? A river, with its waterfalls and meadows, a lake, a hill, a cliff or individual rocks, a forest, and ancient trees standing singly. Such things are beautiful; they have a high use which dollars and cents never represent. If the inhabitants of a town

were wise, they would seek to preserve these things, though at a considerable expense; for such things educate far more than hired teachers or preachers, or any at present recognised system of school education. I do not think him fit to be a founder of a state or even of a town who does not foresee the use of these things, but legislates chiefly for oxen, as it were.'

The bell

This has been a difficult chapter. Building a capacity to understand the big picture is not easy. It is undoubtedly true to say that many of our greatest leaders did not try to do this at an intellectual level. Instead of solely using their head they did it in ways that came naturally to them, also using heart, body and soul. Many *felt* their way to a deep understanding of the whole through instinct. Others were naturally very good at putting together the pieces of the puzzle into a meaningful framework in terms of the work they were doing. At the end of the day, it doesn't matter which qualities of our common humanity we choose to use to see the bigger picture. We remain open and use whatever we've got. It can sometimes be hard to do that in a world where constant activity is worshipped and space is so often seen as evidence of laziness or ineffectiveness. We need to turn this thinking on its head. By thinking differently we can turn our world upside down, putting reflection back at the core of our thinking process.

One of the best ways to get into contact with the bigger picture is to take time out during the day to rest our minds·and open up the space to let new thinking in. I have a confession to make. Like most of us I am not very good at creating space in my life. There are deep constraints within me that cry 'idleness is the devil's work' and make me feel inadequate when I'm not 'productively' busy. So I have to work very hard to create space. Luckily, my young Wiltshire terrier, 'Buddha', forces me to take time out for contemplation in terms of our daily walks. When he informs me that 'nature calls' I have no option but to take him out. When I do so, I often find that nature calls me too. For me, there is no better place to open up to the whole than when I'm surrounded by nature. In fact, I am at my most creative and open-minded when I am rambling across the Wiltshire Downs with my faithful dog. It is also where I resolve my most difficult and practical problems. We can all find different ways to create space that works for us. The specifics don't matter very much.

Two good friends of mine reminded me recently of the time they spent on a course several years ago in a monastery. Every hour the monks would ring the bell and for one minute everyone was silent. Conversation ceased and telephone calls had to be brought to an end immediately. Far from being a waste of time these periodic silences brought about by the bell proved to be a tremendous catalyst for creative thinking and problem resolution. They cut through the deadweight of clutter like a hot knife through butter. For two weeks after the course my friends continued with their own routine but it quickly gave way to the pressures of life. They are not alone. I think we all struggle with maintaining personal space for reflection and contemplation. It is entirely at odds with our '24/7', 'always-on', culture. But there is no better way to connect to the bigger picture. It's ironic that to see the whole *outside* of us the most important thing is to spend time *inside* ourselves.

5
WE NOT ME

'Hey Daisy darling don't spread your arms so wide,
why don't you keep a little something inside.
I know you think that hands are made
for pulling us through
but there are people in this world
who don't think like you do...'
Karine Polwart, Daisy

Wisdom of the geese

Each autumn we see the familiar sight of geese heading south for the winter, flying in a 'V' formation and occasionally honking along the way. I'm not quite sure what the honking means (other than an encouragement from the geese at the back to keep up the speed!) but I do understand why geese choose to fly that way. As each goose flaps its wings, it creates uplift for the birds following, allowing them to fly more easily. In technical terms, the air flowing over each bird's wings curls upwards behind the wingtips (a phenomenon known as 'upwash') so that the birds following experience less drag and need to use less energy to fly. In simple terms, the geese work together as a team to share the work. By doing so, a flock of 25 birds can extend their flying range by over 70%. If a goose falls out of formation it quickly experiences the greater effort required to go it alone and falls back in line. When the leading goose gets tired, it rotates back into the flock allowing another goose to take over at the helm. Remarkably, if a goose gets sick or wounded by gunshot and has to fall out of formation, two other geese will follow it down to help it and lend it protection. They stay with the fallen goose until it is able to fly or dies. Only then do they make out on their own to return to the flock or join another one. We can learn a great deal by studying the natural world.

Geese have another lesson to impart. They are remarkably adept at 'self organisation'. Natural systems manage themselves for the benefit of the whole through simple rules. The flocking behaviour of birds is an example of an emergent phenomenon; one in which complex events emerge from simple interactions. Craig Reynolds, an artificial life and computer graphics expert, identified three simple self-organising rules that underlie the ability of birds to flock together effectively.   He called these three rules 'separation', 'alignment' and 'cohesion'. The rule of separation allows birds to minimise the chance of collisions by steering away from those too close to them. The rule of alignment means that each bird matches the velocity of its neighbours by flying in the average direction that the flock is moving. Finally, the rule of cohesion requires each bird to move towards the centre of the flock to avoid exposure at the exterior. If these three rules are put together we can simulate common flocking behaviour including wheeling and turning in unison and even dividing to go round obstacles. The study of natural systems shows us that it is not only vastly more effective to work together but that in doing so we can employ methods of self organisation that are remarkably simple yet effective to produce complex results. In short, it pays to work together.

The value in relationship

'No one – not rock stars, not professional athletes, not software billionaires, and not even geniuses – ever makes it alone.'
Malcolm Gladwell

It is good to have a healthy sense of self. Knowing who we are and what we are about helps us to focus our energies and strengthens our resolve to act. A healthy sense of identity is an essential quality of leadership. We don't, however, exist in isolation; all things are in relationship, both with each other and with the whole. Yet we often lose sight of that connection and the part we play in the whole. Margaret Silf, a writer and retreat leader, uses the analogy of islands in an ocean to make an important point about our connection with each other. To all extents and purposes, we see ourselves rather like those islands, alone and separate from each other. We don't see the deeper relationship that is hidden below the sea, the solid bedrock that connects us. If we look from space that relationship is all too obvious. We are drawn to the sight of the Earth, a beautiful blue ball spinning in space, with its continents, islands and oceans all one.

We have already seen that leaders share some important common characteristics. Firstly, they are able to grasp their personal power by knowing who they are and what they stand for. By doing so, they accept full responsibility for their place in the world and act accordingly. Their clear sense of self acts as a rudder and allows them to focus on those areas where they are able have a unique impact. We might call this the *'what'* question of leadership. Secondly, they address the question of *'where'* to act by being sensitive to what is happening in the bigger picture. This gives them a deeper sense of perspective and guides them where best to direct their energies. In the next couple of chapters we will be looking at the question of *'how'* strategic leaders act but right now we are concerned with an equally important issue, *'with whom'* should we act. No leader operates alone. In his book, *Outliers*, Malcolm Gladwell takes a different look at how highly successful people became so, emphasizing the context in which success took place. 'It's not enough to ask what successful people are like,' he writes, 'it is only by asking where they are from that we can unravel the logic behind who succeeds and who doesn't.' This means exploring family and relationships, friendships, cultural aspects and accidents of birth, history and geography, as well as focusing on the individual. Strategic leaders recognise, develop and harness their relationships with others because they know that effective action is predicated on the power of relationship.

At a very obvious level, close relationships are fundamentally important to leaders and often influence them significantly. Denis Thatcher played a critical supportive role when his wife, Margaret, was Prime Minister in the United Kingdom. He also had the wisdom to minimize this role in the public eye. He kept himself out of the limelight by a blanket refusal to give media interviews, once commenting, 'I have spent some 15 years or more "keeping my head below the parapet"; that this is misunderstood from time to time is understandable but on balance the policy has paid off.' No one would ever accuse Margaret Thatcher of not knowing her mind or lacking the energy and commitment required for leadership. However, the support of those close to her, Denis in particular, should not be underestimated. Gordon Reece, who worked with Mrs Thatcher on softening her image, observed:

> 'One of the great triumphs of Denis is what he did not do, not just what he did. That is the basis of why he was so valuable to Margaret. He would do everything to advance her interests but wasn't up to being her Svengali... He always said what he thought because he had confidence in what he thought. But look at the things he didn't do: the capacity for interference was limitless; he could have tried to be a policy-maker, he never tried to do that. He just gave his point of view. He didn't do anything more.'

Leaders are often only able play their roles *because* of the support and help of close friends and relationships. Karl Marx is an excellent case in point. Marx first became friends with Friedrich Engels in 1844 and the two worked very closely together for most of their lives. In fact, the contribution of Engels to Marx's masterwork, *Das Kapital*, was immense. Although they were both Rhinelanders, and at one point jointly edited the Rheinische Zeitung, they came from very different backgrounds. Karl Marx was a Jewish lawyer who had converted to Christianity, whilst Engels was a prosperous protestant cotton-mill owner who lived for much his life in England. They initially collaborated together on *The Communist Manifesto* and then travelled across Europe in the 1840's as revolutionary fever swept the continent. Domesticity then entered the picture when Marx acquired a German aristocratic wife and found that he had children to support. How could he continue to write *Das Kapital* and yet live in the comfortable lifestyle to which he had become accustomed? Characteristically, it was Engels who generously provided the solution to this dilemma, despite the fact that it involved him doing something he detested. He agreed to go back to the family cotton business in Manchester so that Marx could continue his work unfettered by financial worries.

For the next 20 years Engels handed over half his income to Marx, as well as collaborating with his friend by providing ideas, business examples and invaluable editorial support. After Marx died, Engels continued to support his family and then played a major role in pulling together the chaotic notes that Marx had left behind for the further volumes of Das Kapital. His contribution in this regard was enormous. In the third volume, Marx originally discussed the 'shaking' of capitalist production caused by the tendency for profitability to fall. Engels substituted the word 'collapse' instead, a far more radical concept that was later seized upon by twentieth century Marxists to convey quite a different story. His contribution to Marx's legacy was immeasurable. Yet, Engels was always happy to play the supporting role, declaring after his friend's death that 'Marx was a genius; we others were at best talented.' There are plenty of people who agree with the sentiment expressed by Engels and are happy to play a supporting role, often working behind the scenes, contributing to a cause that is important to them. In the United States alone, non-profit organizations now employ close to ten million people with a further five million full time volunteers. And this is merely the tip of the iceberg when we look more closely at the importance of relationships.

Family and close friends play a particularly important role for many leaders. Rob Parsons, Executive Chairman of Care for the Family, a charity committed to strengthening family life, talks of the family as the 'bulwark to the storms of life … a place of training, security and safety.' But, he adds, 'it also has another vital function. It gives us a sense of belonging – of roots; it helps us know our place in the world – perhaps, even, the universe.' Where family ties are not strong close friends often step into that place. Many entrepreneurial businesses have two structures; a formal hierarchical one for operational purposes and a small group of long standing friends who play an informal, but often highly influential, role in making key decisions. Both entrepreneurial and family based businesses place a high premium on loyalty. They frequently reward employees who joined the business at the beginning or those who played a supportive role during the early, frequently tough, years. These close ties play an equally strong role in other businesses, although they may not be as transparent. Personal relationships are fundamentally important to us and we fool ourselves if we believe that they do not exert significant influence on business decision-making.

Go deep not broad

When I was fifteen I had one or two good friends and a group of others who I would hang around with. I felt happy and my social 'connectivity' was just about the same as everybody else. My fifteen-year old son has hundreds of 'friends', mostly on Facebook, and classifies his entire class at school (bar one or two individuals) as his 'friends'. Given the power of relationship surely this must be a good thing? I think, perhaps, we had better look a little deeper. In February 2009, *The Economist* asked Cameron Marlow, the 'in-house sociologist' at Facebook, to crunch some numbers. Mr Marlow agreed and, at that time, the average numbers of friends for a Facebook user was 120, with women having slightly more friends than men. I'm sure it has grown since then. The range, however, was large, with many individuals having networks of more than 500 people. Mr Marlow then drilled further. He found that the average man (with 120 friends) only actively responded with seven of those friends by leaving comments on the friend's wall, message or photo. The average woman came in slightly higher with ten active friends. For two-way communication by email the numbers dropped still further, to four friends for men and six for women. Users with very large numbers of friends posted higher numbers but these too were a very small fraction of their overall network. Lee Rainie, Director of the Pew Internet & American Life Project, comments that people using online social networks are not so much 'networking' as they are 'broadcasting their lives to an outer tier of acquaintances'. Evidence suggests that we have the same small number of close friends as we have always done.

Many of my clients have a poor opinion on the value of 'networking' and I must confess that I agree with them. Having spent considerable time as an independent consultant I have been to many networking meetings in my time, including some that appeared to consist entirely of consultants! For me, it is far more important to know *what* I am about and to be focused on achieving it. I can then arrange to make contact with those people who are important in that context. I have learned to my cost that in my line of work unfocused networking meetings are, at best, a huge distraction of time and energy. In fact, the larger our networks the less the value of the individual relationships tends to be. Small friendship groups encourage the exchange of favours, whereas larger networks convey too little personal information and are too fragile to do this. It is not surprising, therefore, that beneath the clutter of online social networks our close friendships remain small in number. At the end of the day, a small number of deep relationships is far more effective than a broad palate of superficial ones. Quality is far more important than quantity.

We are not who we think we are

The importance of relationship goes far beyond the supportive roles that those who are close to us sometimes play, and the power associated with working together. When we see ourselves as separate individuals with little connection to the world around us, we deny the greater part of our humanity. When we lose this connection we also lose much of our power to make a real difference in the world. If we see ourselves as part of the whole, however, we lose that sense of a divide between 'us' and 'them'.

We stop judging others and begin to look more deeply at the role *we* play in determining how our lives turn out. This is often the point when our lives turn around. Instead of trying to 'push' things out into the external environment or marketplace, we create the space to meet the needs of those who are drawn to us (a 'pull' strategy that recognizes that we are part of the whole). Because we speak with authority others begin to listen to us. We no longer have to exert lots of energy to make things happen, we learn instead to move out of the way as events occur of their own accord. Rick Jarrow, author of *Creating the Work you Love,* suggests that when we start a business or follow a new career path, we don't start by analyzing our potential market. Instead, we ask 'what is my community?' By knowing who we are, where we are from and what we stand for, we align ourselves with those who are naturally drawn to the products and services that we wish to provide.

As we move beyond the artificial division between 'them' and 'us', all kinds of barriers and obstacles dissolve because we have placed ourselves in a position of service to the whole rather than the more familiar competitive 'zero sum' game (if I win you have to lose). This community orientation provides access to deeper roots and relationships, to like-minded people within the community at large, which translates into practical help, advice and access to resources. The concept may appear to be philosophical but the application is entirely practical. At a deeper level, placing ourselves in the context of serving others, rather than using them primarily to meet our own needs, opens us up to the power of synchronicity and serendipity in our lives. This is the fortunate coming together of events and people in unforeseen ways to our advantage, often combined with fortuitous timing.

We are also able to build on solid foundations, on rock rather than sand, because our roots go deep and we intuitively sense the best place on which to build. We are able to plan for the long term because we have clarity in purpose about what we are seeking to achieve and our intentions have been 'sense checked' by others (who are objective and may have valuable knowledge in the area of our endeavours). Other advantages quickly follow. We are open to multiple perspectives because we are not overly identified with our own, allowing us to be more creative and innovative in our approach. Knowing that our work is part of a common vision allows us to draw on the ideas of others because we are no longer directly in competition with them. We can remain focused and are thus less likely to be distracted. Distraction is the destroyer of many ideas, concepts and plans. As the old adage says, 'if you want to defeat them, distract them'. To put it most succinctly, we come into our power because we are using that power for the common good. We recognise that we are not who we think we are. We are not the limited self that is defined by our ego. We are more than that. Much more than that. We are an intrinsic part of the whole. We are one.

Let me be honest. I am no nearer to acting without self interest than anyone else I know. In fact, almost all of my time is spent in a state of limited self-awareness with sturdy barriers that I have erected between myself and other people. I am not alone in that. But here's the good news. We don't have to be perfect to tap into the power of relationship. We simply have to be aware of its existence. That is enough to change our world. One day at a time. Little by little. Bit by bit.

The blind spot

We do not exist as simply ourselves. We exist 'in relation to'. That is our true identity. Author, Laurie Beth Jones, explores this aspect of our greater selves in her book, *Jesus, CEO*, where she talks about what made Jesus' 'management style' effective. She concludes that Jesus incorporated and transcended the best of Alpha ('masculine') and Beta ('feminine') leadership styles by harnessing spiritual energy. She calls this Jesus' 'Omega' leadership style. Critically, for our purposes here, this leadership style incorporates three key strengths; self-mastery, action and relationships. We have explored all these aspects in this book and *all* are necessary for a leader to make profound and lasting changes. The great leaders of history understood this. If we look at the lives of leaders such as Mahatma Gandhi, Nelson Mandela and Martin Luther King, we see the importance of relationship to the community, and to the world as a whole, as the foundation of their work. This is not to say that they were 'perfect' people. On the contrary, when we read their biographies we find that they were very human. As was Margaret Thatcher, the former Prime Minister of the United Kingdom, whose legacy we are going to explore here. Given her sense of 'rightness', I suspect she shares her Enneagram personality profile (*Chapter 3*) with quite a few of the other strategic leaders explored in this book (Howard Schultz, CEO of Starbucks, Steve Jobs, CEO of Apple and Oskar Schindler to name but a few) and this lens provides some insight into her character. In fact, it is not in the least surprising that the lady 'would not be for turning' and showed such extreme fortitude and persistence in achieving the aims that she so passionately believed in.

Margaret Thatcher

'The problem with socialism is that eventually you run out of other people's money.'
Margaret Thatcher

Margaret Thatcher will almost certainly be remembered as one of the great leaders of the twentieth century. She created an extraordinary legacy in economic terms, albeit one that was spectacularly painful at the time in her native country. The impact of 'Thatcherism', as it became known, was profoundly felt throughout the world. She also wielded considerable political influence as a result of her close relationships with both President Reagan and Soviet leader, Mikhail Gorbachev. She forged warm personal friendships with both leaders and her impact on world events, political and economic, was considerable. There are many, however who disagree that she should be remembered as a 'great' leader. For them, it is not Thatcher's economic legacy, or her influence on world events that is important, but her social impact, particularly in the UK. Those who suffered as a result of her policies, when whole communities were torn apart, are often not prepared to forgive the former Prime Minister for her actions, irrespective of whether the country as a whole has prospered. For those directly affected, the wounds run deep, very deep indeed. As is often the case, we can capture this best in the words of a song. In *Please Sir*, written by Welsh singer-songwriter, Martyn Joseph, a miner's son asks the question 'why?':

> *'She stood there with her arms around him and she said*
> *She promised him a better day*
> *But after twenty years of working underground*
> *It's not just your job that they take away.*
> *Sometimes he'd walk to the edge of his world*
> *And stare at the valley below*
> *He thought about leaving, maybe running away*
> *But knew there was nowhere to go*
> *Please sir can you give me an answer*
> *Please sir you know I just can't see*
> *Please sir when you make these decisions*
> *Do you have a vision of what happens to me?'*

Discussing the impact of Margaret Thatcher is always going to be controversial. The twenty-year period of prosperity that spans the centuries' divide is largely attributable to the Iron Lady's refusal to be swayed from her economic agenda. But even as the country as a whole has prospered, some communities have suffered immensely. Was the price worth paying? To answer this question we need to look at the bigger picture, and at the nature of relationship in particular. This is an exercise well worth undertaking because it also provides a very vivid example of why relationship is so important to leadership. Few would argue that Margaret Thatcher's economic legacy was not predominantly positive in the long term. Her economic policies, no matter how unpleasant they were at the time, restored the competitiveness of the United Kingdom in the global economy, and the country has consistently moved back up the international economic ratings over the past 20 years. Undoubtedly, some of her primary reforms were inevitable in the long term, and the pain of economic dislocation would have happened sooner or later. If these decisions had been postponed, the consequences would have almost certainly been far worse.

Yet, in 2010, Britain is once again in economic crisis, partly due to global recession in the developed world but also, in many ways, of its own making. Some of the features of this crisis (not all) would be familiar to Margaret Thatcher during her first years in office. These include large budget deficits, increasing and dangerous levels of debt, trade deficits, a high degree of government intervention in the economy, an ever-expanding role for the state and a declining currency among them. What went wrong? Why hasn't the Thatcher legacy held more firmly in these areas?

Margaret Thatcher possessed extraordinarily strong 'masculine' leadership qualities including certainty of purpose, authority and control. No one could tell her that she was wrong. Arguably, it was these very leadership qualities that were so critical in 1980's Britain to force through the difficult changes that were long overdue. She was also gifted in certain aspects of 'feminine' leadership, particularly in her appreciation of the whole; the nature of British economic decline in relation to the global economy. She knew what needed to be done from the perspective of the big picture and she was capable of action, more than capable in fact. But she had a blind spot. Convinced about the 'rightness' of her policies and acting as she did without self-interest, she didn't feel the need to pay attention to the importance of relationship. When we 'know' what needs to be done it is hard to listen to the viewpoints of others. They simply get in the way of our ability to get things done. They impede progress. Besides, we 'know' we are 'right' and they are 'wrong', a point that Mrs Thatcher reiterated many times during her years in power. So, we often fail to notice the potentially 'toxic' side effects of our actions until it is too late. We have cut off the feedback process. In this case, it caused not only Mrs Thatcher's personal downfall but also led to the unravelling of some of her most important policies over the years. In addition, it has bedeviled British society with an inability to separate out the healthy aspects of Mrs Thatcher's legacy from the mythology of her person, depriving the nation of some of the long lasting benefits from her time in office. Ultimately, it was the *way* in which Mrs Thatcher achieved her aims that has proved to be fatally flawed.

There is no doubt in my mind that history will be predominantly kind to Margaret Thatcher and she will be viewed as an important *strategic* leader because she instigated a sea change in British economic thinking and laid the basis for twenty years of prosperity. The powerful 'masculine' aspects of her leadership style were key to her success because she was operating within the political process. A 'weak' leader in this area is unlikely to have had the personal power and authority to push through the changes that were necessary. Indeed, others tried on a smaller scale and failed. Conciliatory policies do not necessarily work well in government. When Michael Foot, who later went on to lead the Labour Party, was Employment Secretary in 1974-75, he was given the task of trade union relations. A fellow cabinet member later remarked, 'the relationship was one of give-and-take. The government gave and they took.' What marks Margaret Thatcher out as different from, say, Mahatma Ghandi and Martin Luther King, is that she operated *within* the system, while they both operated *outside* it. Her failure, however, to fully appreciate the importance of the relationship dimension did have serious long-term repercussions. It has left Britain with a fractured social landscape that has never been healed. Mrs Thatcher did not invent these fractures. They existed long before her tenure as Prime Minister and are deeply embedded into the British psyche. But her particularly abrasive personal style and confrontational policies (so necessary at one level to effect change) exacerbated these tensions by destroying long-standing communities at grass roots level. Ironically, the later attempts by government to safeguard community infrastructure from above has precipitated the very interventionist mindset that Mrs Thatcher fought so hard to reverse.

Over the years a consensus emerged in the UK that would be quite foreign to Mrs Thatcher's way of thinking. In economic terms, mainstream opinion supported the notion that 'greed is good' and that markets should reign supreme. As a counterbalance we also accepted that it is in the public interest for the state to control an ever-increasing share of these economic benefits to ensure that community structure is maintained. As a result, government spent ever-increasing amounts of money on health services, education and other public services. Unfortunately, both assumptions are seriously flawed. Margaret Thatcher never believed that 'greed is good'. On the contrary, she believed that hard work and enterprise are the basis for wealth and that strong financial disciplines are essential (including spending according to our means, one of the lost golden rules of Thatcherism). And community is built from the bottom up not the top down. The result of an over weaning state and lavish spending is not healthy community but the squandering of wealth on an unprecedented scale and the build up of high levels of debt, something that was happening in the United Kingdom long before the credit crunch precipitated a global crisis. Too late, the established consensus is now disintegrating and trust in the state has slumped (from 41% to 35% in 2009, compared with a comparable increase in trust in business from 45% to 47%). The UK now faces up to two decades of austerity to pay off the debt burden. It is an expensive lesson.

It is a risk to write about somebody who carries such emotional weight as Margaret Thatcher. Like many leaders she is imbued with a disproportionate amount of 'hero or villain' mythology. In reality she is neither. It is always fascinating to read her biographies because they are full of very normal and very human incidents. As Prime Minister she remained uncannily rooted in reality and kept personal egocentricity and self-aggrandizement at bay (how many celebrities and politicians can say that?). Carol Thatcher, her daughter, remembers visiting Number 10 at the beginning of the Falklands crisis. Her mother had gone round the flat a few months earlier with little sticky dots, marking family possessions apart from government property. The idea was that if the Thatchers had to move quickly it would make the job of the removal team easier. It wasn't that her mother expected to leave her position but that she was practical and ordered and knew that 'prime ministers don't last forever'.

Relationships in business

The very first step in becoming a great salesperson is to value relationships. A salesperson with no relationship skills is simply an 'order taker'. Good businesses value relationships just as much as good salespeople do. They are the heart of a successful business. Waitrose, part of the John Lewis Partnership, takes its community ventures very seriously indeed. As a premium food retailer, product quality is at the very core of its business proposition. Supermarket retailing is fiercely competitive and Waitrose has built a value proposition that goes far beyond the tangible quality of its food offer. A community orientation and 'win-win' philosophy are built into its relationships with suppliers and other partners, its commitment to its own people and to the local communities around its stores. The Waitrose Foundation, for example, helps communities in supplier regions around the world (including South Africa, Kenya and Ghana) by paying for health, education and social projects. So far, the Foundation, which is run in collaboration with key suppliers, has set up more than 100 projects including crèches, adult education schemes, community medical centres and bursaries to fund workers' children through college. In my local town, Marlborough, the Waitrose store gives money to local charities on a weekly basis, allowing customers to choose between three alternative causes at a time. St John's School in Marlborough was one grateful recipient of funds when the store raised £308 to help equip the new school that was being built. And, as the school newsletter reports, 'the mood turned to celebration when the Waitrose Community Investment Committee announced that it would donate a further £15,449 to sponsor one of the three Food Technology Classrooms at the new St John's School.' This is not fluff. This is a deep commitment to local community that supports the supermarket's premium business proposition.

Waitrose understands that consumers will be reticent to pay over the odds for products where the perceived quality is little different from cheaper competitors. As a result, the chain has introduced an extensive range of over 1,000 'essential' products at competitive prices. This is a shrewd, even essential, move in recessionary times. Waitrose also knows, however, that people will pay for better quality, especially if they feel a sense of relationship and connection. As a result, it provides customers with information on individual suppliers, with brochures and leaflets showing pictures of individual farmers and business proprietors. 'Meet our Waitrose Food Heroes', reads one brochure, while another explains 'why Waitrose pigs are happy.' In 2009, Waitrose teamed up with Duchy Originals, which donates all its profits to the Prince's Charities Foundation set up by the Prince of Wales. The Foundation has already donated over £7 million to charitable causes throughout the UK and overseas. The new partnership gives Waitrose the exclusive right to originate, manufacture, distribute and sell Duchy Original products in the United Kingdom, recognizing that Waitrose is its oldest and largest customer. There are many other signs that Waitrose 'walks the talk' in its community ventures. When I shop at our local store I am immediately aware of how welcoming the environment is. People who work in the store are friendly, helpful and take time out to chat to customers. The result is a much more personalized and pleasant experience for the customer (and a major stress reduction given our modern overly busy lifestyles). This is core to the Waitrose proposition.

Unlike many corporate social responsibility initiatives, Waitrose has embedded its community and sustainability commitments deeply into its business processes with tangible targets across all areas. The John Lewis Partnership is very open about where it stands on all these key issues. It provides a wealth of information on its current position on key environmental issues (including sustainable sourcing, packaging and waste policies, energy efficiency and so on), ethical trading policies, health and nutrition, construction and regeneration projects and building sustainable communities. This is further *direct* evidence that community and relationship thrive in many areas of the business. But I am the kind of person who likes to seek *indirect* evidence too. The Leckford Estate in Hampshire is about 25 miles due south of me. It was purchased by the John Lewis Partnership in 1928 and is beautifully located on gently rolling chalk hills alongside the River Test. The working farm is 4,000 acres and provides Waitrose with cup mushrooms, fresh milk, flour, apples, apple juice and chickens. From 2014, it will also be providing English wine, grown on the local chalky slopes around the river valley. I drive through this idyllic scene twice a year on my way to the Isle of Wight and I am always struck by how well maintained the area is. It is not just within the farming operations, which are open to the public on special occasions, but also the very positive impression of the place as a whole. I noticed last year that the trees by the side of the road had been trimmed. When I looked more closely I realized that the ivy, which is profuse in such a lush area, had been carefully removed from the tree trunks. Such sensitivity to nature and attention to detail is almost unheard of alongside public roads. I have no idea whether Waitrose or local people initiated this action. But it speaks volumes about the positive effects of business and community working together.

Many other businesses are expressly committed to community. Howard Schultz, the CEO of Starbucks, sees community relationships as core to Starbuck's proposition at every level of its business, from equitable relationships with suppliers to local store initiatives. Other retailers such as Whole Foods Market, Innocent Drinks and Pret A Manger run charitable foundations that funnel back profit from the business into the communities associated with it. Like Waitrose, they also integrate their community values into their operational policies and core business models. Pret A Manger, for example, runs a fleet of electric and LPG vans in London, which collect and distribute leftover food at the end of every day to charities for the homeless. It has become known as the 'Pret Charity Run'. This is wonderful but the company is restless and doesn't feel that it is doing enough. Good quality food is still going to waste. As a result, it promotes the issue of waste in its stores, reaching out for suggestions from customers as to how they can reduce wasted food still further. Each year Innocent Drinks gives at least 10% of its profits to charity, mostly through the Innocent Foundation. The Foundation is a grant giving organization that works with NGOs to deliver its vision of building sustainable futures for the world's poorest people. It currently has 15 partner organizations, working on projects primarily in countries where it sources its fruit. It maintains an agricultural focus because Innocent believes that it is essential for communities to get the most out of the natural resources available to them, in order to build a sustainable and better future.

Not all businesses are so overt about recognizing the power of relationship. But our best businesses know that they are only as strong as the relationships that define them. Relationships are key to core purpose and to an organization's sense of identity and are vitally important in guiding the strategic decision-making process at top level. As Ikujiro Nonaka, leading author on knowledge management, and currently Professor Emeritus at the Hitotsubashi University Graduate School of International Corporate Strategy, in Tokyo, writes:

'A company is not a machine but a living organism, and, much like an individual, it can have a collective sense of identity and fundamental purpose. This is the organizational equivalent of self-knowledge – a shared understanding of what the company stands for, where it's going, what kind of world it wants to live in, and, most importantly, how it intends to make that world a reality.'

Foundation in community

*'Let everyone sweep in front of his own door,
and the whole world will be clean.'*
Goethe

Community is not built from the top down by well-intentioned planners. It develops organically from the bottom up and is best understood as a 'complex ecology'. In other words, many things that happen together make the community much greater than the sum of its parts. These 'many things' are often simple when taken individually, but together they provide a strong foundation for our identity, security, health and sense of wellbeing. They are best understood at ground level and they require work. In our society this often translates into a lot of work for a few people, but healthy communities actually thrive on the reverse, a little bit of work from lots of people. Although we fret continuously about the disappearance of our communities, the truth is that most of us don't value them enough to actually get involved. Community work is mostly unpaid, often thankless and, for some, goes against the grain. If we pay for our children to be educated privately surely it is not right to expect us to help our local state school on a voluntary basis? Since we all pay municipal taxes why should we pick up litter that somebody else has discarded? I have some sympathy for questions such as these. But community begins with responsibilities and not with rights. The basis of community is the good of the whole and not the translation of that common benefit into personal gain. Ironically, when community is strong we all gain, sometimes in very unexpected ways. But we have to put aside our self-interest in the short term if we are to benefit from community in the longer term.

We have so many opportunities for building community, provided that we don't mind rolling up our sleeves and doing a bit of work. Government is keen to push down responsibility (if not authority) to volunteers in a vast range of services including health, education, caring for people in the community, local government and drug and alcohol addiction. Charities make a very direct contribution to almost all areas of community life, from protecting the environment to combating illness, poverty and social exclusion. Even infrastructural projects (such as restoring canals, refurbishing local heritage buildings and planting trees in urban areas) have a strong volunteering orientation. Never before have volunteering organizations been better organized and funded and this is a profoundly positive development. Some areas of community life, however, seem to evoke our community spirit more than others. Animal welfare does well in this regard. Areas that pose more intractable social problems, such as drug and alcohol addition, struggle to make headway. Yet, they would also benefit hugely from similar involvement, or access to additional funding. In fact, the power of relationship in the community can be seen in almost any area that people are passionate about. The local cricket team is a fine example, one that invigorates the community in sporting terms but also normally makes a healthy contribution to the local pub!

There is a very real connection between the environment in which we live and our own health and vitality. If some of our communities are dying of neglect it is because we have forgotten how to care for them (or no longer regard it as our responsibility). Building community comes down to our mindset and to seeing ourselves as part of the whole. When we lose this we lose our communities. No government, no matter how well meaning, can possibly substitute community from above. Indeed, the very best thing that government can do to benefit community is simply to get out of its way by removing bureaucracy and red tape.

Conservation and creation

Looking after community also means taking conservation seriously. This is not simply a matter of preserving our old 'stuff' for posterity because it is unique, rare or beautiful (although that is important too). It is about looking forwards by maintaining and reinvigorating valuable parts of our communities as living and working 'social ecologies'. The National Trust is at the forefront of this work as we saw in the last chapter. But there are many other organizations that are doing equally valuable work including English Heritage, The Churches Conservation Trust and numerous smaller charities looking after individual properties, restoring canals, maintaining steam railways and many other activities. If we notice that we have a tendency to shrug these efforts off as 'quaint but hardly relevant to modern life', we should look a little deeper. As we have seen, Winston Churchill once remarked, 'the further back you look the farther forward you are likely to see.' But it is about more than that. The sustainability of any system depends on the health of the whole. This in turn depends on the intricacies of all the relationships within the system, how each relationship supports, enhances and extends the others. Conservation and creation are inextricably linked. In relationship terms they are bedfellows not enemies.

In simple terms we might start with a redundant church and open it up as community centre with café, craft centre and facilities for live events. Each of these has the capacity to thrive on its own account as well as add value to the community as a whole. The centre also acts as a relationship hub for others seeking to start new social endeavours, small businesses or community enterprises. And so it goes, in time creating a virtuous cycle of growth and renewal. Ultimately, the ripples of the new activities spread wider and deeper into the broader community. Local tax revenues, for example, may rise, giving the municipality the opportunity to fund key infrastructural improvements in the area. Sensible tax and planning regulations will also allow the community to capture some of the value of what economists call 'externalities' (for example, the additional income of a café that is situated in a market square next to a magnificent cathedral). It is another example of a potential 'win-win' scenario, provided that we can bring together interested parties with a common community vision and allow them to act upon it. This does not require great intellectual prowess, vision or creativity. It is normally a series of practical simple steps agreed upon by people who come together as part of a common cause.

Reversing the tragedy of the commons

Relationship is not just about our ability to get on with others. It is also about understanding the nature of relationships within the whole system. It is about connection. *How* we connect, and how we manage the relationships within an overall system, really matters. In 1968 Garrett Hardin, a professor of biology, published an article called '*Tragedy of the Commons*' in the journal, *Science*. He found that although it is in the interests of everyone to manage common property well, it is also in each person's individual interest to use more of it than is good for the whole system. Hardin used the example of a common pasture open to all the local herdsmen. Each individual herdsman, he argued, had:

'an incentive to add another animal to his herd. And another; and another ... But this is the conclusion reached by each and every rational herdsman sharing a commons. Therein is the tragedy.'

This analysis has struck a chord and the term 'tragedy of the commons' has now become common parlance, used to explain everything from overfishing in the oceans to the destruction of the rainforests. There is, thankfully, a 'but' and it is this. It all depends on how the common asset is managed. It turns out that there are many examples of commons that *are* well managed and last for decades. They include Swiss Alpine pastures, Japanese forests and irrigation systems in Spain and the Philippines. These common resources don't necessarily survive forever, but disaster is not inevitable. Mr Hardin was sufficiently convinced that before he died he admitted that he should have called his article 'Tragedy of the Unmanaged Commons'. And here's the rub. It is the quality of management that is key and this depends critically on an understanding of the whole system and the key relationships that underpin it. The good news arising from this is that the destruction of common assets is not, necessarily, inevitable.

Elinor Ostrom, an American political scientist, won the Nobel Memorial Prize in Economic Sciences in 2009 for her work on economic governance, particularly in relation to the commons. Her work over the years has demonstrated that commons can be maintained when informal rules for their usage exist. Successful informal systems almost always have elaborate conventions over who can use resources and when. They include making sure that what users take out of the commons is proportional to what they put in and ensuring that the overall use of the commons is compatible with its underlying health. In addition, all users need to have some say in how the rules are set and the emphasis is usually on monitoring abuses and resolving conflict rather than on sanctions and punishment. Ironically, informal systems tend work better than formal ones. In fact, tragedy often occurs when governments trample over informal systems and substitute their own rules, especially when they are highly politicized.

Elinor Ostrom has also formulated eight 'design principles' that help manage common resources in a stable condition. By showing how resources can be managed successfully by people who use them, rather than by governments or private companies, she has overturned conventional wisdom and opened up new possibilities for tackling climate change and other key issues of the twenty first century. 'There for a while, we had scientific ideas that there were economies of scale, so you always had to go big,' she says, 'but some of them were wrong.' She points to the 'miracle of the Rhein', Europe's busiest waterway, as an example of what can be done. It was only when all the interested parties (local pressure groups, government and non-government organizations and polluters) got together that progress could be made. By working together on a common cause polluters finally began to recognise the costs they were imposing on others and agreed to make changes. The 'miracle' had begun. Interestingly, the International Commission for the Protection of the Rhine, an inter-governmental body, failed to have the same effect. Community works from the bottom up. Always.

Beginning in service

I think it is appropriate to end this chapter by quoting somebody who has dedicated his life to service in the community, the Prince of Wales. In his book, *The Radical Prince, the Practical Vision of the Prince of Wales*, David Lorimer summarises the core principles that are essential to understanding the Prince of Wales's philosophy: the centrality of the sacred, of wisdom and of spiritual vision; the significance of living tradition; and the practical application of spiritual insights to life. Under the principle, 'service, community, consensus, partnership', he writes:

> 'The motto of the Prince of Wales – and one wholly appropriate to the nature of his work – is Ich Dien, meaning "I Serve". The Prince understands service in the widest sense to include the duties imposed by his position. The sheer number of his charitable patronages – over 380 – bears witness to his sense of

service. At the centre of his socially-oriented work lies the importance of community. And this in turn is related to the building of partnerships and consensus within and between communities. The Prince's work is focused on enabling communities to help themselves.'

6
TRAVELLING LIGHT

*'In the next century
or the one beyond that,
they say,
are valleys, pastures,
we can meet there in peace
if we make it.
To climb these coming crests
one word to you, to
you and your children:
stay together
learn the flowers
go light.'*
Gary Snyder, For the Children

It's a gift to be simple

We moved into our current home in Wiltshire nearly 20 years ago. I remember vividly coming to see it for the first time and the impression it made upon me. We were leaving London to live in the rural southwest and I could feel the pressures and stresses of life flowing out of my body as we took in the villages and surrounding countryside. The vendors of our home-to-be were moving to Yorkshire and they too were excited about their move. It was a big hike up the property ladder and their new house was, apparently, very grand indeed. 'It has fourteen bathrooms', the lady excitedly told us, 'and that's just the beginning'. Perhaps I should have been jealous or happy on their behalf but I must confess that only one thought went through my mind. 'Who on earth would want to clean fourteen bathrooms?'

It seems to me that nothing is more difficult to obtain in life than simplicity. Even when we find it, or work hard to obtain it, the malevolent spirit of complication is lurking around the next corner. My life in rural Wiltshire is every bit as chaotic and busy as my previous existence in the 'big city', but with one important difference. Within five minutes I can be walking in the beautiful hills, downs and valleys that surround our home and it is as if I have entered a new world. I sometimes walk my faithful terrier from Silbury Hill, built nearly 5,000 years ago, to the ancient stone circle at Avebury. At once, I feel the weight drop from my shoulders. Here, in the heart of the prehistoric world, I make the practical decisions to simplify my life. I think carefully about what I should be doing and what I should not. I shed responsibilities that are not mine to take on, so that I *can* be effective in those areas where I can truly make a difference. I learn to say 'no', which for me is the hardest thing of all. I practice living light.

The discipline of simplicity

When I wrote *The Strategic Mind*, I developed seven key disciplines that I believe help us to think strategically (*chapter 2*). As a holistic discipline, it made no sense to me to attempt to prioritise these disciplines; they work together as a whole. As the years have gone by, however, I have come to see one of them as particularly important. It is simplicity. Simplicity will unlock all the other disciplines. It opens up pathways to strategic thinking that are 'hidden' from the mind, by providing us with the most valuable thing we can possess; space. I have also learned another lesson. Simplicity does not come easily. In our modern world, most of us require some kind of 'simplicity practice' to maintain the benefits of an uncluttered lifestyle. This may seem a bit over the top for something that we probably think should flow naturally, but simplifying our life *does* take a little work initially. Almost all of us need to find ways to bring it to our conscious attention on a regular basis. I do this by walking, but there are an infinite number of other ways to achieve the same thing; meditation, active sport, yoga, the martial arts, dancing, being in nature, community service, caring for others and many more. All these activities help to take our attention away from ourselves (and our day-to-day worries) and focus it elsewhere. By doing so, we are able to put events in our own lives into perspective and prune away the excess. After a while we don't need to work quite so hard at it because simplicity is integrated into our way of thinking and it becomes second nature.

Simplicity is first and foremost a state of mind and it is available to all of us. We live in a world of excess, so much so that the word 'extreme' is now used as a branding device for consumer products rather than as a warning sign. There is a price to be paid. We are often hassled and stressed, which results in illness, emotional imbalance and depression. Some of us are like firecrackers, ready to ignite at the slightest provocation. In technical terms, we suffer from what is known as 'free floating hostility'. Any situation in which we do not feel respected, listened to, or get our way, is likely to set us off. For others, it is as if we are carrying the weight of the world on our shoulders. No wonder we are often distracted, unfocused and ineffective. So here's the good news. It doesn't have to be this way. When we begin to simplify our lives consciously, to live a little lighter, many of these burdens drop from our shoulders. Focus, clarity and effectiveness follow and we feel a good deal better too.

Removing clutter

In February 2009, Howard Schultz, CEO of Starbucks, inadvertently upset Britain's Business Secretary, Peter Mandelson, by remarking in a US television interview that Britain's economy was in a downward 'spiral' with soaring unemployment and 'very, very poor' consumer confidence. Mandelson responded angrily, reportedly asking, 'why should I have this guy running down the country? Who the **** is he?' Schultz gently backed down. He pointed out that the minute-by-minute coffee sales at Starbucks' stores act as a good barometer of the economic mood of a country. He was, in fact, expressing his concern about many Western economies. He finished by saying that he had not intended to single out the UK. Referring to his family's British roots, he added, 'I wasn't talking down the country and I had no intention of doing so.' Why didn't Schultz behave more confrontationally? Perhaps self-interest is part of the answer. It makes sense to limit the damage to Starbucks' interests that might be caused by further antagonizing the British political administration and media groups. However, I think there is another, more important, reason. Schultz knows where his focus lies and sees an ongoing argument as a distraction from central purpose. He possesses the self-awareness to acknowledge that he made a mistake in speaking out a little too forthrightly, but also the dignity to explain why he made that mistake. He is capable of eating 'humble pie' but maintaining his integrity and authority. This is a 'simple' solution that quickly leaves behind the distraction of an unintended remark and puts him back on track for more important matters. How many of us find ourselves going down quite a different pathway in similar circumstances?

I like to think of clutter as baggage, stuff that weighs us down. This helps me visualize a 'simplicity practice' as a way of removing some of this excess weight so that I can walk a little easier. In *The Strategic Mind*, I recommended a number of practices to eliminate physical clutter, one of the most satisfying being a good clean out. There is something very rewarding about the physical work of clearing out our junk and knowing that charity shops can make a good return from our old and unused possessions. This not only creates space, it also allows opportunities and possibilities to come to us. There is an old adage, 'nature abhors a vacuum'. This invariably plays out as soon as we create the space for it to do so, which is particularly useful if we find ourselves stuck and don't know what to do next. A good clear out is rarely finished. Something new inevitably enters into our life in mid-process. As we get rid of the old, so space is created for the new.

We tend to think of clutter in terms of physical things but the same principles operate at an emotional level. Consider, for example, all those past hurts and resentments that we just can't seem to let go. Emotional burdens may be more difficult to deal with than physical clutter, but they act just as effectively as thieves of our space and time. All of us carry historical resentments, hurts and relationship issues within us. Some are too deep (or unconscious) to deal with easily or quickly. For these we need time, healing and, more often than not, help and support from others. But we *can* learn to stop taking new stuff on. We start by letting go of the small things. All those irksome moments (or people) that bother, aggravate and frustrate us. We can still get angry and express ourselves where necessary but we don't carry the hurts, grudges and resentments forward with us. Like Howard Schultz, we deal with the issue and move on. Gradually, over time, we also learn to shed some of the more serious stuff that's anchored in the past and is preventing us from moving forward. The reward is well worth the effort. We travel a good deal lighter and experience the freedom and space that this brings with it. And the less baggage we carry, the more intense our focus and clarity of purpose will be. I often sense the gods of fate laughing as they tangle our personal lives into knots and complicate our working lives. Now is a very good time to begin to untangle these knots.

Reversing the illusions

> *'Any fool can make things complicated it requires a genius to make things simple.'*
> **E. F. Schumacher**

When we simplify our lives we are able to really commit to our choices. Strategic leaders often live incredibly busy lives but their activity is focused around a central purpose. As a result, they are able to move forward, even when they make mistakes and have to begin again. Mistakes become part of the learning process rather than merely a point of distraction. Simplicity is also a vital process in decision-making. No other area in this book presents such large and immediate opportunities as simplifying our society at every level. Complex environments suit simple rules, which underpin flexibility and adaptability, and result in long term sustainability. When H.L. Mencken wrote that 'every complex problem has a simple solution that doesn't work', he was not arguing for complicated solutions. Complicating matters offers us the false certainty of control, which is one of the central illusions of our society and our thinking. Mencken was, in fact, warning us of the dangers of resorting to simplistic assumptions instead of thinking at a deeper and more holistic level.

Complex systems are best managed by simple rules. Many of the most important issues that we face in the twenty first century are complex in nature, so we need to think deeply but act simply. Simplistic thinking, on the other hand, tends to result in complicated solutions, that are, invariably, ineffective. This should give us good cause to breath a collective sigh of relief. But there is a 'problem'. We cannot continue to hold dear the illusions that we are in control, that bigger is better and that we are independent of the world in which we live. As we have seen, none of these beliefs is true. In reality, we have a limited degree of control, which we should learn to use wisely. The most profound solutions begin small scale and grow organically, rather than being imposed from above in grand gestures. And, we are most certainly not apart from our world. We are, in fact, one with it. The time has come to dispense with these illusions, which drive us into ever more complicated solutions that are, at best, ineffective, but often turn out to be more problematic than the original issues that they were intended to resolve. Worse still, the energy that is required to maintain these complicated 'solutions' is so great that we are beginning to suffer from collective exhaustion just trying to maintain them.

Simplicity in action

Simplicity may be a way of thinking but it is also a very powerful and practical tool. It is not necessary to go very far in today's world before we see examples of everyday practices that could be streamlined, eliminated or redesigned using simplicity principles. These range from common nuisances (too many confusing lines and safety paraphernalia on our roads springs to mind) to our response to key global issues such as climate change and environmental degradation. Satish Kumar, editor of *Resurgence* magazine, talks about the simple solutions that would allow us to move towards climate stability. He advocates using energy much more effectively, minimizing waste and using resources more carefully. He also suggests eating less meat to reduce the amount of methane emitted by intensively reared cattle. It is his fourth suggestion, however, that I find the most interesting because it is the simplest of all. 'We need to plant trees', he writes, 'Many, many trees. They will help to absorb our carbon emissions.' 'If every family in Britain,' he adds, 'and there are 20 million of them, planted five trees in 2010 there would be 100 million trees – how much carbon would they absorb? How simple it is.' Satish Kumar has a point. In the nineteenth century, 40-50% of the UK was covered in trees, but this has been reduced to just 6-7% over the past 200 years. Planting more trees alongside other simple environmental practices is key to developing long-term solutions to living sustainably.

Naturally, we are not going to resolve an issue as complex as climate change solely by planting more trees. But it is important. By becoming more aware of the deep source of value that trees bring, both to the earth's environment and to the quality of our lives, we move into harmony with our world. And this *is* an excellent place to begin to tackle climate change. The root of positive change often lies in the cumulative effect of small acts taken by large numbers of people. The simpler and more intuitive the change the more likely it is that we will act. Make something complicated, on the other hand, and it is guaranteed that most of us will switch off. Perhaps, this is why the former British administration decided to portray the dangers of climate change using highly simplistic advertisements that portrayed the potential future for British children as a sub-Saharan nightmare. This is to confuse being simple with simplistic. If we deny the complexity inherent in climate change we cease to treat people as intelligent adults and we fail the 'common sense' test. Even before the Advertising Standards Authority stepped in and formally expressed its disapproval the approach was bound to fail. Sometimes, we need to be honest and admit that we do not know all the answers, something that is very difficult for all of us, especially politicians. As *The Economist* concluded in March 2010:

> *'Rather than feeding voters infantile advertisements peddling childish certainties, politicians should treat voters as grown-ups. With climate change you do not need to invent things; the truth, even with all those uncertainties and caveats, is scary enough.'*

Simple solutions are not about pretending we have all the answers. They are about removing the dead weight of unnecessary complication that is choking our world. And there are many areas where simplicity principles can have an immediate and very positive effect. The reduction of waste throughout all aspects of our consumerist society is one area that is ripe for the application of simplicity principles. We currently light our offices '24/7', pay scant attention to the real cost of energy in our industrial, commercial and domestic activities and throw out a very sizeable proportion of the food that we grow. Tackling this immense waste provides some of the biggest opportunities of our times. A particularly good example is the way in which we deal with the ultimate disposal of waste in our world.

Waste not want not

At the moment, waste tends to be dealt with downstream through recycling policies, many of which are neither economic nor cost effective. It would be much better to move our focus upstream to concentrate on reducing waste at its source. This means redesigning products and services with minimal waste as a key objective upfront, potentially a powerful source of competitive advantage. There are particularly big opportunities to reduce excess packaging (which has the additional benefit of saving money throughout the entire supply chain) and redesigning products to increase their re-use (for example, making more use of modular technology so that only the non functioning elements of a product need be discarded). Sometimes, technology is on our side. The digitalization of media product and the migration of software onto 'cloud servers' are good examples. It is quite possible, however, to apply simplicity concepts to the design of such basic products as industrial carpeting for offices and commercial premises. In this case, the carpet is supplied in squares so that it can be replaced piecemeal in areas of high usage. These strategic approaches to reducing waste are invariably 'high value added' in competitive terms, offering significant long term advantages in competitive positioning to those firms that are able to adopt innovative and creative approaches.

There is scope for creativity and innovation in other areas too, particularly when it is combined with long-term sustainability principles. Rene Gisbers, a heating-systems engineer from the Netherlands, provides one good example. He has invented a collapsible plastic shipping container. It offers many advantages over the conventional steel variety. Plastic containers are more resistant to corrosion, easier to float and clean and produce only 25% of the carbon dioxide that would be generated by the manufacture of a standard steel container. As the containers are made of a fibreglass composite, they weigh three quarters of a standard container when full but only one quarter when folded down. The problem, as always, is persuading existing industry players to change. Edgar Blanco, a logistics expert at MIT, summarises the dilemma nicely when he points out that, 'everyone is vested in the current system. Introducing a disruptive technology requires a major player to take a huge risk in adopting it. So the question will always boil down to: who pays for the extra cost, and takes the initial risk?'

Simple policies do not, of course, eliminate risk, although they may make it more transparent. Neither does 'simple' necessarily translate into 'easy'. That is why there is plenty of scope for competitive advantage through superior implementation of new product and service technologies. The power of simple solutions lies in the depth of understanding that underlies them, the ability to challenge existing industry assumptions and to be able to disrupt existing ways of doing things. This is most certainly *not* easy but the potential rewards of doing so are immense, both commercially and environmentally.

Clarity and focus in business

Airdrie Savings Bank, based in Lanarkshire in Scotland, is Britain's only independent bank. It is small, very conservative and safe. In our times the last word is particularly important. The bank grew out of the nineteenth century savings-bank movement and is still owned by its customers. Even today, this heritage is clearly visible in its current ethos and Airdrie continues to be run on 'simple', straightforward and very conservative principles. It is a minnow in banking terms with just seven branches, 60,000 customers and just over 100 employees. However, it is also doing very well by sticking to simple principles and rules. It limits its profits to £500,000 to £750,000 a year, all of which is used to build reserves. The underpinning values of the business are refreshingly traditional and free of contemporary business jargon. There are just five statements and they include transparent banking, a people-based approach, good service and 'a wish to meet our customers' needs at a fair price.' The bank does not sell its customers insurance or mortgages and it does not issue credit cards, preferring to stick to debit cards. It also adheres rigidly to the rule that only a third of customers' deposits should be advanced in loans, a third kept on deposit with other British banks for liquidity purposes, and the remaining third invested in government bonds. Its core capital (the deposits with other banks) is roughly three times the increased level required by the British Government after it rescued the 'big banks' during the credit crunch crisis. It is not surprising to hear that the bank also takes on no currency risk. These traditional banking rules have served the bank well. In 2007 bad debts amounted to just £53,000 on loans of £33.5 million. Jim Lindsay, the bank's general manager, comments that 'we'd only be in trouble if the whole British banking system collapsed.' 'But then,' he adds, 'everyone would have a lot more to worry about than us.'

A simple approach brings focus and clarity to a business. Simple rules make it easier for firms to make conscious decisions about the scale and scope of their activities by identifying boundaries and trade-offs. Food retailers such as Pizza Express, Starbucks, Pret A Manger, Lidl and Waitrose all have clearly defined offers that leave managers free to concentrate their energy on maintaining and enhancing the unique aspects of their core retail propositions. The complexity in these businesses lies in delivering the offer in the competitive marketplace. Execution is key. The aim is to give customers a special experience in a world where so much of what sets businesses apart can be copied and replicated easily. In short, the energies of the business are focused on those areas that matter most to customers. A similar example is the comeback of the humble American diner in the United States, particularly in the North Eastern states. The largest diners now make millions of dollars each year in earnings. Part of the reason for their success is that customers know exactly what to expect when they go to a diner. But a major factor for their continuing popularity is that they also tend to be family run businesses, with high levels of attention to detail. Their charm is a mixture of nostalgia, good delivery and the idiosyncratic touch of their owners, which gives them a special character so lacking in many of the fast food chain restaurants.

Many environmental charities and voluntary associations also benefit from having highly focused remits, which can be communicated easily to potential members. A case in point is the Royal Society for the Protection of Birds, a British charity that works to promote the conservation and protection of birds. There is nothing small or inconsequential about the RSPB. It has over one million members (including 150,000 youth members) making it the largest wildlife conservation organisation in Europe. At the other end of the spectrum lies Action for the River Kennet, a Wiltshire-based charity dedicated to protecting the health of the River Kennet, particularly from over-extraction of water: By being tightly focused on its purpose it is able to punch well above its weight. The Wiltshire Wildlife Trust, which is based in the market town of Devizes, provides another excellent example of the advantages of focus and clarity of purpose.

At first sight, the Wiltshire Wildlife Trust appears to have a very general remit. It is concerned with 'all aspects of the environment in Wiltshire'. What really matters, however, is how the charity translates this mission into concrete local initiatives. The answer is 'very well'. It is particularly adept at identifying specific opportunities for projects and then executing them extraordinarily well. One such project is the creation of a unique habitat and walking area at Langford Lakes Nature Reserve in the south of the county. The lake was created on a site of former gravel pits and has now become a beautiful tranquil area for breeding and wintering birds such as mallard, gadwall and tufted duck. With the Wylye Valley close nearby, it is a perfect example of meeting both the environmental and recreational needs of the county. Specific projects such as these make it very easy for local people to see exactly what the Wiltshire Wildlife Trust is seeking to achieve and how this impacts on the local environment and their lives. This creates a powerful sense of community and belonging as well as a clear sense of identity for the Trust. One of my favourite annual rites is the spring 'Sarsen Trail' walk, which raises money to 'keep Wiltshire rich in wildlife'. The walk begins in Avebury and ends 26 miles later at Stonehenge after traversing across a good portion of Salisbury Plain. The expression 'to keep the county rich in wildlife' may seem rather general at first glance. But it becomes very personal when you witness that potential first hand. As a result, the event is hugely successful (and I might add exhausting!).

Travelling light

'Do not say a little in many words but a great deal in a few.'
Pythagoras

This is the shortest chapter in this book but in many ways it is also the most important. We live in a society that values 'doing' rather than 'being'. We are constantly distracted by too many activities, experiences and choices. There is a price to be paid for that. We have little time for reflection and scant chance to hear our own inner guidance. But isn't leadership all about the capacity to act? So what's wrong with an emphasis on doing? 'Quite a lot' is the short answer. The ability to make things happen in the real world *is* a vital aspect of leadership. The word, entrepreneur, for example, literally means 'one who undertakes'. But action that is unfocused and not based on a clear sense of purpose and identity is likely to translate into energy wasted. The result of wasting our energy over a continued period of time is that we become worn out, dispirited and resentful. We begin to blame the world for our woes and move away from the central tenet of leadership, taking responsibility for where we stand *right now*. Becoming a leader is often exhausting in the first place, so it's important to use our energy wisely.

Simplicity allows us to maintain clarity and focus in what we do. When we travel light we protect ourselves from distraction and loss of focus; simplicity acts as our bulwark for protecting central purpose. It plays a critical, largely unacknowledged, role in our ability not just to act, but also to do so decisively and effectively. A simple approach to life allows us to remove unnecessary baggage from our shoulders. We stop taking responsibility for things that don't concern us and we resist the urge to meddle in other people's business. We get on with what *does* matter to us with a simple approach that reinforces our intensity of purpose and gives us the inner strength to stick to our path when the going gets tough. We learn to let go of the clutter that we have accumulated and we find, to our surprise, that we never needed it in the first place. This not only makes us more effective as leaders. It also gives us real freedom, perhaps for the first time in our lives.

7
GOING WITH THE FLOW

*'Just a green olive
In its own little egg-cup:
It can feed the sky.'*
Kit Wright, Acorn Haiku

Acting in the moment

When Wesley Autrey, a construction worker from New York, leapt in front of an oncoming subway train to save a man who had fallen onto the tracks, he probably didn't think too much about it. If he had, he may well have changed his mind. The young man had had a seizure and Wesley acted on instinct, knowing that the train coming into the station would kill him. He covered the man with his body to keep him still whilst the train passed over them and they survived. The grease on Wesley's cap told him how close a call it had been. Without doubt, Wesley's actions required great courage and he was dubbed the 'Hero of Harlem' and the 'Subway Superman' after the event. Donald Trump called his actions 'an astonishing act of bravery and selflessness' but Wesley is far more modest and self-effacing. 'I don't feel like I did something spectacular', he comments, 'I just saw someone who needed help. I did what I felt was right.' Perhaps, but he had the courage to act in the moment and he was able to use his skills as a construction worker, used to working in confined spaces, to save somebody's life. This is the stuff of leadership.

Marek Edelman, the last military commander of the Warsaw ghetto uprising, was also a 'hero who didn't like heroism' in the words of Bronislaw Geremek, another ghetto survivor. In April 1943

Mr Edelman held off 2,000 Nazi soldiers who had been sent to liquidate the ghetto. As deputy commander (and later leader) he had 220 untrained 'boys' under him, armed only with pistols and home-made explosives. The soldiers who faced him were the pick of the Wehrmacht. Yet, the Jewish fighters stood their ground for almost a month before the Germans burnt the ghetto to the ground around them. Marek and a few remaining comrades escaped death by travelling through the sewers to join the Polish underground outside. He went on to take part in the larger Warsaw uprising in August 1944, which was brutally crushed after 63 days and resulted in the city being razed to the ground. Mr Edelman did not fear death. For him it was far more important to make a stand so that the world would know what the Nazis were doing to the Jews in Poland. He never regarded himself as a hero. 'Others who were sent to Treblinka,' he remarked, 'their death was far more heroic. We didn't know when we would take a bullet. They had to deal with certain death, stripped naked in a gas chamber or standing at the edge of a mass grave waiting for a bullet in the back of the head.' 'It was easier to die fighting,' he summed up, 'than in a gas chamber.' After the war, Mr Edelman stayed in Poland where he continued to stand up for human rights and promote the causes of minority peoples until his death in 2009. He never compromised his principles even when, as with his open letter to the Palestinian resistance leaders in August 2002, he attracted both criticism and controversy in doing so.

In their acts of heroism Wesley Autrey and Marek Edelman shared a capacity to act instinctively in the moment. Both men knew who they were and what they stood for. This gave them the courage to act on their beliefs when the opportunity presented itself, no matter how dire the consequences might be. Both were capable of facing death because they were in service to something they valued far more. Wesley Autrey did not think twice when it came to saving another human being because it was simply the right thing to do. Marek Edelman was determined that the world should know what the Nazis were doing to the Jews in Poland. Like many leaders it was this sense of purpose that enabled them to grasp the opportunities that presented themselves in the moment, regardless of how desperate the situation appeared to be. Thankfully, not all of us will have to deal with such extreme circumstances. But if we are to be leaders we do need to develop the ability to go with the flow of life and take full advantage of what presents itself to us, whether good or bad. We build for the long term but we also need to be fully conscious in the moment of all that is around us.

Heart of New York

Knowing who we are and what we stand for is essential to becoming a leader as we have seen. It allows us to put down strong roots and build for the long term, knowing that our foundations are secure. And, naturally, planning is good. It helps us to prepare for what lies ahead. It is healthy, however, to remind ourselves that we can never fully anticipate the pathway before us. If we believe that we are fully in control of our lives we will never be able to grasp fully the opportunities that present themselves to us because our focus will be elsewhere, either in the past or the future. It is wise, therefore, to remain open to the present moment and accept what is directly in front of us right now. Nobody has ever planned their way into leadership. In fact, quite the reverse is true. It is the way in which we deal with the unexpected that determines whether we are a leader in the eyes of others. We are judged most often by how we deal with unplanned events, how we act when things go wrong. That is the acid test of leadership. As leaders, we need to learn to let go sometimes and surrender to the natural flow of life. Even though we may have rock solid foundations none of us knows how our future will unfold.

Singer-songwriter, Benny Gallagher, often tells the story of his song, *A Heart of New York*, when he performs in concert. Benny wrote the song in 1977 whilst he was part of duo, Gallagher and Lyle, and pushed his label repeatedly to release it, but his pleas fell on deaf ears. This might have been the end of the matter, except that Art Garfunkel (who had previously had a big hit with *Breakaway*, also penned by Gallagher and Lyle) picked up the song for his 1981 album,

Scissors Cut. Garfunkel's version of *A Heart of New York* was even released as a single but it failed to make much of an impression at the time. Once again, it looked as if the song was destined to fade into obscurity. Fate then intervened in the form of Simon & Garfunkel's reunion concert in Central Park in September 1981. Apparently, the duo had planned to perform Frank Sinatra's, *New York, New York*, in honour of the city, but Paul Simon had second thoughts on the night and asked Art Garfunkel if he knew of any other suitable songs. As a result, they substituted *A Heart of New York*, which they sang as part of their set in front of more than 500,000 people. The album of the event made the Billboard Top 10 and achieved multi platinum sales. But even this is not the end of the story. Benny Gallagher tells of how he was travelling on the subway train during a visit to New York and heard the song playing on the transit system. Aware that he had not been asked permission for its use he called the New York Transit Authority. He apparently had to work quite hard to convince them that he was the rightful author of the song! *A Heart of New York* is now inextricably linked with the Big Apple and one of Benny Gallagher's biggest songwriting successes; the big hit that never was.

Strong foundations

There is nothing wrong with being opportunistic. It is, in fact, an essential prerequisite of leadership. On April 30th 2008 over one thousand people packed into Colston Hall in Bristol to witness a gala celebration of their roots. *A Passage to Bristol* was a spectacular staging of the diversity of the city, both in terms of talent and of people's stories of how they came to be in the city. The show brought together many of the strands from the city's rich mix of 89 nationalities and ethnic origins, featuring everything from Tibetan Overtone Chanting to Somali Wedding ceremonials. Perhaps, more importantly, it was a rare chance for many to celebrate their personal journeys and share their stories of how they came to be in Bristol. The event was put on by the Pierian Centre, a training and development conference facility based in St Paul's, which has a strong focus on community development. June Burrough, founder and Director of the centre, was delighted with the success of the event. The audience 'embraced 60 nationalities, and showed how diverse communities can come together to enjoy an evening of shared fun.' It was the stories, however, that made the evening so special. With 30,000 people coming through the doors of the Pierian Centre every year, June hears a lot of stories. 'They're funny, moving and often inspiring,' she says, 'I wanted to celebrate them in some way – and I wanted to see what other stories, what other journeys are out there.' 'I wanted to find somewhere big enough,' she continues, 'to share the different stories that make up Bristol.' This is just one aspect of what the centre is all about.

June Burrough is one person who has had plenty of experience in both planning for the long term and dealing successfully with unanticipated events. As a social enterprise with a not-for-profit ethos the centre measures its success by its capacity to affect positive change in the communities it serves. This necessitates a very wide remit and current activities include events such as the Ann Frank exhibition, Refugee Week and centre's role as a leading partner in the Bristol programme for European Year 2010: Combating Poverty and Social Exclusion. These events, together with a strong social, cultural and arts programme, are held together by a very strong sense of core purpose, which the centre defines as 'serving the wider community of Bristol, especially marginalized, excluded and disadvantaged people'. The Pierian Centre trades as a conference facility to generate income to meet this broader social purpose, which is incorporated into its structure as a social enterprise and community interest company. This is the robust foundation upon which everything else stands. Because the centre has such a clear and compelling vision, June has been able to forge strong partnerships and collaborations with organizations such as the University of the West of England, Bristol Cathedral and Bristol City Council to help it achieve its broad objectives. Strong foundations, a clear sense of purpose and a compelling vision for the future of Bristol are imperative for building support. Yet, this is still only half the picture.

Since June Burrough founded the Pierian Centre in 2002 it has had an amazing impact within Bristol and beyond. June is very adept at seizing opportunities and transforming unfavourable circumstances, making the very best of what lies directly in front of her in the present moment. Without this ability the centre would certainly not have achieved all that it has done. Indeed, it is unlikely that it would have survived this far. I have had the pleasure of working with June since the beginning of her venture. I remember vividly being shown around a beautiful, but semi-derelict, Georgian building in Portland Square in the heart of St Paul's after June first purchased it. This was to be the Pierian Centre and June did a wonderful job of bringing her vision to life as we stumbled across rubble and builders' mess. Like many others at the time I was positive and supportive on the surface but part of me wondered how on earth she was going to put these wonderful plans into effect. Surrounded by rubble and chaos there seemed every reason for things not to work out despite her strong intentions. Would the centre even be open on schedule I wondered as I surveyed what looked like a six-month building project. I needn't have worried. It opened a couple of months later on time, to the very day.

At the time I didn't know June quite as well as I do now, but when we meet I still sometimes find myself pondering quite how she is going to execute her latest plan! Experience tells me she will succeed and I am used to witnessing her achieve the 'impossible', often clutching victory from the jaws of defeat. It is this ability to transform the everyday chaos that accompanies an entrepreneurial venture, combined with her steely determination, resilience and persistence that marks her out as such a powerful leader. She has the capacity to stay true to her principles, yet be open to opportunities in the moment, even if they would normally be called 'challenges' by the rest of us. Although she has never wavered from first principles in terms of core purpose she has shown remarkable flexibility in other aspects of the venture including structure, funding and staffing. Her vision is long term but she lives in the present. She gets things done. And how!

Step by step

Going with the flow might best be described as the ability to be in the moment or, more precisely, to be fully *conscious* in the moment. This may sound obvious until we consider how little time most of us actually spend in the moment; when we can truly say that we are consciously present *right now*, not anticipating some future event or looking back on the past. Some people use the word 'opportunistic' as a form of abuse, implying that no serious foresight or integrity is required to be good at it. But what if opportunism is born of an intuitive ability to see advantage in something that others cannot because they are not 'present' enough; because they are either too invested in the past or too busy escaping into the future? Strategic leaders are not only good at seeing the 'big picture', they are able to deal with the grimy reality of day-to-day experience. As it happens, this is where we live most of the time, so being connected with the 'here and now' is vitally important. Far more critical, in fact, than most business texts would have us believe.

When *Time Magazine* ran a series of articles on leadership in 2009, it concluded that 'charisma is overrated and that nothing matches the power of getting things done.' And we can only get things done in the moment. When we are present in the moment we are connected to our intuitive nature and to the world around us. Strategic leaders may be visionary to a greater or lesser degree, but they all have the capacity to act, which means being grounded in the here and now. Simon Burke, currently Executive Chairman of Superquinn, and formerly CEO of both Virgin Entertainment Group and Hamleys, puts it this way:

> *'It's all about mind-set, the way in which you receive ideas, suggestions, opportunities, threats, events, you name it. If you know what you want to do and what sorts of things you want to take advantage of, then little lights will go on in your head when the right sort of particle hits you. And that's what it's about. That's where you get the vision from. It's actually out of the dust and miasma of everyday life and conversations. If, at the end of*

the day, you don't have a belief in what you want to do, and that It is going to work, all the data around you is ultimately meaningless.'

The ability to go with the flow is one of the 'secrets' of how leaders succeed. It is often ignored because it seems pedestrian and obvious. In reality, it is anything but. Here's a good exercise to do. Observe your reactions when your day does not go to plan. If you are anything like me, you will note how much resistance you put up when even the simplest of things goes awry. This is an over-attachment to the past and a state of mind that is, to say the least, not very conducive to seeing the opportunities that so often lie within the challenges we face. Some of us are fortunate to be more forward facing. You may be saying to yourself, 'well, I am always willing to change my plans.' This is a good characteristic to have in this fast moving world where adaptability and flexibility are key. A word of caution is, however, appropriate here. Because some of us live in the future, creating all kinds of exciting prospects for tomorrow, we may prefer to change our plans when the going gets tough rather than remaining committed to the path we are on. This is escaping into the future and it prevents us from making a difference in the world because we don't have the perseverance and persistence to follow through.

I have known both Simon Burke and June Burrough in a leadership context for many years. As a result, I am able to observe that they share an essential quality of leadership. They have the tenacity and commitment to work through tough challenges in the present, often very tough challenges indeed, by being open and opportunistic in the day-to-day but firmly committed to core long-term principles. They can be visionary at times but they live and act in the present. They can make difficult and tough decisions and carry people with them because they are trusted as leaders. As a result, they both routinely achieve results that others would deem to be 'impossible'.

Think small and go slowly

Two of the key disciplines that I outlined in *The Strategic Mind* are intimately connected with our ability to go with the flow. In that book I termed them *'think small'* and *'go slowly'*. Both are counter-intuitive because we are trained to believe that 'big is best' and that success in our world requires us to think and act quickly. There is no truth in either of these beliefs. It is simply not possible to build a robust business or social enterprise if it does not have solid foundations. And this takes time and patience. Organizations that grow too quickly often unravel when things get tough. Indeed, when we look closely at some of our most successful organizations we find that they have largely grown organically by an incremental step-by-step process. Amazon began life as an online bookseller not an online department store. It added other product categories later. It also developed its information technology infrastructure (one of its core competencies) over time through a process of continual improvement and extension. At first it sold products on its own behalf, only later replicating the market trading structure of eBay, by moving to also acting on an agency basis on behalf of third party buyers and sellers. eBay itself is another good example of an organic approach to growth.

It is true that eBay grew very quickly in its early days but it also did so incrementally. The company's first priority has always been to support the unique relationship that it has with third party traders and it was the natural growth of the trader community that powered the company's early rise. eBay's biggest misstep was its $2 billion purchase of Skype, a leap of faith that resulted in a large write off on disposal and little else. Both Toyota and Honda are further examples of an incremental step-by-step approach. Toyota's well-publicized quality control problems in 2009 are a very rare example in the company's history, when the goal for growth has overridden the established incremental culture of the company. Toyota is determined to redress the issue as we saw earlier in the book and was still placed seventh in Fortune's list of the most admired companies in 2010. Naturally, there is a time and place for big moves. BP under its former CEO, John Browne, was successful partly because of the audacity of his vision, which required some big strategic moves. We should, however, be careful here in our interpretation. There are some industries where economies of scale and scope are critically important and the energy industry is one of them. Ownership of energy sources and maintaining reserve capacity (finding more resources than are being used up) are critical strategic dimensions in the industry, so acquisition and mergers are often key.

Going slowly does not mean dithering and being unable to make a decision. It is the ability to reflect deeply before we act. When we take time to make decisions, we not only make better ones, we also become much more aware of our unconscious assumptions and beliefs, including the boundaries and trade-offs that underlie our decision-making. Ironically, by making these assumptions more conscious we are actually able to speed up our decision making in the longer term. Simply put, we know what we are about, what we do and what we don't do and why this is so. We can react swiftly in the moment when things go wrong because we have sorted out our priorities and understand the consequences of our actions. By thinking slowly we are able act quickly and spontaneously. And we don't have to reinvent the wheel so often!

Apple

Apple is the quintessential success story and the world's most admired company. In 2010 it topped *Fortune Magazine* prestigious list for the third year running, this time by the highest margin ever. Indeed, 51% of corporate leaders surveyed in 2009 said that they admired Apple, an unprecedented majority. It has powered its way through the recession, reporting record earnings and celebrating an undiminished stream of new consumer products and services. How has the company achieved its iconic status and enviable profitability record? CNN, Fortune and Money suggest that one explanation is that the company has 'single-handedly changed the way we do everything from consume music and access information to design products and engage with the world around us'. There is no question that Apple has a powerful vision for the role that technology will play in the years ahead through its integration in everyday products and services. That's why I used the company in *The Strategic Mind* as a case study to illustrate the power of dreaming, one of the seven disciplines of strategic thinking. But what clearly differentiates Apple from the many other dreamers in the world is the *human scale* of the application of that technology, and the ability to make products *work*. It makes products and services that work for us in our everyday lives and it does so effortlessly. As Steve Jobs, CEO of Apple, is the key driver, the company reflects his key beliefs and aspirations and it is almost a mantra in Steve Job's personal philosophy that technology serves us and not the other way round. It is for this reason that Apple products have consistently revolutionized the industries within which they operate, including computing, music, telecoms and, with the introduction of Apple's new tablet computer, the iPad, potentially also publishing.

If you use Apple products this will not be anything new. The combination of the iPod and iTunes brought order into the world of digital music by integrating hardware and software seamlessly into a product that worked. The iPhone has played a similar role in mobile telecommunications. Cell phones were already a revolutionary application of technology when Apple entered the market but they were largely stand-alone devices. Apple has not only 'humanised' the phone by increasing functionality and improving its design but it is also playing a vital part in reintegrating mobile technology back into everyday life (synching phones and computers together so that information can be accessed from any device for example). Apple computers have done something for me that I would not have thought possible before I made the switch; they have brought back the 'joy' of computing into my life. Don't get me wrong. I am primarily a functional user. But for years I had become accustomed to dreading every change to my computer configuration. No matter how simple the upgrade, chaos and confusion always seemed to threaten. Gradually, I adopted the policy of 'no change, good change' or 'upgrade only when absolutely necessary'. My world has now altered. Each new application that I learn (when I have the time!) adds genuine utility to my life, whether it is in managing my photos, organizing music, editing songs or keeping in touch with my colleagues and friends. For me, Apple's greatest achievement is to have put back the human being at the centre of technology, which, I believe, is where we belong.

Apple offers a particular challenge for a writer. It is such an iconic company and it is so widely admired that it has attracted more commentary than, perhaps, any other business organization. So what's new to add? Certainly not that it is hugely profitable and successful (it posted a *quarterly* profit of $1.7 billion on sales of almost $10 billion at the end of 2009). Few can be unaware of Apple's continued ability to churn out a seemingly endless series of highly innovative world-beating products. In 2010 it launched the first version of its new tablet computer, the iPad, but there are countless other examples such as the introduction of the wireless mouse earlier in the year. We can certainly note the relentless march of Apple into application software (users downloaded more than 1.5 billion applications from the Apps store in the first year alone and that number had topped 2 billion by September 2009). We are in even more interesting territory when we look at Apple as a major disruptive force across a wide spectrum of industries ranging from computing to publishing. The iPad, introduced into the UK in April 2010, has considerable potential for gaming applications in addition to spearheading a breakthrough in e-book sales through Apple's iBooks online store. At the same time, by March 2010 the number of 'apps' for books on the iPhone had apparently exceeded those for games (previously the largest category), which is surely a sign of things to come. In short, Apple's ability as a major industry disruptor is phenomenal. Suddenly the technology is not only feasible from a technical perspective but it looks simple, appealing and intuitive. *That* is what Apple is so good at doing. The more important question for me, however, is 'how' Apple has managed to achieve all this. Part of the answer is that it is a particularly good example of a company that is fully present in the moment but also charged with a powerful mission. It is, perhaps, the supreme example of an organization that knows how to go with the flow.

As we have seen to 'go with the flow' is to be connected in the moment to the possibilities around us. When this is combined with a powerful sense of meaning and purpose, it is anchored into a long-term mission and becomes an unstoppable force for change. Apple has deep meaning and purpose encoded into its DNA and it comes directly from Steve Jobs. It's about making products and services that best serve customers in new and innovative ways, but within a human context. This is not the same as meeting the needs of customers. Apple goes beyond meeting existing needs because it is operating at the boundary of possibility; one that lies beyond the comprehension of many of its customers. These are the perfectionist and inspirational qualities of Steve Jobs translated into practical and functional products and services that currently do not exist. Just as Henry Ford did not ask customers what new form of transport they wanted, because they would have chosen an improved horse buggy, so Apple is not interested in solely addressing existing customer requirements. Instead, it is looking over the shoulders of its customers into a better world where technology and consumer products combine in exciting and revolutionary ways that connect with deep human desires. At the same time, innovation must be functional, practical, empathetic and exhibit a unique sense of design. It must serve human beings not be the master of them. This is an inordinately tough remit. The fact that Apple so regularly succeeds is what makes it such an extraordinary organization.

Understanding Apple means understanding Steve Jobs. One of the major reasons why the company has succeeded is his remarkable persistence, commitment and endurance through some very tough times indeed. I covered Steve Jobs' personal story in *The Strategic Mind* and it includes being dismissed from the company he helped to found, major illness and significant market reversals. Apple even warranted a jibe in *The Simpsons* during its early years, the implication being that Apple computers had had their day. It is no exaggeration to say that it is something of a minor miracle that Apple has made it through to today. Far from weakening Steve Job's resolve, however, all these experiences have simply made him stronger and more determined. In his Commencement Address at Stanford University in 2005 he talked of his brush with death and called it 'the single best invention of life... it clears out the old to make way for the new'. As for his firing from Apple, it was the 'best thing that could have happened to me... it freed me to enter one of the most creative periods of my life'. In fact, it is Steve Job's failures that have been the making of him as a leader. 'Sometimes,' he says, 'life hits you in the head with a brick. Don't lose faith.' 'It was awful-tasting medicine,' he concludes, 'but I guess the patient needed it.' Many leaders face similar trials and tribulations and these invariably constitute an initiation into real leadership. It is 'trial by fire' and we emerge stronger, more resilient and, most importantly, more grounded than before. In the case of Apple, Steve Job's experiences have made the company tremendously receptive to the opportunities that exist in the moment.

There is no doubt that Apple has strong foundations, a clear long-term vision and a strong sense of identity and purpose. But it is its ability to be open to the moment, receptive to possibility and capable of decisive action that underlies its formidable innovative prowess. It many ways Apple is not a revolutionary organization that invents afresh but one that takes existing technology and improves it relentlessly, seeking out new opportunities to apply technology within new perspectives. In this respect it is similar to Toyota and Honda, which pioneered lean manufacturing practices and 'kaizen' (incremental improvement) and thereby revolutionized the world's automotive industry. Apple shares much with these companies including an incremental 'step by step' approach ('*think small*') and a capacity to think deeply before acting ('*go slowly*'). Over time, however, these practices have become fully integrated into Apple's culture allowing the organization to act quickly and decisively. Building on strong foundations also means that incremental but consistent growth can become a powerhouse. Perhaps, Apple is currently enjoying a 'golden age', but right now all these things have come together to push it to the top of the corporate league. There is no doubt that Steve Jobs is a perfectionist and that even the best is not really good enough. While he remains head of the company, it is unlikely that it will slow down or that its relentless stream of innovative products and services will falter. When he decides to step down it will be interesting to see how the company evolves. But for now, there is no better place to understand Apple than by reading or listening to Steve Job's Commencement Speech at Stanford University, which captures his life experience and philosophy so well and is freely available on YouTube.

Intent

> *'Our perception of the world is transformed through the awareness that we bring to simple experience.'*
> **Joseph Goldstein**

There is one thing that makes all the difference to whether we succeed or fail in the long term. It is our intention. It is intention that links our sense of purpose and destiny in the world with the ability to be open to the possibility inherent in the moment. It is this that underpins our ability to act decisively. Yuzaburo Mogi is Chairman and CEO of Kikkoman Corporation, the world's largest maker of naturally brewed soy sauce. Kikkoman is one of Japan's oldest continuously operating businesses, tracing its origins back to the early seventeenth century, when the Mogi and Takanashi families first began soy sauce production along the Edo River in Noda, a small city located not far from Tokyo. Mr Mogi is descended from one of those founding families. It is also one of the most recognizable Japanese names outside the automotive, electronics and banking industries. Kikkoman's success in overseas markets is a product of being open to opportunities and willing to adapt where appropriate. Not only has this generated annual overseas sales growth of nearly 10% for 25 years, but it has also been vital in keeping the company healthy in the current recession. 'Without international expansion, Mr Mogi notes, 'a major part of our sales and operating profits would have evaporated.' Markets outside

Japan accounted for 30% of the company's total business in 2009 but 60% of its operating profits. The US alone generated 80% of overseas sales and more than three quarters of its overseas operating profits.

Mr Mogi spent many years heading up the company's American division. The United States was the perfect springboard for international expansion as the country was open to new things and willing to try new ingredients in its cuisine. During the early days there were few Japanese restaurants in the US so Kikkoman had to adapt. It hired cooks to incorporate its sauce into American recipes and began to position soy as 'all-purpose seasoning' rather than a Japanese product. It also went one stage further by introducing teriyaki sauce (a mixture of soy sauce and other ingredients) specifically for the American barbeque market. In Europe, it has followed a similar strategy, encouraging the use of its soy sauce as flavouring for rice, despite the fact that this is not done in Japan. Kikkoman has consistently demonstrated a willingness to be opportunistic, yet it has never wavered from its long-term commitment to healthy eating. Fostering health is a core company mission and the 74-year-old Mr Mogi practices what he preaches. Each morning, apparently, he rises at 5:30 and walks for more than half an hour, irrespective of the weather. 'Staying healthy has two meanings,' he says, 'one is to promote personal happiness and the other is the contribution health makes towards society.'

This long-term purpose acts as an anchor to Kikkoman's ability to be opportunistic in the moment. Indeed, the name Kikkoman is derived from the Japanese folklore that the tortoise lives for 10,000 years and is thus a symbol of longevity (In Japanese, 'kikko' means 'tortoise shell' and 'man' is '10,000'). The company both looks back to its tradition of brewing high quality natural soy sauce and forward by developing new and better products through biotechnology, a key element of the brewing process. It takes pride in promoting the exchange of food culture, even when this means moving beyond traditional Japanese use. This is the deeper intent that underpins Kikkoman's success. There are many other similar success stories to that of Kikkoman and they come from all sectors;

commercial, not-for-profit and the public sector. One of the best is the Schulich School of Business at York University in Toronto, which has consistently moved up the international business school ratings.

In 2000, the *Financial Times* placed Schulich School of Business 45th in the global ranking of the world's best business schools. By 2009, *The Economist* ranked it as the top business school in Canada, #7 in North America and #12 in the world. In just under a decade it entered into the business school elite alongside MIT, Yale and INSEAD. This ascent has been 'steady and unbroken', marked by innovative programmes, large investments in facilities and, most important of all, a commitment to the importance of globalization in management education. Schulich launched one of the world's first international MBA's in 1989 and this became the catalyst for the internationalization of the school, allowing it to differentiate itself from its older, more established, competitors and giving it a powerful source of competitive advantage. The Dean of York University, Dezsö Horvárth, who is also a strategy professor, recalls that 'there was no way that we could adopt a me-too approach and hope to compete with any of the leading schools in Canada or abroad.' 'But,' he continues, 'international business was an area where we truly could be among the best in the world.' This was the powerful statement of intent that started the ball rolling.

It would be easy to underestimate the considerable amount of work at ground level over the past decade that has happened in order to make Schulich's dream come true. Implementation plays a vital role in successful strategy and without this consistent commitment the school would not have been able to achieve its strategic objectives. Along the way, it has established a management centre in the downtown area of Toronto, compensating for its location north of the city. It has also built a $104 million state-of-the-art Executive Learning Centre, which has helped propel its executive division into the top tier. In 2006, Schulich was one of only four education providers to attain the Economist Intelligence Unit's award of excellence in both in-house and public programmes. And, there is much more in the way of innovative programmes, global alliances and satellite centres, and a truly diverse student body supported by world-class professionals. All of this is impressive and it was also hard work. However, as with Kikkoman and Apple, Schulich is also able to seize the opportunities in the present moment because it is anchored with a strong identity and sense of purpose. It is this that has allowed the school to achieve those features that define a leading management school: attracting first-class students, recruiting world-class faculty, developing cutting-edge programmes, building strong alumni relations and cultivating strong corporate linkages. This is possible because Schulich is defined by its core intent, equipping the leaders of tomorrow to manage global issues. Mamdouh Shoukri, York University's President and Vice Chancellor, expressed this in February 2010, in a comment that is tellingly long on responsibilities and short on self-congratulation:

'In a world characterized by challenges and opportunities of global proportions, universities are key agents of change. The great global issues we face – climate change, poverty, epidemics, war – cannot be addressed by great technological advances alone. Technology provides us with important tools, but we also need to develop social innovations that allow for a better exchange of information between cultures. We need to install in our students a sense of our shared citizenship. Our students are the leaders of tomorrow... It is our responsibility to respond with educational programs to help prepare them for that future – and involve them in becoming global citizens.'

Our intention also links us with the free flow of life and the serendipity and synchronicity that lie within. York University was able to fulfil its dreams for its business school partly because of the significant support of Canadian entrepreneur, Seymour Schulich (after whom the business school is named). This leads us to a classic 'chicken and egg' question. Would the school have been able to attract this support if it had not had a clear sense of its identity and core purpose? My guess is that the two are inextricably linked. Once we commit to something we become connected to the natural flow of life, and thereby benefit from to all manner of unanticipated support, whether it be favourable circumstances or help available when we need it most on our journey. For those of us who are naturally practically minded and like to control our lives this is often a difficult concept to accept. The illusion of control is a very powerful one to break. But take some time out and talk to those who have travelled a leadership journey and you will be amazed at the tales they have to tell. To truly align ourselves with the flow of life is to recognise the power of everyday miracles. As Einstein observed, 'There are two ways to live your life. One as though nothing is a miracle. The other as if everything is a miracle. I choose the latter.' Receptivity is the key. Nancy Gibbs, an essayist and editor at large for *Time Magazine*, expressed the paradox of miracles by saying, 'For the truly faithful no miracle is necessary; for those who must doubt, no miracle is sufficient.'

Small is beautiful

It is a useful skill in life to be able to observe ourselves without judgement. I know that when I talk about the discipline, *'think small'*, I inevitably find myself using 'big' examples. Usually my central argument will coalesce around the concept that the cumulative effect of many small steps can be very significant indeed. Some of the business examples in this chapter certainly fall into this category. There is much more to thinking small than this but I, like so many of us, have been trained to think that 'big' equates with 'important' and my presentations often reflect this unconscious bias. The truth is that our sense of what is important is often deeply flawed and we are also rather poor at 'connecting the dots' to the bigger picture. The result is that we fail to see the intrinsic importance in small things and place far too much weight on the advantages of size.

One of the very interesting characteristics of strategic leaders is that they reach a point in their lives when they accept that they will be doing what they do regardless of what the world thinks. It's not that it is no longer important for them to be successful or make an impact. Neither do they stop having dreams about what they would like to achieve. It's a lot subtler than that. They come to a place within themselves where they accept their area of influence, be it big or small, and put their heart and soul into what is immediately in front of them. They may achieve success in their own lifetimes, but often it is much later when their true contribution and influence is appreciated. The naturalist, Henry David Thoreau, is a good example. 'For many years', he once said, ' I was the self-appointed inspector of snowstorms and rain-storms and I did my duty faithfully.' His love of nature took precedence over everything else in his life, regardless of whether others understood his actions or not. 'I frequently tramped eight or ten miles through the deepest snow,' he noted, 'to keep an appointment with a beech tree, or a yellow birch, or an old acquaintance among the pines.' Indeed, it was a late night excursion to count the rings of tree stumps during a rainstorm in 1859 that led to him being ill with bronchitis. His health declined over the next three years and he died in 1862, aged 44. Surely the man was a kook? Certainly, even his mentor, Ralph Waldo Emerson, had his doubts. He once commented that Thoreau could have been a great man if he hadn't been so obsessed with nature. History, however, tells a different story. Both Martin Luther King and Mahatma Gandhi were heavily influenced by his life and beliefs and their influence in turn is beyond measure.

Thankfully, we are beginning to appreciate that small is beautiful in its own right. The Prince's Trust makes a significant impact on the lives of thousands of young people through its policy of making small loans available to help youngsters establish businesses and create their own careers. Microfinance, providing financial loans to people who would not normally be judged creditworthy by the banking system, is making an increasingly important contribution to lifting people out of poverty in developing countries. Microfinance also provides credit in amounts that would normally be considered to be too small to be administratively viable in the financial system. Online micropayment systems provide a similar role in the developed world. Many charities are pioneering the 'small is beautiful' model. Small actions can make a big difference to very large issues. Books such as *100 Ways to Make Poverty History* by

John Madeley and Oxfam's *Change the World for a Fiver* are examples of this trend. The same principles underlie the '10:10' climate campaign (where people sign up voluntarily to reduce their carbon footprint by 10%), and the Fairtrade 'swap' campaign (encouraging people to swap their 'usual stuff for Fairtrade stuff').

There is even more power in bringing together like-minded partners and cross promoting such initiatives. Not surprisingly, Starbucks was heavily involved with the Fairtrade 'swap' campaign, but it also participates in many other issue-related causes. It worked with the Prince's Trust, for example, to promote the 'Inspired to Change' campaign, offering a free beverage to all those agreed to support the work of the Prince's Trust in specific ways. We have begun to realize that depending on top down solutions is ineffective and potentially very dangerous. By taking responsibility for our actions and making small changes we can make a big difference. This is particularly true of areas such as changing our impact on the environment, for which I would recommend the excellent book by Archie Duncanson, *Ecology Begins at Home, Using the Power of Choice*. We really can make a difference from our own back yard.

Connecting with the flow

To be able to 'go with the flow' is to connect with the moment, to be *conscious* of all that is going on around us. Most of us, for most of the time, are living either in the past or the future. There is nothing wrong with going back to know who we are and where we came from. And there is certainly nothing wrong with dreaming of a better future. But our point of power is in the now. Right now. At this very moment. Unfortunately, all our self-wisdom and our desire to make the world a better place will come to very little if we remain unconscious in the moment. Becoming more conscious in the now requires awareness. When we use the expression 'to become aware of something' our focus tends to fall on the 'something', the object of our awareness. This is safely out there in the environment, outside of us. In fact, we need to look inside of us to cultivate a state of awareness. It is an inside job and that's what the next chapter is all about. To be in a state of conscious awareness changes everything, what we are able to see and how we see it. As singer songwriter, Bruce Cockburn, observed:

'Little round planet
In a big universe
Sometimes it looks blessed
Sometimes it looks cursed
Depends on what you look at obviously
But even more it depends on the way that you see.'

8
AN INSIDE JOB

'I wish I'd realised then
That all we have is Here and Now,
That One Day may be one day
More than time allows.'
Jane Miles

As within so without

There is an old story of Asclepius, the Greek God of medicine and healing, meeting two travellers on their way to Athens. Asclepius had stopped by the side of the road to enjoy a drink of cool clear water from a nearby spring. As he sat there quietly enjoying the warmth of the day a traveller appeared. It was a hot dusty day and the weary traveller was only too glad for the chance to stop for a chat and a rest, time enough to recuperate for the remaining journey ahead. 'I'm on my way to Athens', he said, 'do you happen to know what it's like?' 'Well,' replied Asclepius, 'Where are you from?' 'Piraeus' came the response. 'What's that like?' asked Asclepius. 'I wouldn't recommend it,' the traveller replied, 'it's a noisy, busy town, full of dirt and dust'. 'And the people,' he continued warming to his theme, 'are dreadful, very unfriendly and unwelcoming.' 'Well,' said Asclepius, 'I expect you will find Athens just the same.' The traveller sighed as he got up and trudged wearily on. Asclepius took a deep breath and relaxed. 'Time for lunch', he said to himself, but before he could reach for his food a second traveller appeared. 'Good day,' said the new arrival, 'do you mind if I sit with you and rest for a while?' 'Not at all,' replied Asclepius. 'I'm on my way to Athens,' said the man cheerfully, 'do you know what it's like?' 'And where are you from?' replied the Greek God. 'Piraeus,' beamed the man, 'a lovely place, so vibrant and exciting – never a dull moment!' 'Well,' said Asclepius, a wide smile on his face, 'I expect you will find Athens just the same.'

As we think so do we see. Yet, for most of the time, we are oblivious to this basic truth. The belief that the world around us is an objective reality, independent of the observer, is a strong one and we forget that our perceptions colour the way we see external reality. 'We are always paid for our suspicion,' noted Henry David Thoreau, 'by finding out what we expect.' What we believe is what we experience. 'As within so without' as the old saying goes. We fall under the illusion of independence. As the ninth century master of Zen Buddhism, Huang-Po, astutely observed, 'the foolish reject what they see, not what they think. The wise reject what they think, not what they see.' 'Observe things as they are,' he recommended, 'and don't pay attention to other people.' Marcel Proust was referring to the same thing when he said that 'the real voyage of discovery lies not in seeking new landscapes, but in having new eyes.' The Japanese Zen master expressed the same principle as 'don't seek the truth – just shed your opinions.'

Strategic leaders have those 'new eyes'. It is true that they are passionate about what they believe in. They are fully committed to what they believe, often obsessively so, and they possess the persistency and resilience to translate ideas into action. But there is something more, something that enables a leader to connect to, and transform, the reality around them. Strategic leaders possess the awareness to see things as they *really* are, to observe the world around them as it is. They are also acutely aware of how the external world is connected to them by what they believe and they act accordingly. Put another way, they have the capability to reflect *before* they act (the seventh discipline of strategic thinking), to go deeply within themselves before passing judgment on what is before them. By doing so, strategic leaders come into their own power. It is in knowing how to transform our inner reality that we learn how to change the world around us.

The power of stillness

There is a traditional story of three brothers who lived with their father. After the old man had died they pondered over their future. All wanted to make a positive contribution to the world. The oldest brother decided to become a doctor and went off to medical school, founding a successful practice in a busy city. The second brother had always wanted to become a teacher. So he enrolled on a teaching course at a big university and, upon qualifying, began to teach at a large high school in that city. The third brother stayed at home. 'What are you going to do?' asked his siblings. 'I'm not sure,' replied the youngest, 'I'll wait and see what comes to me.' After ten years the oldest brother returned home for a break. 'I'm exhausted,' he said, 'It has been non-stop ever since I left and I don't think I have the energy to carry on like this.' With both of his siblings at home, the second brother also took the opportunity to pay a visit. His brothers greeted him warmly but they noticed that he looked tired and pale, with a disconnected and slightly harried look in his eye. 'I seem to working on automatic pilot these days,' he confessed, 'it's all I can do to get through the day sometimes.' 'Well, it's good to see you both,' said the youngest, 'wait here and I'll bring some water from the stream to make us all some tea.'

When the youngest brother returned he had a bowl of thick brown murky water with him. 'Surely we are not going to drink this', thought his older brothers. The youngest, however, asked his siblings to sit silently around the bowl and watch it. Gradually the mud fell to the bottom and the water became clear enough for them to see their reflections in it. They looked at the clear bright water and the way that the sunlight reflected on its surface, and they felt the peace of stillness fall on them. 'You see,' said the youngest brother, 'it's only when we are still enough to see our own faces that we know how best to make our way in the world.'

Cultivating awareness

My youngest son, Jamie, has always loved reptiles. When he was still very young a friend in the neighbourhood recommended the

Cotswold Wildlife Park to us, and one visit was enough to make it Jamie's favourite Sunday outing. Whilst most children of his age headed straight for the farmyard animals, Jamie would make a beeline for the Reptile House. Here was the home of the Park's reptile and amphibian collection, and as far as Jamie was concerned it was sacred ground. Once he had entered the hallowed enclosure he was immediately entranced, spending hours staring intently at the beaded lizards, iguanas and Morelet's crocodiles. It would often take him the best part of an hour to make it through the relatively small exhibit and, if he got is way, we would then have to return to the entrance and begin all over again. Never in my life has an hour seemed like such an eternity! I quickly became an expert in locating and identifying every single frog in the enclosures, if only with the vain hope of moving Jamie on more quickly to the next one. I think it was only the contemplation of afternoon tea in the nearby Cotswold town of Burford that got me through those days.

The result of Jamie's intense scrutiny of the animals, however, was that he saw a good deal more than me. Unlike me, he could draw animals with a remarkable sense of proportion and detail. It is no exaggeration to say that he surpassed my drawing ability by the age of five or six. He was learning how to see the natural world in a way that I have never mastered. It is no surprise to me that as a teenager he has gravitated to biology and environmental science, and has taken up wildlife photography as a hobby. In short, he has cultivated a deep awareness of the natural world that few adults possess. Interestingly, he has been able let this deep awareness emerge naturally rather than having to work at it consciously through discipline or practice. It just happened. He was young enough not to place blockages in the way of his learning so the intuitive knowledge simply emerged naturally. And, he is now building on this consciously through his formal school education. Jamie's awareness is also marked by openness and sensitivity, an ability to look at things from new perspectives. He sees things differently. It is this sensitivity and openness that will be his point of power for effective action in the future.

Like my son, John Thorbjarnarson, the 'saviour of crocodiles', loved reptiles as a boy. As a child, he collected snakes and frogs from a the bog behind his house in suburban Norwood, New Jersey and had a little spectacled cayman in a glass cage in his bedroom. Apparently, he was absolutely captivated by the cayman and used to stare at it for hours upon end. There was even a pet boa constrictor that used to swim regularly across the family pool. John worked for the Wildlife Conservation Society in the United States for over 20 years and spent most of his life trying to persuade people to view crocodilians differently, as friends rather than pests. 'I guess you could say,' he once commented, that 'I was obsessed to some extent with reptiles.' John Robinson, Chief Conservation Officer of the Wildlife Conservation Society, called him 'the most well-known crocodilian guy around the world,' and in 2004 he was awarded the Castillo Prize for crocodilian conservation by the world Conservation Union for 'multiple and long-term efforts in crocodilian conservation.'

Dr Thorbjarnarson has played a major role in warning the world how scarce crocodilians are becoming, cataloguing them as a postgraduate and then drawing up plans to save them in 1988. He liked to explain that they were more like birds than snakes, hoping to reduce some of the fear and prejudice that people feel against them. He worked with locals to collect eggs and tried to train them to hunt only adult males under legal quotas, leaving the females to breed unharmed. He preached that man's role should be one of stewardship for these precious creatures, and he put theory into practice by helping to preserve habitats and convince famers and other native peoples that they had a real stake in the animal's survival. When he first began to catalogue the 23 species of crocodile, no less than 20 were teetering on the edge of extinction. Today, this has been reduced to seven. Despite dying early at the age of 52, he has made a big difference in his world. This is all the more impressive, given the deep-seated fear of crocodilians and the immense prejudice against them. John also faced significant practical challenges in trying to save them, including dealing with the illegal trading of their skins for luxury leather goods. He was only able to take on this leadership role because of his deep awareness of crocodilians, based on his early passion and reinforced by years of experience, reflection and observation.

John Thorbjarnarson may have been immersed in the world of crocodiles but this did not make him any less of a 'doer'. He travelled all over the world, studying crocodilians in over 30 countries from Brazil and Venezuela in South America to the mouth of the Yangzi River in China. He was never happier than when punting through waters full of crocodiles, collecting DNA samples or simply massaging their scaly necks with a six-foot poll. Indeed, he probably contracted the malaria that killed him whilst he was looking for dwarf crocodiles in Uganda. John's work is certainly not the preferred choice for those of us who are squeamish, as crocodiles can move very quickly when they want to and no species has stronger jaws. 'You have to be out there in the swamp in the dark in a boat that can easily get capsized,' notes John Robinson, before adding, 'that's what John just loved to do.' With strategic leadership it is not a question of reflection or action; it's both.

The power of reflection

'When a man does not know what harbour he is making for no wind is the right wind.'
Seneca the Younger

It is one thing to contemplate how John Thorbjarnarson's passion for reptiles developed into his rewarding life as one of the world's leading authorities on crocodiles and alligators. There is a direct thread to John's life that we can follow, and we also have the benefit of being able to view it retrospectively using hindsight. It can be quite another to see the same process in ourselves. We are intimately involved with our own life and this tends to make us the *least* objective observer of what happens to us! While we shake our heads in disbelief about the exigencies of life, those around us often have to suppress a smile because they see our patterns far better than we do. Many of our core beliefs were formed when we were very young, often before we acquired verbal communication skills, and they are deeply unconscious. As a result, the only way we can really be sure about what we believe is to observe our reality in the here and now. Witnessing what is actually happening in our lives in the present moment is always the acid test when it comes to understanding our beliefs. Only then, can we start to explore how our perceptions colour our world in a practical sense. This is, however, where things can get a little tricky.

We are trained to think in terms of 'good' and 'bad', 'positive' and 'negative', 'success' and 'failure', so we can quickly run amok establishing plausible reasons for why things happen to us and placing a judgment upon them. This may even involve beating ourselves up and attempting to change our attitudes through force of will. If, like me, you have tried this route, you will know that it doesn't work. Despite the plethora of self-help books that promise 'quick fix' remedies, making that kind of deep change at the head level isn't going to happen. Period. Life is a great deal more complex than we sometimes care to believe and we rarely, if ever, have access to more than a fraction of the whole picture. It is wise to take heed of Hamlet's powerful observation to Horatio that 'there are more things in heaven and earth... than are dreamed of in your philosophy,' and set our expectations accordingly. Luckily, there is another route to working from the inside out and it is a great deal simpler. We begin by detaching from the result. We stop judging ourselves from the perspective of how we think our life *should* be and we simply accept it for what it *is* – right now at this very moment of time. We accept the wisdom contained in the traditional Zen 'koan' or proverb:

'If you understand, things are just as they are;
If you do not understand, things are just as they are.'

For most of us this is counter-intuitive because we are steeped in the illusion of control. We have been taught that if we want something to happen we have to *make* it happen. Surely this state of acceptance is a recipe for indolence and inaction? Well, actually, no! We have already seen the importance of working with a clear intention of what we want to achieve and the hard work that is necessary to make any dream, endeavour or enterprise a reality. This is our commitment to making something happen and it remains firmly in place as our foundation stone. What we are really letting go of is the illusion that we are fully in control of the *mechanics* of how our intention manifests in reality. Unfortunately for us, we are *not* in control. We are only *part* of the process. An important part, true, but only part nevertheless. Instead of charging forward in semi-darkness through sheer force of will, we are taking the time and space to establish a connection to the whole, to the very flow of life. It is here that we will find the intuitive wisdom that lies within us, and it is here that we learn to 'see' the opportunities that lurk in the challenges, issues, problems and full-blown crises that emerge in our lives. The practice of reflection is a precious opportunity to clear our mind of day-to-day clutter and connect with our 'whole' selves: mind, body, heart and soul. We are then able to fire on all cylinders, from the fully integrated human consciousness. That is when things begin to happen. This is the point when our ideas begin to manifest in reality.

When we take time to reflect we deepen our awareness over time. We *slowly* become more aware of how the connection between our inner and outer realities plays out in our lives and we are able to make changes. These will often be small and incremental but, as we have already seen, the effect of incremental change over long periods of time can be very significant indeed. We learn the wisdom in the words of James Allen, the nineteenth century writer and philosopher, that 'we do not attract that which we *want* but that which we *are*.' Gradually our sense of who we are deepens and we begin to connect the dots. Because we are not judging outcomes at a simplistic level, we are less likely to set unrealistic expectations on how much we will achieve, often in the very shortest period of time. We allow the natural flow of life to take its course. This does not mean abandoning our deepest, most heartfelt desires, those that lie at the core of our being. Quite the contrary. We are freeing those desires to express themselves in the best way that they can, including those that are beyond our ken because we don't see the full picture. We are also removing many of the obstacles and conditions that we unconsciously place in our way, so that our deepest sense of purpose can flower in the way that is optimal for the whole.

Reflection in business

We are not all, by nature, reflective. For some us any philosophical discussion about awareness grates. It may seem too far removed from the job of actually making things happen, and thus a couple of stages removed from our understanding of leadership. But if we think about some of our greatest leaders for a moment, we quickly realize that they invariably spent a good deal of time in reflection (especially those who found themselves deprived of their freedom by being placed under house arrest, in gaol or otherwise incarcerated). Mahatma Gandhi, Nelson Mandela, Martin Luther King and Barrack Obama are some of the more obvious examples but many leading business executives also have a strong reflective stance. We have seen examples in Steve Jobs, CEO of Apple, Howard, Schultz, CEO of Starbucks and John Browne, former CEO of BP. It is also true of John Mackey, co-founder and CEO of Whole Foods Market, Akio Toyoda, President of Toyota, Yuzaburo Mogi, Chairman and CEO of Kikkoman and the 'Google twins', Larry Page and Sergey Brin, co-founders of the mighty Google.

The capacity to be reflective is not the opposite of being practical in life or being capable of making tough decisions when necessary. Far from it. Awareness and reflection are essential qualities that underpin the capacity to act effectively. They are the bedrock of effective decision making, rather than a limiting factor. As we saw in the last chapter, when a reflective practice becomes ingrained into strategic decision-making and we learn to 'think small' and 'go slowly', we actually speed up day-to-day decision-making. We know who we are, what we are committed to do and why we are doing it. We know our boundaries and our trade-offs, what we do and what we don't do. As a result, we can deal far more effectively with the crises, chaos and confusion that inevitably hit us from time to time. Taking space for reflection in the business world offers many practical everyday benefits. It reduces the temptation for us to judge every event and every person who enters our lives and it can be a major step forward in reducing the power of our self-limiting beliefs, whether or not we become fully conscious of what these are. Over time, we learn to meet the problems and challenges that inevitably enter our lives with a more accepting and measured stance, rather than reacting out of fear. As a result, we are able to see the hidden opportunities that so often lie within the situation presented to us. This state of mind not only makes us more effective managers who people want to be around. It is also the making of us as leaders.

By becoming more aware, we avoid the fate of Henry Ford in the late 1920's, when he allowed GM to overtake Ford because he failed to see that car buyers were looking for more than the cheapest and most basic model available. Whilst GM, under the celebrated leadership of Alfred P. Sloan, began to cater for the emotional needs of customers (style, prestige and power), Ford continued to concentrate on wringing further cost economies out of the manufacturing process. As Richard S Tedlow, Professor of Business Administration at the Harvard Business school and a specialist in the history of business, concludes, 'Ford elected to be the CEO who "knew but did not know". Ford "acted by not acting". The sales department told Ford that the Model T was slipping, Ford said the car was fine – the problem was an incompetent sales department.'

An alternative plan

It's my guess that those of us who are reflective by nature are already on a path that recognizes the value of reflective space, even if we are not always diligent about our follow through. For others, it may seem easier to act first and learn from our mistakes as we go along. This is a time-honoured path, which even has a name. It is an iterative approach (learning by doing) and, in many ways, it provides an alternative path to the same destination. In fact, we all do this, at least some of the time. Even the very best leaders sometimes have to adopt a practical, 'suck it and see' approach to life. And, whilst it is true that we sometimes change as a result of increased self-awareness, more often than not we make those changes because it has become painful *not* to do so. In a personal context, this may be ill health, relationship problems or a business failure. As Marcel Proust pointed out, 'to goodness and wisdom we make only promises. Pain we obey.' In an organisational context, this is most likely to find its expression in financial problems, which persuade us that it is time that changes are made. There is nothing as powerful in business as the reality check caused by the flowing of red ink. Naturally, we learn a great deal in our lives through experience, sometimes referred to as the 'university of hard knocks'.

The downside of this approach is that it can be exhausting and debilitating, and our daily experience often feels like 'one step forward and two steps back' (with the hope that the ratio is reversed in the long term!). And, whilst *we* may be able to muster the energy and commitment to pull through personally, we face a different kind of challenge when we take up the mantle of leadership. Those who support us may value stability and consistency a great deal more than we do. Unfortunately, making life uncomfortable for people is a very good way to lose them. Business leaders often demand a great deal from their people including commitment, loyalty, creativity and the ability to work together effectively. Using a reflective approach allows us to give something back in return; a clear sense of purpose and long-term vision, consistency in our approach to day-to-day decision making, decisiveness in times of uncertainty and, most of all, our own commitment to 'walk the talk'. Naturally, we can consciously decide to do all these things without any reflective practice at all, but just taking that space does wonders for our powers of observation. It grounds us in reality. We see clearly again. Often, we are then able to observe the same picture as those around us see only too clearly, but are often loath to communicate to us. No one wants to be the messenger of bad news, particularly if they feel they are going to be shot. We are able to connect, recalibrate and take the appropriate action and then move on. And, crucially, we take action before the problems become more serious and debilitating.

I have been fortunate to work with many leaders who do this in practice. They share strong reflective qualities but, interestingly, none would wish to be identified primarily as a 'thinker'. They are too rooted in reality for that. They may have strong strategic skills but their leadership abilities are also founded on their capacity to act, to make a real difference in the world. They are, by nature, 'doers' as well as thinkers. Without exception, they are strong personalities with a belief in themselves and what they stand for. John Tucker, founder of the International Centre for Families in Business and June Burrough, founder of the Pierian Centre in Bristol, both fall into this category. They have strong, driving personalities and a hard-headed, proven record for making things happen, sometimes in the least promising situations. They are very good at uniting people behind them, which is critical to successful execution. As the old proverb says, 'a house divided against itself cannot stand.' Yet they both possess the ability to reflect deeply and change the way they do things when necessary, even if it means almost starting again. This is the central paradox of leadership. Leaders often need a strong ego to be able to drive through change, whilst their connection to deeper purpose provides the rudder in their lives, keeping them on track in the right direction. Reflection and the capacity to act go together hand-in-hand.

Reflective practices

'If you think that peace and happiness are somewhere else and you run after them, you will never arrive. It is only when you realize that peace and happiness are available here in the present moment that you will be able to relax. In daily life, there is so much to do and so little time. You may feel pressured to run all the time. Just stop! Touch the ground of the present moment deeply, and you will touch real peace and joy.'
Thich Nhat Hanh, Walking Meditation

Cultivating a state of awareness is not like turning on a light switch. It isn't either 'on' or 'off' and it doesn't happen immediately. John

Thorbjarnarson did not go from being a geeky kid with a pet cayman to the world's best authority on crocodiles and alligators overnight. He spent his life paying close attention to crocodilians. He combined formal study with years of practical experience and, I'm guessing here, he probably spent most of his days (and plenty of nights too no doubt) in getting there. He had a passion for the subject area and that helped him but it was the combination of close attention and discipline that made him what he was. As we have seen, as a rough rule of thumb we need to practice for 10,000 hours (roughly ten years at 20 hours each week) to build sufficient skills to master something. The author, Malcolm Gladwell christens this the '10,000 hour rule'. Just as John was able to 'see' things about crocodilians that would be invisible to rest of us, we can learn to do the same in our areas of endeavour. The key is attention and regularity. Let me be very honest here. I am no better at maintaining this sort of discipline than anyone else. But I do know that I am far more effective when I pay attention to creating space to reflect. When I become consumed with a whirlwind of activity and I neglect to take time out I suffer. In my case, it is a sense of exhaustion that tends to bring me back to my practice, although my Wiltshire terrier is good at doing the same thing. When he stares up at me with his big brown eyes, I know it is time to stop what I am doing and take him out for a walk, or play a brief game of ball in the backyard. I often come back, full of new ideas about how to complete my task and, occasionally, with the knowledge that I should not be doing it in the first place.

When we think of reflection, our first thought is probably of a passive practice of some kind such as meditation or prayer. But reflective practices can also be active. Dancing, running, singing and playing an instrument can also lead to the same calm state of mind, particularly if we become absorbed totally in the activity. By slowing down the constant stream of our thoughts we open up space and allow in new ideas, insights and inspiration. Often, we are also able to connect the dots between the many areas of our lives, our different experiences and the huge wealth of information and knowledge that we digest every day. In this interconnected world, we don't lack information and stimulation, but we do lack the time to digest it properly. A reflective space gives us the time to connect all that input as well as the pleasure of simply 'turning off' for a brief time. As a result, it makes us more effective and also does wonders for our health and sense of wellbeing. Naturally, different things work for different people. Some of us are able to get 'lost' in the genius of Mozart or Beethoven, whilst others prefer a ten-kilometre run or a martial arts work out. We learn what works by experimentation and intuition. Rock climbing may not appear to be a reflective discipline but, in practice, it is an ideal way to still the mind because every step taken requires the utmost concentration. The key is that whatever we chose to do, we become absorbed into the moment to such an extent that we calm our mind and slow the steady stream of thoughts. It's all about creating space.

There are many books on reflective practices, covering all areas from meditation and breathing exercises to yoga and Tai Chi. The aim of any practice is to still our mind, to enter a state of 'mindfulness', which is simply a calm awareness of ourselves in the present moment. But what if we are inevitably 'on the run', rushing from place to place and a regular discipline or practice is not possible? Well, there are two possible answers to this question. The first is that we would do well to assess our priorities and ask why we are so busy that we cannot spend any time doing something that is so important. Perhaps, we need to reassess our life and create this space and time as a gift for ourselves. The second is less testing, but equally important. There is one reflective exercise that we can do at any time in any place for any duration. It is simply to become conscious of our breathing. When we slow and deepen our breath, it helps us to be focused and calm, which is particularly useful in stressful situations (when our breath naturally quickens and becomes shallower). A simple breathing exercise helps to let go of stress, physical tension and negative emotions. It increases our sense of wellbeing by becoming more conscious of our basic connection to life, our own breathing. It is the most powerful reflective discipline and the foundation of all meditation practices. By letting go we allow in. It can be done in a matter of minutes and it opens us up to opportunity and possibility in the moment. By focusing our awareness, we open up to new ways of seeing and being in our lives.

Freedom from fear

Jon Kabat-Zinn is Professor of Medicine Meritus and founding director of the Stress Reduction Clinic and Center for Mindfulness in Medicine, Health Care and Society at the University of Massachusetts Medical School. 'There is nothing particularly unusual or mystical about meditating or being mindful,' he says, 'all it involves is paying attention to your experience from moment to moment.' 'Knowing what you are doing while you are doing it,' he continues, 'is the essence of mindfulness practice because the present moment, whenever it is recognized and honoured, reveals a very special, indeed magical power: *it is the only time that any of us ever has.*' This is the still point and it a very special place. When we are in this place, completely in the moment, we are neither anticipating the future nor beholden to the past. We are free and no longer ruled by fear, worry and anxiety. There is only peace in the moment. It is the place where we know 'all is well' and it is our point of ultimate power. This is not power defined by dominance over others, but power in relation to the whole, our individual role in collective experience. When Albert Einstein was asked by a reporter what the most important question facing humanity was he replied, 'Is the universe a friendly place?' The answer to this question lies inside of us. It cannot be answered in our headspace alone but at the core of who we are. In other words, it is found at the still point.

Fear exists for a reason. It is our safety mechanism, the emotional response that alerts us to threats in our environment and prepares us to face or escape from these threats. The physiological response to fear includes our heart-rate and blood flow increasing, muscles that are used for physical movement tightening and the quickening of the flow of oxygen and other nutrients through our body to prepare for a 'fight or flight' response. It is thus essential to our survival as a species and it is healthy and useful in our everyday lives. But whilst, strictly speaking, fear is a response to a one off event, the associated emotional states of anxiety, depression, apprehension and worry are something that many of us live with almost continuously. They can be particularly debilitating because, whereas fear is a response to a situation we hope to avoid, anxiety results from situations and circumstances that we believe to be uncontrollable or unavoidable. Many of us live with a permanent sense of anxiety and stress that wears us down and leaves us feeling drained and exhausted. This also affects our capability to make long-term strategic decisions because our focus inevitably shifts to the short term and our actions become crisis driven when we feel threatened. This is quite a different situation from the positive biological effect of the fear response in a genuinely threatening situation. In this case, we begin to feel and act as if life itself is threatening, and this is not a good foundation to becoming a leader. It is much harder to summon up the courage to act in difficult situations when we feel like this, when we have, in essence, answered Einstein's question in the negative.

When we spend time and space in reflection, in whatever way works for us, we access that still point where anxiety does not exist. There is no worry, apprehension or stress in the moment. As a result, we are able to find an alternative response to Einstein's question, one that is deep inside of us. And it is this that gives us the courage to act, the critical difference between having the ability to think strategically and becoming a strategic leader. This is the point where we can say we are 'free' of fear, not because we have overcome our biological hardwiring but because fear no longer impedes our decision-making outside its natural useful remit. We cannot overcome fear by will. We gain freedom by acceptance and this acceptance is found when we are completely still in the moment. That's an inside job.

The Prince of Wales

One person who lives by the mantra 'as within so without' is the Prince of Wales. 'We are told constantly that we have to live in the 'real world', he says, 'but the "real world" is *within* us.' 'The reality,' he continues, 'is that "Truth, Goodness and Beauty" in the outer, manifested world are only made possible through the inner, invisible pattern – the unmanifested archetype.' This directly mirrors the discussion in this chapter but it is a belief that has been an easy target for the media over the years. It takes a great deal of courage to walk the path that the Prince of Wales has chosen, and I believe that few of us have what it takes to do so. As he says, 'It seems to be becoming harder and harder in this age to stick to what we believe – or feel.' It is particularly so when we are in the public arena and any ill-advised word is likely to be pounced upon and exploited to the full.

Yet, the Prince of Wales has not faltered. Instead, he has resolutely continued his journey and held to his beliefs, persistently putting them into action over many years to build a formidable legacy. He has risked being considered 'an eccentric; at worst a dotty crank' and emerged unbowed. I don't think that the Prince of Wales is a man to gloat. However, if he were so, I suspect that he might take some pride in the fact that so many of his endeavours, which were considered 'naïve', 'alternative' or 'unworldly' when he began them, are now seen as mainstream. This is certainly the case with the work of the Prince's Trust and his considerable body of charitable work as we have seen earlier in the book. It is just as valid with regard to the Prince's views on organic farming, care for the environment and the importance of the human scale of living communities. The world appears to be finally catching up with the Prince of Wales. And from my point of view this is a very good thing.

There is no doubt that the Prince of Wales is a strategic leader in my mind. Not only does his work embody all the disciplines of strategic thinking outlined in both this book and *The Strategic Mind*, but he also has a phenomenal capacity to act. You don't build the kind of legacy that the Prince has, simply by espousing good theories. Indeed, one of the key principles underlying the work of the Prince of Wales is the practical application of his beliefs and spiritual insights into everyday life. He not only talks about the importance of truth, sustainability, humanity, education, values, stewardship, tradition, harmony, balance, integration and beauty. He does his best to live these principles in all his endeavours. As we discussed earlier in the book, the motto of the Prince of Wales is 'Ich Dien', meaning 'I serve'. In many ways, this is the most fitting summary of his life. There is something else, however, that marks the Prince of Wales as an important strategic leader, more than either his beliefs or his capacity to put them into effect in a practical context. It is his courage. It is so very easy to underestimate this if we are not in a public position ourselves. We can all pontificate on what we *might* do under these circumstances but I wonder what our true capacity would be in reality. Living a life in public is quite a different matter to sharing a few pints and lively conversation in the local pub. In reality, few of us have the personal qualities that are required to tread the Prince's path, which include fortitude, resilience, persistence, courage and humility. Without the latter, the Prince of Wales would not be open to the degree that he is, and many of his endeavours may well have faltered.

The characteristics exemplified by the Prince of Wales are found in many great leaders and we will be looking at how we build these strengths in the next chapter, 'Wake Me Up'. I suspect that the Prince of Wales has been able to develop these character traits partly because they were necessary for him to do his work. As the saying goes, 'needs must'. It is also, undoubtedly, the result of his extraordinarily strong motivations and aspirations, which are so core to who he is. In many ways, he is a modern day mystic, a 'seeker', whose awareness, as he says, 'comes from my heart and envelops my whole being.' As a result, he does not think solely through his head but through the core of his whole being. What he hears and feels, he translates directly into service in the world. He captured this central motivation in a speech in 2002 given to the Temenos Academy, which is committed to fostering a wider awareness of the practical relevance of the world's great spiritual traditions in everyday life:

'As I have grown older I have gradually come to realize that my entire life so far has been motivated by a desire to heal – to heal the dismembered landscape and the poisoned soil; the cruelly

shattered townscape, where harmony has been replaced by cacophony; to heal the divisions between intuitive and rational thought, between mind, body and soul, so that the temple of our humanity can once again be lit by a sacred flame; to level the monstrous artificial barrier erected between Tradition and Modernity and, above all, to heal the mortally wounded soul that, alone, can give us warning of the folly of playing God and of believing that knowledge on its own is a substitute for wisdom.'

Beginner's mind

It is much easier to read about developing a reflective state of mind than to do it. Much of what we do in life is automatic and we naturally take the path of least resistance. It's simpler that way and a great deal more useful too. We wouldn't want to have to ponder over every small decision we make. Some neuroscientists differentiate between the *automatic brain*, which is fast, unconscious and associative and the *reflective brain*, which is slower, deductive and more controlled. For many of our day-to-day tasks we are on automatic mode and that's how it should be. To be a strategic thinker, on the other hand, requires us to be in reflective mode and to be able to access this mode on a regular basis. We may have observed, for example, that we need to exercise more regularly because we have put on weight and we feel heavy and stodgy. We may even have marshalled evidence (that hill that we climb with the dog is getting steeper by the day!) to help us make a conscious resolution to do something about it. But we don't. Why? Because in the day-to-day, we seek the comfort of the path of least resistance, the domain of the automatic brain, and this tells us that we are too busy dealing with the chaos and confusion of daily life to take any time off for exercise. As Winston Churchill once observed, 'Giving up smoking is easy. I've done it hundreds of times.' We make our resolve in the reflective state but the pressures of daily life quickly push us back into automatic pilot.

Naturally, we have devised many clever ways to get around this dilemma. One of the most popular approaches is to provide positive (or negative) incentives to move from aspiration to reality. Unfortunately, incentives rarely work as we imagine they should. Our automatic behaviours are normally far too entrenched for any real change to occur without exerting a great deal of willpower, and this requires a corresponding degree of effort on our part. Automatic mode quickly claims victory and, before we know it, our resolution is quietly shelved until next year! Real change requires commitment and this is born inside of us. No amount of external planning (or wishing) can act as a substitute. As Dr David Freemantle, a leading authority on motivation and customer service, puts it, 'Motivation can only be sustained over a long period of time if it comes from within the individual.' If this is not the case, good intention aside, we tend to give up as soon as things get difficult. Perhaps, the time is not right. Perhaps, when I am less busy. These issues are as true at an organizational level as they are in our daily lives. Dan Millman, a former world champion trampolining athlete, inspirational speaker and author, observes that:

> 'Everyone wants to change, but not everyone wants it enough to go through the period of initiation and discomfort. We may think we have the will to change, but we really have the **whim** to change... Change doesn't happen until we commit to it... Commitment means no matter what. When we commit to a relationship, we stop wondering if someone else out there might make an even better partner for us. If we commit to a career we give it our best and waste no time toying with other possibilities. The feeling of commitment doesn't come naturally. We have to develop it, and earn it.'

The power of a regular reflective practice, however simple, is that it clears the space for us to recalibrate. We put our automatic responses on ice for a moment and think again, but this time we link back into the reflective brain. We return briefly to 'ground zero' where we can look at and see things afresh. This is why Zen practitioners advocate approaching every situation we meet with a 'beginner's mind', or ''beginner's eyes', as if we encountering it for the very first time. This way, we put our existing beliefs and preconceptions to one side and look at the situation as it really is, as somebody else might if they were totally unfamiliar with the circumstances. Our mind is open to what is possible in the here and now, rather than operating through the automatic response that limits possibilities and opportunities according to our experiences in the past. Developing a 'beginner's mind' sounds easy, but it isn't. Like all useful disciplines it takes a bit of practice. We are used to operating primarily on automatic mode. This why rest, relaxation and 're-creation' are important. Time off is *not* time wasted. Time off fuels our creative process. Opening up space for reflection is essential if we wish to become a strategic leader. It is, in fact, the very lynchpin of strategic thinking.

Hearing the call

We began this part of the book on the process of becoming a leader by thinking about *what* leadership means to us in the context of *who* we are ('Taking Responsibility'). We then looked at *where* we can act ('Seeing the Whole') and *with whom* ('We not Me'). The last three chapters ('Travelling Light', 'Going With the Flow' and 'An Inside Job') were concerned with the all-important question of *how* strategic leaders make a difference. In the next chapter ('Wake Me Up') we are ready to examine that very special point when we actually *become* a leader. This is the point where we decide that what we want to achieve is so important that it is worth the rollercoaster ride that is likely to ensue. Steve Jobs, CEO of Apple, is just one of many business leaders who answered that call:

> *'Your time is limited, so don't waste it living someone else's life. Don't be trapped by dogma — which is living with the results of other people's thinking. Don't let the noise of others' opinions drown out your own inner voice. And most important, have the courage to follow your heart and intuition. They somehow already know what you truly want to become. Everything else is secondary.'*

9
WAKE ME UP

*'There came a time when the risk
to remain tight in bud
was more painful
than the risk it took to blossom.'*
Anaïs Nin

Courage to act

Van Jones and Craig Sorely share the most difficult of tasks. They are working to build bridges between different worlds that are divided as much by lack of mutual understanding as anything else. This can be hazardous work as economic, social, cultural and religious differences often mean that emotions run high. Van Jones is an African-American activist based in Oakland, California. He is leading the way in changing public perception of what a green economy could mean for working people. His mission is to link economic and environmental issues, recognising that it is the poor and disenfranchised that often suffer the most from environmental change. Traditionally, environmentalism has largely been seen as the preserve of the white middle classes, those who are economically better off and can afford to make choices that are good for the earth. Van Jones' insight is that 'we can beat pollution and poverty at the same time' by providing a 'path to posterity' for blue collar workers in a low carbon economy. It comes from seeing the contrast between his Oakland constituency, which suffers from high unemployment, urban issues and pollution and its more prosperous neighbour, Marin County, which has created jobs in new 'green' industries such as organic food and solar panels. 'He's trying to convince America's minorities and working class,' wrote *Time Magazine* in October 2009, 'that building a green economy is the opportunity of a lifetime.'

Craig Sorely is a similar bridge builder, an 'eco-evangelist', whose passion for the environment has resulted in his personal mission to bring 'creation care' into the forefront of the conservative Christian agenda in the United States. Traditionally, environmentalists and evangelicals have come from very different backgrounds, but Sorely is working to change that from his base outside Nairobi in Kenya. Evidence suggests that he is achieving his aim. Many Christian colleges now offer degrees in Environmental Science and in 2007 the National Association of Evangelicals (a grouping of 45,000 American churches) formalised its commitment to 'creation care' as a key priority. Van Jones and Craig Sorely succeed partly by recognising common interests and emphasising shared values, so that different groups can learn and benefit from each other, with significant gains to society as a whole. We see the same process in many other walks of life.

At York University in Toronto, two very different students set up a society in 2003 called 'Shalom Salam', the Hebrew and Arabic words for peace. Hina Khan is a Muslim student from a privileged Pakistani family and Miriam Yosowich is Jewish with grandparents who fled from the former Soviet Union. Although the students could not be more different, they are united in building a bridge between the Muslim and Jewish communities at the University. With the help of James Murayama, a Japanese Canadian, they have made a profound difference on campus as peacemakers. Their object is not to force people to change their opinions but simply to open up to the possibility of listening to each other. 'We want people to come together and heal from the difficult past,' they say, 'to see how we're for peace.' They are both galvanised by past racist experiences. Hina Khan, who grew up in Toronto, witnessed the increasing suspicion of Muslims and Ismalophobia following 9/11. Miriam Yosowich was badly injured when she was pushed down the stairs by an anti-semitic youth at her school in Germany, necessitating six months off school and contributing to her family's decision to move to Canada. They have met plenty of resistance along the way but it has only spurred them on. 'We're not here to make people happy, says Khan, 'we're here to present an alternative.' 'We are peacemakers,' says Yosowich simply.

Answering the call

> *'From a spark may burst a mighty flame.'*
> **Dante Alighieri**

Leadership is an inside job. It is not simply the courage to act but to act wisely. Wisdom implies more than knowledge and the capacity to make use of it. It is associated with the qualities of judgement, compassion, reflectiveness, commitment, deep understanding, sagacity, responsibility, intuitive reasoning, vision, appreciating significance and a great deal more. Wisdom is always connected with the desiring of good for the greater community. A leader is somebody who acts on behalf of the whole. If we work with this simple definition we no longer have to worry about the significance of our actions, whether they are 'big' or 'small'. We are concerned primarily with intention, not with immediate outcomes. Mary Baker Eddy, founder of the Christian Science Movement, captured this when she said, 'A deep sincerity is sure of success, for God takes care of it.' Author and teacher, Wayne Dyer, is blunter still, 'our intention creates our reality.' For me, however, this skips a little too lightly over the courage that is required when we make the commitment to become a leader. Warren Bennis, Founding Chairman of the Leadership Institute at the University of Southern California and a pioneer in contemporary leadership studies, gets the balance just right. 'Leadership is the wise use of power.' he says. 'Power is the capacity to translate intention into reality and sustain it.' Our intention may be critical but we are also required to do some work!

We have seen that leadership is initiated by taking responsibility and acting for the benefit of the whole rather than for ourselves. It is built by learning to see the bigger picture, developing the ability to go with the flow and seeing and seizing opportunities along the way. It helps to travel light, to focus on our most important priorities by eliminating unnecessary clutter. And, most importantly of all, we become leaders by being able to connect regularly with the deeper intuitive wisdom that is inside of us, in whatever way that makes sense to us. When we act in this way, we signal that we are ready to hear the call of leadership. And, we are ready to commit to the rollercoaster ride that it may entail. This is not, necessarily, the big stuff that appears in magazines, on TV and in countless movies and stories. It is our *personal* leadership call. The unique call that has been with us since the day we were born. We are at that very special point when we actually decide to *become* a leader. We make a commitment, however small, that often, many years in the future, we see as being a critical point in our journey. We *answer* the call. As the American poet, Robert Frost, wrote:

> *'Two roads diverged in a wood, and I –*
> *I took the one less travelled by,*
> *And that has made all the difference.'*

When we talk to people who have chosen a leadership role they are often able to remember a special point in their lives, one that has had a profound and dramatic impact on their path. For Miriam Yosowich it was her experience of being severely hurt at school as a result of an attack by an anti-semitic youth. At the time she had no idea of how this event would play out in her life. But it sowed a seed. A very deep seed. It is only much later, when she met Hina Khan at York University that it become apparent how that seed would begin to flower.

Crucibles of change

In September 2002, Warren Bennis and Robert Thomas wrote a landmark article in the Harvard Business Review called 'Crucibles of Leadership'. In it they pinpointed the importance of intense, and often traumatic, events that transformed the lives of leaders. These were never planned and, in hindsight, could be seen as the source of their 'distinctive leadership abilities'. They called these experiences 'crucibles' after the vessels that medieval alchemists used to turn base metals into gold. 'The crucible experience,' they wrote, 'was a trial and a test, a point of deep self-reflection that forced them to question who they were and what mattered to them.' The leaders that Bennis and Warren studied were able to take a deep look at their core values and the assumptions that underpinned them to emerge from the experience 'stronger and more sure of themselves and their purpose – changed in some fundamental way.'

Many of the business leaders featured in this book have had experiences that have provided them with the courage and energy to pursue their dreams. Howard Schultz, CEO of Starbucks, is on a mission to create a company that provides for its people in way that his father, Fred, never experienced. The Prince of Wales remembers vividly how he felt in the 1960's when he experienced the 'frenzied dismemberment of what was left of the traditional framework of our existence.' He has dedicated his life to 'finding ways to bring back the 'baby' that was inevitably thrown out with the bathwater.' For the Prince of Wales that 'baby' is 'the recognition that man has a dual nature beyond the scientific reductionism of modern thinking.' His vision is one in which man has 'his feet on the ground and his head in the clouds... a microcosm of what lies at the heart of the Universe.' Steve Jobs, CEO of Apple, has faced a series of very significant trials, including being sacked from the company he founded and facing death itself. These experiences, painful as they were, have only made his resolution stronger. For John Tucker, founder and Director of the International Centre for Families in Business, it was the experience of personal bankruptcy and its effect on his family that provided him with the 'fire in the belly' to pursue his dream. And, for June Burrough, founder and Director of the Pierian Centre in Bristol, it is a search for justice based on her own painful experiences of injustice.

Warren Bennis and Robert Thomas concluded that great leaders possess four essential skills, which allow them to find meaning in events that others would merely find traumatic or painful. The first is a sense of integrity and strong values. To be a leader is to know who we are and what we are about. Secondly, leaders develop a distinctive and compelling voice; they are able to express this inner knowledge and purpose to others. The third skill is to create a sense of shared meaning, which allows others to support them whilst remaining true to their own beliefs and sense of self. We have explored all these skill sets in this book. They emerge when we take full responsibility, learn to see beyond the limited perspective of ourselves and act from the communal interest rather than our personal one. The fourth skill set is 'adaptive capacity', which the authors define as the 'ability to grasp context' and 'hardiness'. We have already noted how resilience and persistence are key characteristics in leadership. Richard Branson, for example, demonstrates both qualities of adaptive capacity, honed partly by his painful experience of dyslexia. To this day, he likes nothing better than a good challenge, a chance to prove himself anew to the world. The inclusion of the ability to grasp context in 'adaptive capacity' is particularly important. Not all of us, irrespective of the courage and tenacity that we may demonstrate in circumstances of adversity, can channel our learning into our calling or sense of purpose. To do this, we also need a strong sense of context. In other words, we need to be connected to what is happening to the whole, to see ourselves as part of the greater picture. As the Greek Stoic philosopher and former slave, Epictetus, observed, 'First learn the meaning of what you say, and then speak.'

Many of the leaders that I have worked with can identify with the work of Bennis and Thomas and can pinpoint times of adversity, which, in hindsight, represented the opportunity to commit to a deeper sense of who they are. Some of these make dramatic stories (when we survive a life-threatening illness, for example, or decide to quit our job without another one in prospect) but others are too personal to relate to others in a book such as this. They have deep meaning for the person involved but this does not necessarily translate into a good story for others. To understand the significance of an event we always need to know something about context too.

The importance of context

There is a well-known story of the profound impact that seeing a car for the first time had on Soichiro Honda, the founder of Honda. He was eight years old when the Model-T Ford passed through his small village. He heard the car before he saw it and he remembered being engulfed in a cloud of dust and petrol fumes as it passed by. 'I turned and chased after that car for all I was worth,' he recalled. 'I could not understand how it could move under its own power.' 'I found myself,' he continued, 'chasing it down the road, as hard as I could run.' He never forgot that moment and it became deeply symbolic in his life. He saw himself as always chasing something that was just beyond his reach. It was literally a life changing experience. When he discovered some oil that had leaked from the car onto the road, he got down on his hands and knees to smell it. 'It was like perfume,' he said later.

There is something very dramatic about this story but it is only when we have some context around Soichiro's early life that we begin to understand *why* this experience was so meaningful for the young boy. Soichiro was naturally attracted to mechanical things in his childhood and there are many stories of his ingenuity, including the time when he used a bicycle pedal rubber to forge the family seal on an unfavourable school report. There is no doubt that this passion was something deeply within him. But, he was also born into a family where such things mattered and were held to be highly important. His father, Gihei Honda, taught his children the value of hard work and a love of mechanical things. Soichiro quickly developed the ability to work with farm machinery and even made his own toys. His grandfather took him to watch the nearby rice mill in operation every day because his grandson was so fascinated with the small engine that powered it. He grew up working daily with his father at the forge and would go to school with such a dirty face that the other children gave him the nickname, 'black nose weasel' (which is apparently not as derogatory in Japanese as it sounds when translated into English). At the age of eleven, Soichiro 'borrowed' a bicycle and petty cash in order to watch a biplane in action some 20 kilometres away. Instead of punishing him for helping himself to the bike and the cash, Gihei recognised the positive qualities of grit and determination in his young son. It was also in his father's bike shop that Soichiro first practiced his engineering skills. There is, of course, much more to Soichiro Honda's story. But knowing even a little of the context in which he grew up, helps us to understand why a small patch of spilled oil fuelled the passion in a young boy to go on and create one of the world's most successful automotive companies.

Sometimes, of course, it is not one incident or point in our lives that really stands out, but a series of events that build a sense of our deeper purpose over time. It is often something as simple as not accepting a promotion, deciding to go part time, attending our children's football matches every Friday afternoon or signing up to the art class that we have previously never had the time for. Sometimes, even a small decision has much bigger repercussions than we realise at the time. This is a subject much better understood through stories than theory, and a good place to start is with my own.

My own story

My first career was in accountancy at Ernst & Young, one of the big professional services firms. This wasn't a deliberate choice. Joining one of the 'Big 8', as they were called in those days, seemed like a good entry point into the business world and a convenient way of adding an additional professional designation to my university degree. I had intended to 'move on' quickly but 'where' remained an elusive issue. At school, I had wanted to be a journalist but this had met with deep resistance from my parents. Once I was on an accounting career track it acquired a momentum of its own. My energies went into passing the exams and gaining promotion rather than a deeper questioning of whether this was a career that I really wanted. In those days I lived in Hampton, a leafy suburb alongside the River Thames, just south west of London. I travelled into work by train and these journeys provided the perfect space to catch up with my professional reading and continuing professional development. On one such occasion I got off the train and began to walk home, a journey that normally took about 10-15 minutes. I cast my mind back to what I had been reading to make sure that I had 'logged' anything of importance. Nothing. I wracked my brain to remember what I had been reading about. Nothing. I tried to recall the title of the article. Nothing. In fact, I couldn't remember anything at all. Not a single word. My first feeling was frustration; it was bad enough to have to read this stuff, let alone not be able to remember any of it. However, as I walked on a sense of relief came over me. I knew from that point onwards that I wasn't going to spend my life as an accountant. That article was to be the very last one on accounting or finance that I would ever read.

Many years later, I was on a weekend course in London held by Nick Williams, co-founder of The Inspirational Learning Company. At that time, Nick was a Director of Alternatives, which hosts Monday talks at St James' Church in Piccadilly and weekend workshops in spirituality, creativity, wellbeing and self-development. The course that I had booked was based around Nick's best-selling book, *The Work We Were Born to Do*, and I was there to find inspiration on my future path. In certain ways I was happy. I had moved, largely by stealth, from accounting to finance, from finance to corporate finance and from corporate finance to strategy. I was now self-employed as a strategy consultant. I had a good mix of clients and was also in control of my own destiny. What is more, I had worked extensively at executive level, so I had built an experience and networking base that boded well for the future. Yet, something was missing. I couldn't help but wonder if this was all there was. I felt a bit like Chandler Bing in one of the episodes of *Friends*, when he tries to reconnect with a 'cool vision' for his life. Perhaps, this course would lead me in the right direction. One of the exercises that we were asked to do by Nick was to pair up and meditate for five minutes on our vision for life. We would then share what emerged with our partner. I had great difficulty connecting with the exercise. My mind seemed to go blank. Nothing emerged but random thoughts, drifting by aimlessly. When we finished our meditation I quickly suggested that my partner went first. This would at least buy me some time. If I was feeling disconsolate at this point it quickly got worse.

My partner excitedly explained to me all the wonderful things that had come up for her in what appeared to be a fully blown game plan for life. I was being supportive on the surface and yet dreading my turn. How could I compete with this? Perhaps, I mused to myself, I should just make something up. As it happens, fate intervened and I didn't get the opportunity to. At one point my partner mentioned something about her sister and in my response I found myself referring to her sister by name. My partner stopped in mid-sentence and looked slightly startled. 'Have you met my sister?' she asked. 'No'. 'Then, how do you know her name?' This wobbled me. I found myself mumbling that 'it simply popped into my head' and being aware that this was hardly a very satisfactory explanation. As I was taking stock of whether to respond further my resolve to make up a vision quietly slipped away. Honesty looked like the best policy. My partner finished her piece and it was now my turn. 'Nothing came out of my meditation,' I confessed, 'it was completely useless.' 'Well, you must have thought about something,' came the reply. 'Yes, but no matter how hard I tried the only thing that kept coming into my head were my two boys.' My partner said nothing. She just looked at me patiently with eyes that said 'I'll wait as long as it takes for him to get it.' There was a rather uncomfortable period when we simply stared at each other before it hit me. 'How could I have been so stupid?' was all that I could think.

Sometimes the most obvious things are right in front of us but we just don't see them. Since that day I have built my career around my children, sharing the day-to-day parenting role with my wife, with both of us taking time out from our careers and also working part time when necessary. I have said, 'no' to all sorts of exciting projects and roles over the years and have thoroughly exasperated some of my more career-oriented friends and colleagues by my refusal to compromise. My professional role has gradually moved from 'expert' to 'facilitator' and the mix of my work has also changed with mentoring, teaching and writing coming to the fore.

This process has emerged naturally, although it has also been painful on occasions. It has helped that I haven't been hung up about earning less money than some of my successful peers. I consciously made that critical trade-off many years ago. A little while back, I found myself remembering myself as a teenager staring out of my bedroom window in the pouring rain. I could recall exactly what I was thinking on that day as the raindrops ran down my windowpane, all of my hopes and aspirations in that period when I was no longer a boy but not yet a man. How I wanted to make my mark in the world. It struck me forcibly how close I now am to what I hoped for all those years ago.

Making it happen

Clive Farrell, the founder of Butterfly World, remembers watching a hairy caterpillar emerge from its chrysalis as a beautiful moth when he was five years old. 'I have a theory that we all have a magic moment as children,' he says, 'that goes on to change our lives.' Clive has devoted his life to these beautiful insects, opening butterfly houses all around the world. The largest will soon be Butterfly World in St Albans, Hertfordshire, which will cost £25 million and is due to open in 2011. It will be the home to 10,000 butterflies and many other species including hummingbirds and leaf-cutter ants, which will live together beneath a huge central glass dome. Its aim is both to educate people about butterflies and to preserve them. 'It's about ecology, the environment and how people can take a bit of butterfly magic back to their own gardens,' says Managing Director, Angela Harkness. 'We have some of the richest wildflower meadows in Europe,' she continues, 'in an area hardest hit by the decline in butterflies.' Clive Farrell talks of the importance of butterflies as 'the canaries in the coalmine. 'They are very sensitive,' he says, 'to pollution, climate change and loss of habitat.' He has been dreaming of building a 'walkthrough butterfly experience' on the scale of St Albans for more than a decade. It 'represents the climax of my knowledge and work,' he says. He talks of butterflies as 'fragile, beautiful and harmless – a symbol of freedom.' St Albans, he says simply, will be 'my life's work.'

For Chris Spence, leader of the Toronto School Board, it was the combination of a running injury and a job at a detention centre for young offenders that acted as his wake up call. He had won a sports scholarship to Simon Fraser University in Vancouver, but a torn Achilles tendon put an end to his ambitions to pursue a pro-football career. He took the job at the detention centre because 'I had a strong interest in helping kids who had taken a wrong turn', but he wasn't prepared for what he found. In an interview with York University magazine in October 2009, he talked about how the experience changed his life:

> *'Boys 12 to 16 years old locked up, boys whose dads were in jail, boys without hope, boys "society had written off". To this day, Spence seethes at the memory of how routinely he was paged: "got a hanger in Cell 4. Need help." He can still feel the limp bodies he lifted in his arms so a colleague could cut a crudely crafted noose. It happened all the time. And it choked him up. "I decided I've got to get to these kids before they get here."'*

Chris Spence's path took him first to Oakdale Park Middle School, located in a rough neighbourhood in North Toronto where few others wished to teach. On his first day he was looking at class lists in the cafeteria when two black boys approached him. 'Who are you?' they asked. When he replied that he was their teacher he was immediately swarmed by children. 'I told you he's our teacher,' said one, 'I told you he's black.' When Chris arrived at Oakdale the failure rate among black children was 40 per cent. 'Obviously, the status quo wasn't working,' he recalls, 'school was a temporary incarceration. I wanted to find a way to break down the door and make them see education as their future, as a way to realize and recognize their dreams.' He worked hard for six years to make a real change. He shook hands with each child in his class every day and told them what he expected of them. He believed that a 'culture of caring', a mixture of setting high expectations and becoming a caring adult in their lives, would make a significant difference. And it did. He then made history in Toronto by moving on to another 'bad' school and, as Principal, turning it around. He is now leading Toronto's School Board, but despite his obvious success, his basic mission remains the same. 'My philosophy of education hasn't changed from being a classroom teacher to being a director of education,' he says, 'I now have the opportunity to influence the lives of 250,000 kids. I think that's what leadership is about — influence. The future of this city, the future of this province, the future of this country is sitting in our classrooms.'

As an undergraduate, Pernille Ironside organized her courses around her love of equestrian show jumping, which required six hours of training every day. Given this level of commitment it would seem only natural that she would go on to pursue the activity that she so loved as her career. Instead, she took a year off after finishing her undergraduate degree 'to get riding out of my system' and moved to Toronto to do a graduate law degree. She remembers feeling like 'a bit of an odd duck' amongst her classmates, most of whom were set for corporate careers in big law firms. After graduation, she chose instead to become a clerk in Ottawa for a Federal Court judge. This proved to be a decisive point in her life. She was hired by the Department of Foreign Affairs and International Trade as a legal officer and sent to the UN as part of the Canadian team in charge of negotiating an international treaty on children's rights. This had a profound effect upon her and, after a spell with the UN Office for the Coordination of Humanitarian Affairs, she moved to UNICEF to focus directly on children affected by armed conflict.

Pernille chose to go to Eastern Congo, one of the worst areas in the world for humanitarian issues. 'Until you go there,' she comments, 'you don't know whether or not you can handle it.' Despite the obvious physical danger, she negotiated the release of over 500 child soldiers shortly after arriving in February 2005, and several thousand more in the years that followed. 'I feel this work is my calling,' she says, 'Seeing children's lives transformed, seeing them smile and be kids again, seeing their hopes and dreams revive after surviving terrible ordeals – it is incredibly motivating and keeps you going, especially on the tough days.' 'You muster up the courage,' she continues, 'because children are so vulnerable and require protection. It's not about you.' Dealing with violent warlords and rogue militias is a long way from equestrian show jumping, but Pernille recognizes the Congo posting as a defining moment in her career. In many ways, it has prepared her for her current role overseeing UNICEF's child protection efforts in areas of conflict and natural disasters around the world. She is also working actively to help child soldiers and prevent their recruitment. 'Now', she remarks, 'I can make a difference not just on a local level but on a massive scale.' Chris Spence and Pernille Ironside are both emphatic about their sense of mission and calling in life. Interestingly, they both share leadership roles that are very different from the interests they pursued when they were young. The path of leadership is rarely a linear one.

When Robin Lynn Macy, a founder member of the Dixie Chicks, left the band in 1992 after a dispute with her band mates, it was undoubtedly painful. More so, one would think, given the huge success that the band achieved later without her. But life had other plans for Robin. In 1997 she was travelling across Kansas when she stumbled across the Bartlett Arboretum in Belle Plain, 20 miles south of Wichita. It was 15 acres of heaven that had fallen on hard times. She 'saw through the prickly brambles and broken spirit of a once-proud forest,' and 'saw something in it that locals had become blind to – its unique promise and towering soul.' When Robin first came upon it, however, the place that was once touted as 'the only mature arboretum between the Mississippi and the Rocky Mountains' was in a sorry state and its future was far from assured. Glenna and Mary, the granddaughters of the founder of the arboretum, Dr Walter E. Bartlett, had run the gardens until 1995 with the help of Mary's husband, Bob Gourlay. But by 1997, they had come to the decision that they could no longer continue and had decided, regrettably, to sell it. 'Fortunately,' says Mary Gourlay, 'this cute little blond elf, Robin Macy, came knocking at the door. We didn't lose an arboretum, we gained another daughter.'

Since that day in 1997 Robin has dedicated herself to restoring, preserving and renewing the garden, by becoming the Steward of

Bartlett Arboretum. In addition to tending to and restoring the garden, and making the arboretum available for educational purposes, she has introduced sympathetic commercial activities, such as weddings and concerts among the trees. She also hosts corporate events and garden clubs and has attracted important sponsorships. This combination of a love of nature, her experience as a talented singer, and good business skills, has proved to be invaluable for the Arboretum. In 2012, it will be celebrating its centennial, its massive cypress, oak and Japanese maple trees standing as a testament to the dedication of all those involved with its recovery. Naturally, many others help Robin in her work, but there is no doubt that she has made a profound difference by accepting the mantle of leadership. And, she has done this by expressing who she is at the deepest level. As she says, 'For me, to create music and to live deliberately among trees – and teenagers – is the essence of my being.'

No free lunch

Answering our call to leadership is not always an easy experience. We may sense it. We may hear it whispering to us through our restlessness or frustration. We may feel it through our lack of connection, or our sense that something is missing in our lives. Sometimes, we come face to face with it through the most tragic events in our lives. But often, it lies below the surface of our consciousness, like a fish that refuses to bite, waiting for the right timing and circumstances. At this time, our job is simply to listen. And, when we do make that all-important commitment, success does not come immediately. Not at all. On the contrary, things may appear to get worse as we are 'tested' in our resolve. In reality, we have only just started our journey; in much the same way as those who attain a black belt in karate find that this is only the very beginning of their mastery of the martial art. Leadership is rarely an easy path and we are only at the point of signing up. But signing up is critically important. As the nineteenth century theologian and philosopher, William Shedd, once noted, 'a ship is safe in harbour, but that's not what ships are for.' The comedian, Dave Allen, was fond of telling a joke about a man praying to God to win the lottery. After hearing the man's continual pleas for rather too long, God finally appears in person. 'Do me a favour', he roars, 'do your bit by buying a ticket!' Commitment is important. We always have to buy the ticket first.

Sometimes we need a little encouragement to commit to our path. Leadership can be an exciting prospect but it is also a scary one. The journey will take us well out of our 'comfort zone' and into the unknown. I find it useful to look at the trials and tests that we face in life, the 'crucibles' as Bennis and Thomas call them, as the 'encouragement' to turn our attention to deeper things. We have seen this process in many of the leadership stories in this book, the role that unplanned and traumatic events have had on altering the course of a leader's life and moving them towards a deeper calling. Chris Spence's dreams of a pro-football career were ended painfully through injury. At that point, he could not have imagined where this painful event would take him. When Robin Lynn Macy left the Dixie Chicks she had probably never even heard of the Bartlett Arboretum in Kansas. And, when Pernille Ironside felt like 'a bit of an odd duck' amongst her more conventional classmates, it is unlikely that she could have guessed how important this would turn out to be in her choice of occupation after graduating from law school. We don't plan our way to leadership. It is the way that we react to the circumstances that confront us that shape us as leaders.

The leadership journey is not a linear one. We are not privileged to know how our life will turn out, or what our influence will be when we are long gone. It is easy to overlook the most obvious things in life. By providing a secure and loving home for our children, we allow them to make *their* mark on the world. Sometimes, their imprint will be much greater than ours. By lending our support to our family, friends, work colleagues and those in the community around us, we have the same effect. There is really no way that we can be sure of the impact we have on others, the full extent of the influence that we exert on their lives. Leaders often have another story in common. It is the support and influence of a colleague or friend when the chips were down. This was the person who made all the difference, who inspired the leader to carry on and not to give up. Very often the person involved is not a 'major player' but a 'bit part' in the greater scheme of things. Yet, they played a disproportionately important role in that circumstance. We should never underestimate the extent of our influence in these moments, which invariably appear when we least expect them. Our best hope is to remain conscious of our impact on others in the day-to-day, be reflective of what we are doing and maintain our sense of purpose and integrity. Life is too complex to do anything else. This is one reason why a reflective practice is so important in the leadership journey.

National Trust

'Small but … the compostabilities are endless.'
National Trust paper bag

There is another way to look at that special moment when we commit to becoming a leader and that is from the viewpoint of the community. As individuals, our commitment to acting from the deepest expression of who we are can make a big difference. When we act together with others on the same journey we can have a profound impact. One person thinking differently is powerful. Many people thinking differently together can be transformational. One organization that is turning the way that we see things upside down is the National Trust, or simply National Trust, as it is now known. The Trust is one of the few organizations that genuinely thinks long term and is good at it. This is underpinned by a reflective quality to its decision-making process and the consistency that results from a clear and constant sense of core mission and purpose. We can learn a great deal from looking at the National Trust a little more closely.

My eldest son, Scott, was recently on a week's volunteering vacation with the Trust in Carmarthenshire in Wales. His team undertook a variety of physical tasks including gardening, clearing of coastal paths and putting in new wooden benches. There was no TV and contact with the 'outside world' was discouraged unless absolutely necessary. As a result, the team bonded quickly and Scott had a hugely enjoyable time. The utility of the work that he did for the Trust was easily matched by the camaraderie of the group, the breathtakingly beautiful environment, the ability to learn new skills and the space for reflection and contemplation that is so rare in our '24/7' world. This is a simple and unsophisticated statement, but unpack it and something very interesting reveals itself. When we work as a team, begin to look at the whole, spend time in reflection, and are attentive to the small incremental steps that are the building blocks of significant long-term achievements, we are automatically beginning to think and act strategically. When we put this into the context of working on behalf of something greater than ourselves, we are opening ourselves up to becoming leaders. In many ways, these one-week volunteering holidays that the National Trust runs could easily serve as introductory leadership courses. Like the best apprenticeships, best practice is modelled and knowledge is gained from the bottom up. By being engaged at the sharp end, participants are closely connected with the core operational aspects of the work of the Trust and form an intimate relationship with the properties, land and the environment on which they are working. This is part of what makes the Trust so interesting. Its philosophy and approach provide a sustainable template for living in harmony and balance with our environment, but doing so in a way that is commercially viable.

We live in a fragmented, often isolated, world and the way we look at organizations tends to reflect this. If we analyse the work of the National Trust from this perspective we are likely to see the organization as one that looks after old properties and land, provides food and drink for visitors and runs a retail business on the side. We may then focus on something we think needs improvement. 'The prices in the café are too high', we may say, or 'Why aren't the properties open throughout the year?' But these elements of what the Trust does are not the complete picture. The whole is far more than the sum of the parts. At each property and landscape the Trust owns, it is managing both an ecosystem and a community. It runs extensive educational and learning programmes in addition to the volunteering activities that my son was lucky enough to participate in. This includes important local initiatives between National Trust properties, local schools and other educational establishments. There are also wider projects such as the School Arts Partnership, which introduces children to 'creative approaches to learning with specialist arts-based projects' run by National Trust staff and local artists. The 'Small Steps BIG CHANGE' project helps visitors to develop more sustainable habits by exploring 'green choices' and 'food choices'. Like much of the work of the National Trust this is not just theory. 'All of our projects', the organization points out, 'aim not simply to challenge beliefs and change our ways, but to record, measure and support those changes.' At a very practical level, the Trust is involved in a wide range of educational and learning activities that are designed specifically to be integrated within the National Curriculum, and also extend it by deepening the learning experience. This takes time and effort and plenty of it. Just ask any teacher how easy this is or how much work it requires!

To appreciate the value of many of the day-to-day activities of the National Trust we have to reflect a little. Take a simple example. Many properties actively encourage visitors to integrate their walk around the grounds with longer walks using public footpaths that surround the property. These must be maintained and publicized, which has a direct benefit for the local community. It is a small, but important, way of helping to bring local communities together. For many single or older people who live alone, walking their dog (or just taking exercise) becomes a vital way of meeting people in the community. A local Trust coffee shop or restaurant serves as a very handy meeting place, accessible without travelling very far. It becomes a good way to keep in touch with local people or simply a good place to share some neighbourhood gossip. These may be small things but they can also be very significant. Community is built from the accumulation of many small social interactions.

We have also seen that the National Trust plays an important strategic role in exploring the effects of climate change and is actively involved in some big environmental projects, such as the Millennium Seed Bank Project. But, once again, the value of the Trust's work is not simply an aggregation of all its 'good deeds', no matter how great the benefits associated with these activities may be. Its contribution lies also in *process*; the way in which it does things. It is living proof that we can live in harmony with our environment, sustain our communities and meet the needs of large numbers of visitors seeking recreation simultaneously. The number of visitors is significant. In 2008/09, 54 paying properties attracted over 100,000 people. The largest, Wakehurst Place, home of the Millennium Seed Bank in West Sussex, had 427,000 visitors. Catering for the needs of numbers like these is a major undertaking in its own right. As we have seen, however, this only touches the surface of what the National Trust does. In many ways, it is entering genuinely new territory, especially in the area of reconciling the complex needs of very different interest and community groups. This inevitably involves an iterative process of 'learning by doing', which means making mistakes and learning from them. This is particularly important in the areas of environmental and climate change where this learning can be adapted by society as a whole. It is a wonderful example of community sustaining community. As Simon Jenkins, Chairman of the National Trust, points out in the 2008/09 annual report, the work of the organization is only possible because of the widespread support of so many people:

> *'We are indebted to our 3.6 million members, 55,000 volunteers, our many generous donors and all the members of the Centres and Associations, local committees and Friends Groups whose support is so essential to our work, and central to our strategy.'*

My son was very proud of his newfound abilities in bench making when he returned home from his week of volunteering but his voice was full of wonder when he described the badgers emerging from their set in the early evening air in Dinefwr Park. This sense of wonder and mystery has been almost obliterated in our modern world. We cannot solve the great issues of our time including poverty, inequality, environmental destruction or climate change, without first reconnecting with the sacred mystery of life, the wonder of it all. The National Trust allows us to glimpse at this wonder, see fragments of it reflected back to us when we visit the properties, landscapes and coastlines that it maintains. It is there in the attitude of so many who work for the organization, many of them volunteers who do it for the simple reward of being part of a work greater than themselves. It is there in the 'small' acts as well as the 'big' ones. When the Trust had to fell the large trees that stood between the ancient stone circle in Avebury and the main road last winter, it automatically planted new ones. When spring arrived this year the small saplings burst into leaf, still young and vulnerable but beautiful in their delicacy, full of energy, as if aware of their majestic role to come. We would do well to rest awhile and take it all in, reconnect to the rebirth of life each year. Singer-songwriter, Susan Enan, expresses this nicely in her song, 'Bring On The Wonder':

'I can't see the stars anymore living here.
Let's go to the hills where the outlines are clear.
Bring on the wonder, bring on the song,
I pushed you down deep in my soul for too long...
I don't have the time for a drink from the cup
Let's rest for a while 'til our souls catch us up.
Bring on the wonder, bring on the song.
I pushed you down deep in my soul for too long.'

Servant leadership

There is a danger in relating stories of leadership. They are, largely, self-selective. We may read them and be inspired, but also feel that we could not emulate these brave souls. Or we may look at them and note the external circumstances that enabled those leaders to fulfil their calling and conclude that they were simply lucky. When we look at our own lives, only too aware of all the challenges and pitfalls that we face, it is very easy to draw a line between us and them, 'the leader types'. There is plenty of theory to support us in this deception. Are not leaders born so? Is it not the case that some of us simply don't have the 'necessary' charisma to lead others? I don't believe that either of these statements is true. Undoubtedly, our leadership abilities are affected by both nature and nurture. Personal charisma can certainly be an asset. But there are many leaders who exert profound influence without possessing the kind of external 'larger than life' personalities that are commonly associated with leadership. This is the kind of leadership that arises when we put into practice what we most deeply believe. We prove ourselves, not in big colourful acts, but in the small things we do in everyday life. We do so quietly and unobtrusively. Ironically, by doing this, we may have a lasting impact in the long term well beyond our immediate and obvious areas of influence. We can do this yet be virtually invisible. We act in the nature of 'servant leaders', those who lead by putting the highest needs of followers before their own.

Robert Greenleaf introduced the concept of the servant leadership to modern management theory in 1970 in his essay, 'The Servant as Leader'. He described such a leader as 'servant first' and went on to write, 'It begins with the natural feeling that one wants to serve, to serve first. Then conscious choice brings one to aspire to lead.' The key to servant leadership is to 'make sure that other people's highest priority needs are being served.' In fact, the concept of servant leadership is a much older concept than that. It was familiar to ancient Chinese civilization and is one of the defining principles underlying the teaching of spiritual leaders such as Jesus. In fact, many such leaders did not regard themselves as leaders at all. As the Chinese philosopher and founder of Taoism, Lao Tzu, who lived in the sixth century BC, famously remarked:

> 'The wicked leader is he who people despise.
> The good leader is he who people revere.
> The great leader is he who people say, "We did it ourselves."'

Servant leadership is a familiar concept to those of us who are parents. When I run leadership sessions I often ask my audience to select a leader who is special to them in some way, somebody who is their 'hero' or 'heroine'. I am always touched when somebody gingerly puts up their hand and says 'my mom', or 'my dad'. There is often a moment's hesitation as they debate whether they should stick to their decision, or select a 'safer' option! But it is these primary relationships that are often so important in our leadership journey, for it these that give us the courage to follow our dreams. It is our relationships with family, friends and close colleagues that determine how safe we feel in the world, and whether we are prepared to take risks, to step outside our comfort zone. And, for those of us who are parents ourselves, we gain something invaluable too. Despite the drudgery and sheer hard work of it all, parenting is probably the best 'fast track' to personal transformation that there is. It both exhausts us and opens us up to new ways of being and new possibilities. Author, Piero Ferrucci, gives us an unforgettable 'before and after' description of parenthood in his book, *What Children Teach Us*:

> '*Before I had children, I would observe parents and feel a sense of superiority and self-satisfaction. Most parents seemed awkward and pathetic to me. I am a psychologist and, full of my psychological know-how, I used to note their mistakes, secretly criticize them and offer a whole lot of advice. I was sure I could do better.*
>
> *Now, two children later, I am a good deal humbler. All my theories have tumbled like a house of cards. Having fallen flat on my face many times, I have lost all certitude... Like every parent, I have been stung, squeezed out, wounded, reprogrammed, turned inside out, never let off the hook. How often have my children, with a diabolical instinct, touched those weak points I have kept carefully concealed! These episodes have transformed me. In a hard and painful way, they have made me different from the person I was before, like no course of psychotherapy, no spiritual retreat, or meeting with an Oriental guru could have done.*'

Starting small

'Every blade of grass has its Angel that bends over it and whispers, "Grow, grow."'
The Talmud

For those of us who are not parents it is comforting (or perhaps not so!) to know that the daily grind of life can be equally effective as a transformative process. Just as the demands of parenting appear to act as a barrier to becoming a leader so does a demanding job or commitments that leave us with little personal space and time. The paradox is that the exact opposite is also true. It is often when we are worn down or worn out, exhausted, disappointed and sometimes rejected, that we are able to hear our call. Those who grandly decide to take a year off to write the 'Great American Novel' or some other world-changing project, often find that they never quite get their great work off the ground. Energy and commitment is hard to come by when there are no limitations before us. Ironically, it is when we have the least flexibility and room for manoeuvre that we tend to commit. This strong sense of commitment attracts us to others who share similar intentions. We are drawn together as if by magic. The path may be hard but we notice the existence of synchronicity (the meaningful coincidence of events that appear to be unrelated on the surface) and serendipity (making fortunate discoveries seemingly by accident) in our lives and we are able to act upon them.

Naturally, we have to moderate our expectations when we work like this because we are acutely aware of the trade-offs and boundaries that we face. We begin to write our 'small novel' or start a local project because we know that's all we can do for now. We write in the late evenings, or volunteer at weekends, because that's the only time we have. It may not be easy, but our ability to endure is a strong sign of commitment. Our commitment acts as a self-reinforcing anchor and brings other like-minded people into our lives. It is our humility and openness, combined with an intense practicality born of necessity, which becomes the key to our success. As Lao Tzu also said, 'All difficult things have their origin in that which is easy, and great things in that which is small.' The 'Great American Novel' always – *always* – emerges from the first short chapter.

I believe that we all have leadership capabilities within us and that we can all chose to adopt a leadership role. We become leaders when we act from the deepest expression of who we are. This is what Henry David Thoreau meant when he remarked, 'Do what you love. Know your own bone; gnaw at it, bury it, unearth it, and gnaw it still.' We may not hold any position of authority or command any resources. We may not be highly charismatic and have the ability to move hundreds of people from the podium. Instead, we may express ourselves quietly in our own way within our circle of influence. More than anything else, leadership is the ability to influence others for the benefit of the whole. As we have seen, however, the act of becoming a leader, no matter how critical, is only the first of many steps in the leadership journey. Once we have mounted the tiger we have to be able to hang on to it and ride. That is what the next chapter, '*Staying the Course*', is all about.

PART 3

MAKING A DIFFERENCE

'There!' said Eeyore proudly, stopping them outside Piglet's House. 'And the name on it, and everything!'

'Oh!' cried Christopher Robin, wondering whether to laugh or what.

'Just the house for Owl. Don't you think so, little Piglet?'

And then Piglet did a Noble Thing, and he did it in a sort of dream, while he was thinking of all the wonderful words Pooh had hummed about him.

'Yes, it's just the house for Owl,' he said grandly. 'And I hope he'll be very happy in it.' And then he gulped twice, because he had been very happy in it himself.

'What do you think, Christopher Robin?' asked Eeyore a little anxiously, feeling that something wasn't quite right.

Christopher Robin had a question to ask first, and he was wondering how to ask it.

'Well,' he said at last, 'it's a very nice house, and if your own house is blown down, you must go somewhere else, mustn't you Piglet? What would you do if your house was blown down?'

Before Piglet could think, Pooh answered for him. 'He'd come and live with me,' said Pooh, wouldn't you Piglet?'

Piglet squeezed his paw.

'Thank you, Pooh,' he said, 'I should love to.'

A. A. Milne, The House At Pooh Corner

10
STAYING THE COURSE

The Rollercoaster

'Ever tried.
Ever failed.
No matter.
Try again.
Fail again.
Fail better.'

Samuel Beckett, Worstward Ho

Mule's wisdom

There is a traditional story about an old mule, much beloved by the farmer who owned him. The mule had a mind of his own, as mules are prone to do, and the farmer was rather attached to him. One sunny afternoon, the mule came upon an old well and, sensing the cool water within, leaned over to take a closer look. 'Perhaps I can just get to that water,' it thought to itself. 'Just a little further.' Before the mule knew it, he lost his footing and fell in. He brayed relentlessly and finally the noise attracted the farmer. But no matter how hard the farmer tried there seemed no way of getting the old mule out. And so, with a heavy heart, he began to shovel dirt onto the mule, hoping to put it out of its misery quickly. 'Better this way,' he thought to himself, 'than to let my friend suffer a lingering end.' Naturally, the mule kicked and brayed for all it was worth. After a while, however, it noticed something strange. Every time it kicked off the dirt and trampled it underfoot, it was slightly higher up than before. This continued for several painful hours, with the mule enduring one pile of dirt after another. Finally, however, its ears appeared at the top of the well and it let out a mighty bray in celebration. The farmer cried out in joy and renewed his assault, confident now that he could save his beloved beast. A little while later, the mule stepped out of the well and gave itself a good shake.

'That which does not kill us makes us stronger,' is a familiar saying that is actually attributable to the nineteenth century philosopher, Friedrich Nietzsche. It reminds us that life experiences, both positive and negative, help to forge us into who we are. Even the very worst things that life can throw at us, such as those the poor mule had to endure, can bring powerful and entirely unexpected benefits. Indeed, in many ways, it is the least desirable experiences that have the greatest potential impact upon us for good. What makes a difference is not the experience itself but our attitude in dealing with it. It is a given that our leadership journey will have its ups and downs. However, if we look closely within the suffering, we can often find a silver lining. As Mildred Witte Struven reminds us, 'a clay pot sitting in the sun will always be a clay pot. It has to go through the white heat of the furnace to become porcelain.' When we are open to learning from our suffering we emerge stronger. In the worst cases, finding meaning can be essential to our very survival. 'Despair is suffering without meaning,' observed Viktor Frankl, the Jewish psychologist and neurologist, who endured and survived unimaginable conditions in the Nazi concentration camps between 1942 and 1944. This sense of deep meaning provides a rudder in our lives and enables us to build the perseverance and resilience to endure the tests and trials that we face on our journey. At the end of the day, it is not our success in the good times that defines us as leaders. It is our ability to cope with the tough ones.

When we think of jewellery, we tend to visualise something fashioned from precious stones or metals found in the earth. Indeed, 'jewellery' is derived from the word 'jewel', meaning a precious or semi-precious stone. There is one gem, however, that is found inside a living creature and it provides a wonderful metaphor for leadership. Pearls are found on the inner surface of the shell of an oyster or a clam. They originate when a foreign substance slips between the oyster's shell and its mantle, the part of the oyster that produces the shell and allows the creature to increase in size. The foreign substance irritates the oyster so the mantle covers it up with the same substance (called nacre) that it uses to create its shell. Over time this produces the pearl. A thing of great beauty is born from a lengthy series of irritations. Remembering this magical natural process can help us to reframe how we look at those irritating things that, on the surface at least, seem to prevent us from achieving our aims. When we look back later with a deeper appreciation of the flow of our lives, it is often these very circumstances that have provided the grit to forge us into leaders. The more serious the crisis, the more significant the impact is likely to be. As the old Scottish proverb counsels, 'Man's extremity is God's opportunity.'

From success to significance

'When we get older it begins to dawn on us that the rules have changed. Now we want not so much to be seen as successful as significant. We want to believe that our lives have counted for something – that we have made a difference.'
Rob Parsons, Executive Chairman of Care for The Family

In my experience, the single most important factor that sustains leaders on their journey is a strong sense of purpose underlying the work they do. They get through the hard times because they find meaning in their work. They accept the 'bad' things that come their way because they are seeking to make a real difference in the world. It is this that puts a context around the lean times. At the beginning of *Freedom from Fear* we looked at the profound impact that personal bankruptcy had on John Tucker, founder and Director of the International Centre for Families in Business. John has been through many ups and downs on his leadership journey but he has always been anchored by a deep sense of mission, something he calls 'an intense internal belief.' He has run a successful family business and has also been through the wringer and lost everything. In both cases, he has seen first hand the damaging side effects that running a business can have on family life and relationships. After going through the bankruptcy he had to start all over again and quickly found that the starting point was several steps behind home base. The difficulties in getting another business off the ground were considerable. He found he had no access to funding or credit and he carried the stigma of personal bankruptcy with him. Nevertheless, slowly and surely he built again from the bottom up.

These painful experiences have forged an acute awareness of the dynamics of families in business and the potentially devastating effects that running a business, whether successful or not, can have on the family. John's mission is to provide families in business with the space to sort out personal and business issues so that they do not have to endure the painful journey that he has. He has built a reputation for being able to deal with the conflicts, struggles and tensions that arise when family and business matters coincide. That inevitably takes him into the realm of issues such as personal power, ownership, control, status, recognition, responsibility and even greed. He is determined to provide families that are stuck in a place of conflict with other alternatives, the possibility of a different future. The International Centre is an extension of that core mission. It is concerned with building a much greater awareness of the importance of the family dynamic and the core issues that lie at the heart of decision-making in family businesses. John has few boundaries in his work; he is willing to do whatever it takes to bring his vision into reality.

John Tucker's vision is a deeply holistic one, putting together the broad expertise to help, support and heal families in business. He works with professional intermediaries, business advisers and academics as well as family businesses to do so. The International Centre offers conflict resolution, succession planning and generational transition as well as helping family businesses tackle current business and family issues and develop exit strategies. It is easy to list these services and assume that this *is* the Centre. But this is far from the case. In many ways, the Centre's most groundbreaking work is in developing greater awareness of what makes a successful family business work and how external advisers can help to develop leadership skills within this context. It is currently working with the University of the West of England in Bristol on developing future family business leaders and it also facilitated the first Family Business MBA at Gloucestershire University. This is all part of John's mission to spread a more holistic understanding of family businesses, to connect the dots in how the family dynamic directly affects commercial success and family wellbeing.

The truth is that John is never satisfied with his achievements. He remains restless and is always drawn to finding new ways to bring his dream into the world, to create new futures for family businesses that are being debilitated, or even devastated, by struggle and conflict. 'When you care about what you can contribute,' he says, 'it fires you on.' This is the powerful sense of meaning that has sustained him throughout his leadership journey. Interestingly, this sense of contribution and support is not all one way. Over the years, John has drawn to him friends and colleagues who are willing to lend their support in difficult times, from very practical gestures to simple words of encouragement and support. When we talked recently I asked John what was the *one* thing that has enabled him to stay the course. He paused for a moment and gave me a response that I wasn't anticipating. 'Love,' he said, 'the love and support of real friends and family.' 'Without that, I don't know whether I would have made it.'

Prepare for the long haul

'In the beginning, there was no company – it was my little joke with myself. It became a reality over the course of the next 10 years.'
Ani DiFranco, Singer-Songwriter

When we commit to becoming a leader we are in it for the long haul. We tread that paradox of remaining true to our sense of

270 Freedom from Fear

purpose and mission, which acts as a rudder in our lives, and living firmly in the day to day. This means being open to opportunities and not being too judgemental about what comes to us. In 1975 Tucker Zimmerman wrote a delightful song called *The Taoist Tale*, which tells the story of a farmer. The song begins with the farmer sending his son to graze their horse on the mountainside. The lad falls asleep and when he awakes the horse is gone. When he returns without it the neighbours all say, 'What bad luck.' But all the farmer will say is 'How do you know?' The next day he sends his son to look for the horse and the young man finds it grazing with seven other wild ones. When he returns the neighbours exclaim excitedly, 'What good luck.' Again, the farmer replies, 'How do you know?' The following morning the son is given the task of breaking in one of the young stallions. Unfortunately, as he climbs onto the horse's back it bucks and throws him off. The youngster's arm is badly broken. 'What dreadful luck,' say the neighbours. The farmer simply replies, 'How do you know?' The very next day there is great excitement and commotion in the village. War has been declared and the militia is combing the countryside looking for soldiers. When they arrive in the village they take one look at the old farmer and his invalid son and move on. 'What splendid luck,' say the villagers. Naturally, the farmer says only, 'How do you know?'

If we wish to stay the course on our leadership journey it is wise to learn from the words of the farmer. The only certainty is that our journey will not be straightforward. We will never be able to anticipate all eventualities or judge the significance of them. Our best bet is to be open to possibility without judging events as 'negative' or 'positive'. That's why Arthur Rubinstein, the Polish-American pianist, once commented, 'Of course there is no formula for success except perhaps an unconditional acceptance of life and what it brings.' This is why the farmer's wisdom is so useful. We find the same message in many other stories, such as the Zen master whose response to every situation is always 'Is that so?' and the tale of a man who limits his comment to a laconic, 'Maybe'. The moral is the same. All possibilities are contained in the moment. Our job is simply to remain open to that moment. If we are truly going to make a difference, we will meet plenty of resistance and lack of understanding on the part of others. We may even lose friends and colleagues along the way. And sometimes it will feel as if we are going backwards. Hopefully, the core disciplines of strategic thinking and leadership outlined in *Freedom from Fear* will help us to keep on track. But even this will only take us half way. For each of us the leadership journey is our very own and it unfolds in a uniquely personal way. It is often only when we look back on our journey many years later that we find we have the perspective to understand our life as a whole. When we commit to strategic leadership we commit to the long haul. It's always worth remembering, because it inevitably puts things back into perspective.

Eckhart Tolle, the German-born writer, public speaker and teacher, offers us an ancient Sufi story, which helps us put painful events into perspective. There was once a king who found that he was vacillating between happiness and despondency according to the events that happened to him. Alas, his happy moments seemed short lived and quickly turned to disappointment and despair. Finally, the king began to tire of living his life like this and sought advice from a traveller who was visiting his kingdom and had the reputation of being a wise and enlightened man. The wise man was summoned and the king immediately noticed his calm and serene presence. 'What would you want of me?' asked the traveller. 'I would like to be more like you,' replied the king, 'can you tell me the secret so that I may have wisdom and peace of mind as you do?' Although the king was willing to pay dearly for his desire, the wise man would have none of it. 'I will give you something beyond measure,' he told the king, 'but only as a gift.' Some weeks later the traveller returned and presented the king with a ring with an inscription that read, 'This too, will pass.' 'What does it mean?' asked the king. 'You must wear this ring always,' came the reply, 'and when something happens to you touch the inscription and read it before you decide whether it is good or bad.' 'If you do that,' the traveller continued, 'you will always have peace of mind.' This story points to the same fundamental truth as the story of the farmer.

Whatever happens to us, however 'bad' or 'good' events or circumstances appear to be, they will not last. Everything is impermanent. As Scarlett O' Hara says at the end of *Gone With the Wind*, 'Tomorrow is another day.' Tomorrow is *always* another day!

Resilience, persistence and fortitude

'One isn't necessarily born with courage, but one is born with potential. Without courage, we cannot practice any other virtue with consistency. We can't be kind, true, merciful, generous or honest.'
Maya Angelou, American Writer, Artist and Poet

Most of us have a tendency to underestimate the problems of others and overestimate our own. It's only natural given that we have to *live* with our issues and challenges. Equally, it is easy to gloss over the trials and tribulations that others have experienced on their journey once they have become successful. The reality is that it takes a great deal of courage and self will to make our dreams a reality. Steve Jobs and Howard Schultz are good examples of leaders who are virtually synonymous with the companies they founded, Apple and Starbucks respectively. They both derive enormous personal meaning from their work, which is far more important to them than success itself. This is the foundation of strategic leadership. As Henry David Thoreau noted, 'success usually comes to those who are too busy to be looking for it.' Steve Jobs and Howard Schultz have survived and prospered on their leadership journeys because they have developed the three principle characteristics that define entrepreneurship and leadership: resilience, persistence and fortitude. All three of these qualities relate to our ability to endure, the word 'fortitude' being derived from the Latin, *fortitudo*, meaning courage.

In April 2010, Stephen Fry interviewed Steve Jobs in relation to Apple's launch of its new iPad. Stephen was the second person in the United Kingdom to own an Apple (the first was Douglas Adams, creator of *The Hitchhiker's Guide to the Galaxy*) and he wrote of being more nervous of interviewing Steve Jobs than in meeting five British Prime Ministers and two American Presidents. 'I do believe Jobs to be a truly great figure,' he wrote, 'one of the small group of innovators who have changed the world.' His chance to enter 'Steve's reality-distortion field' left him overwhelmingly excited, just like a young kid meeting his hero for the first time. Stephen Fry's piece was part of a euphoric celebration of the launch of the iPad by *Time Magazine*. 'Jobs likes nothing better than frolicking in the graveyard of other companies' dead products,' it wrote and concluded that 'the iPad is merely the tangible component of a much larger device, an entire Internet ecosystem that extends out to the horizon in every direction.' 28 days later Apple announced that it had sold one million iPads, a considerably quicker takeoff than the iPhone, which took three months to sell this number. Within 60 days, the company announced that it had sold two million, prompting a delighted Steve Jobs to thank customers for their patience and assure them that 'we are working hard to build enough iPads for everyone.' Apple looks as if it has another iconic winner on its hands.

With all this success it's very easy to forget that Steve Job's leadership path has been anything but easy. As we have seen, he was fired from the company he founded, faced off the doubters in the IT industry who saw Apple as a perennial 'also ran' and coped with very serious health issues. In fact, there is nothing linear or straightforward about his journey at all. Having been thrown out of Apple in 1985 after a struggle with the company's Board of Directors, he went on to build not one but two companies. He turned Pixar into a major force in the movie Industry and he founded NeXT, a computer platform development company. In a twist of fate, NeXT was subsequently acquired by Apple in 1997 and Steve Jobs found himself back at the helm of the company he founded over 30 years before. Howard Schultz, CEO of Starbucks, has also been experiencing a similar 'trial by fire' over the last three years as he has struggled to turn the company around and convince sceptics that Starbucks has a serious long-term future. It looks very much like he has succeeded, which is a very significant achievement on his part. However, it was a very different story in 2008 when detractors were only too willing to pronounce Starbucks a finished force. As service and fashion-based industries are notoriously fickle, it is certain that Howard Schultz will be given no time to rest on his laurels. The leadership journey tends to be marked by the exchange of one set of challenges for another. The pressure on leaders can be relentless.

One of the least demanding activities for a business academic is to reverse engineer success. Armed with the benefit of hindsight it is relatively easy to establish why an individual or company has been successful, at least at a superficial level. Unfortunately, this knowledge is often 'time specific' and adds very little transferable value in the real world. In reality, of course, even highly successful organisations have been through tough times, often staring failure directly in the face. At the point of crisis it is normally far from obvious what the outcome will be. When we talk to successful leaders they will almost always tell us that the path they followed was far more circuitous than is apparent in hindsight, filled with synchronicity and serendipity. Academics tend to airbrush these 'irregularities' aside because they don't fit well with our deep-seated reductionist mind-set. But we find countless examples of 'happenstance' when we read the biographies of successful people; fortuitous meetings, offers of funding and support arising from the unlikeliest of places, to name but a few. This is what the Scottish mountaineer, W H Murray, was referring to when he said, 'The moment one definitely commits oneself then providence moves too'. Leaders are not simply strong self-determined individuals on a mission to battle *against* the world. They are also open to opportunity, ready to fight *with* the world. Aligning ourselves with others with similar values and aspirations makes a big difference to the possibility of success.

St John's school, Marlborough

In February 2010, The Duchess of Cornwall officially opened the new St John's school in Marlborough, the culmination of nearly 14 years of work for its Head teacher, Dr Patrick Hazelwood. Over 1,500 pupils had entered its doors for the first time in December 2009, my youngest son amongst them. Quite exceptionally, parents heard nothing but praise from their offspring, a minor miracle in itself! The design of the school is stunning. It is built in the style of a university campus and is enhanced by its dramatic setting, perched on the hill above the town. It is designed to be eco-efficient. There are plenty of glass walls to attract as much natural light as possible and it boasts an environmentally friendly roof that supports natural vegetation. There are wonderful views all around, looking over the surrounding downs and forest, which complement the enhanced learning facilities that include purpose built science and music rooms. It is a wonderful environment for learning. The local community has certainly taken the new school into its heart with considerable civic pride, especially the 'Theatre on the Hill', which is used regularly for community events. This overwhelmingly positive reaction to the finished school is lovely to see. But it has not always been this way.

The new school has been a labour of love for Patrick Hazelwood. Denied public funding, the governors decided to go it alone and the school team raised £25 million to rebuild the existing school facility, which was spread over two different sites. The money was secured by selling one of the school sites and by further fundraising efforts coordinated by the school. By the time the new buildings opened in December 2009 funding appeals had raised an addition £1 million for furniture, equipment, theatre and sports facilities, with efforts continuing to raise a further million to eliminate the remaining financial shortfall on the project. This is a huge achievement. St John's is quite possibly the first time that an entire state school has been rebuilt in Britain without access to public funds. If this is all there was to the story it would 'merely' be one of fortitude and willpower. But there is much more. Far from welcoming the new school, local politicians repeatedly refused planning permission. Opposition also came from other bodies such as the Charity Commission, English Nature and the National Playing Fields Association. At times, the project hung on a knife-edge. The inevitable delays meant that the school faced escalating costs and very difficult budget decisions. Moreover, the existing facilities, which were built in the 1960's, were in need of considerable repair and the needs of pupils were beginning to suffer as a result of dilapidated conditions. At times, the situation looked particularly bleak.

Dr Hazelwood never faltered in his belief that the new school would finally get the 'go-ahead', a vital commitment that energised the will to move forward during the most difficult times on the journey. Throughout, St John's maintained its enviable reputation for academic excellence. There was never any question of the school 'taking its eye off the ball' or letting its high standards in teaching and learning slip. St John's remained 100% committed to offering pupils the best learning experience possible, one that cultivates the ability to learn independently rather than simply accumulating knowledge. This was achieved despite the considerable 'handicap' of ageing facilities, the stress of an uncertain future and the considerable additional workload supporting and leading the new project (not to mention the practical distractions when the new build finally began). Eventually, the political deadlock was broken and the pupils watched building contractors work around the clock for 78 weeks, as fundraising for additional facilities simultaneously kicked into high gear. The result is not only a stunning new school with a first class learning environment but also a 'benchmark' project that can inspire others to take the future into their hands.

Building the new St John's school was very much a team and community effort but it would not have happened without the dogged perseverance of Patrick Hazelwood. It is so very easy to underestimate the sheer determination and strength of will that was necessary to make it happen. When Dr Hazelwood was first interviewed for the post of Head teacher in 1996 he said that he would not leave the post until he had successfully established a new school on a single site. It is this commitment, and the educational values that underlie it, which have provided the deep sense of purpose and meaning that has enabled him to pull through, even on the darkest days. It has been quite some journey. When my oldest son, Scott, started at St John's in September 2002, I was concerned that Dr Hazelwood would move on as the project was then, apparently, well underway (little did I know at that time what actually lay ahead!). When I asked him directly on this his reply was very simple. 'I have always said that I will remain until the new school is built,' he told me, 'and I will. You have my word.' Like all good leaders he is a man of his word. There was simply too much at stake for him not to be.

Humility and selflessness – the anchors of leadership
It's nice to be seen to be effective, clever, a 'mover and shaker' in this world. It's lovely for our ego. What better way to enjoy life than sharing a few drinks with our friends and colleagues and having the opportunity to talk about *our* achievements, particularly the part about how *we* made them happen? Surely there is no harm in that? It grates a little to have to acknowledge that we are not fully in control of what happens to us and that, more realistically, our successes are created in relationship with others and with the whole. This is not *nearly* so satisfying for our ego. The interesting thing about strategic leaders is that they rarely take personal credit for their achievements and when they do they tend to downplay their role. It's not that leaders don't believe in celebrating their success. They do. But they rarely personalise their achievements in the self-centred sense. We often find leaders using 'we' in the communal sense, rather than 'I' in the personal one. They are humble, not because they lack self-esteem, but because they realise that achievement and 'success' is the result of a dance with the universe. This is the great paradox of leadership. We become fully ourselves by realising that we are part of the whole. Both are necessary for effective leadership. Far from making us 'weak' as leaders, humility and selflessness come from an inner strength and openness, which is directly related to our ability to make a difference in this world. They are bedrock qualities in strategic leadership.

Try this exercise. Write down a list of the leaders that you would regard as being amongst the 'greatest' of all time. It doesn't really matter how you decide to classify 'greatness'. I tend to use influence as a proxy for effective leadership. So I look for leaders who have not only influenced people in their own time but continue to do so, such as Henry David Thoreau, Mahatma Gandhi, and Martin Luther King. Alternatively, some leaders, such as Albert Einstein and Charles Darwin, have contributed to a permanent shift in the way that we see things, which is still very much evident in our world today. There are no set rules here. Do what you consider is most appropriate. Once you have assembled a 'first pass' list of names, try to distil them to ten leaders who imbue the best qualities of leadership from your point of view. Naturally, preparing such a leadership list is both an impossible and a rather pointless task. We cannot realistically compare leaders on this level. Nevertheless, something rather interesting inevitably arises as we attempt to do so. The leaders who come out at the top are invariably defined by their humility and sense of selflessness. Whether we select spiritual leaders, philosophers, scientists or those involved with the affairs of state, the result will tend to be the same. The exception appears to be highly creative people, such as artists, musicians and writers, who live deep within the creative process. When they are immersed in their creative pursuit they often exhibit the same lack of ego as other leaders, but it is undoubtedly true that many also lead very colourful personal lives. Perhaps, this principle holds true of all of us to a greater or lesser degree. We are capable of great humility and selflessness within our role as leaders, but that doesn't mean we are not fully human in other aspects of our lives. The idea that leaders are more 'perfect' than the rest of us is an illusion and a rather dangerous one at that.

When I present this to a working group there are inevitably some protests that not all 'great' leaders fit this mould. Interestingly, military generals, politicians and business executives seem to be singled out as popular exceptions; leaders who are the very epitome of the ruthless, often masculine, leadership style, which appears to be the opposite of humility. At this point, I normally encourage the group to dig a little deeper, with the caution to avoid confusing selflessness with a lack of strength, determination or courage.

When the groups do this they often find hidden depths to the leaders that they have chosen. Leadership is foremost a question of attitude of mind. Winston Churchill is a particularly good case in point. Churchill was capable of unbelievable fortitude and strength in the direst circumstances imaginable, but he was also very human, openly weeping at the human realities that lay behind the war. No one would argue that he was perfect. Far from it. But he was engaged completely in the task at hand, not for his own glory but for the good of the greater community. That is the very definition of selflessness. It was this core purpose that enabled him to draw on the qualities of courage, perseverance and sheer doggedness that he needed to pull a wearied nation through the very toughest years of the Second World War.

When we listen to Churchill's speeches his language is direct and truthful, and almost always spoken from the perspective of the greater community. In his first speech to the House of Commons on May 13th 1940 he claimed he had 'nothing to offer but blood, tears and sweat,' hardly the talk of a contemporary politician. His landmark speech on June 4th later that year laid out the choices of the nation in particularly stark terms and included the famous declaration of intent that 'We shall defend our island whatever the cost may be. We shall fight on the beaches... we shall fight in the fields and in the streets... we shall never surrender.' His early speeches are peppered with references to 'doing our duty' and 'standing together', the emphasis always being on communal responsibilities rather than individual rights. Yet, Churchill always gave credit to others when due, never more so than in his famous speech after the Battle of Britain in August 1940. 'Never in the field of human conflict was so much owed by so many to so few.' After the surrender of Germany on May 8th 1945, he addressed the crowds in Whitehall in similar terms by saying, 'This is your victory. It is a victory for the cause of freedom in every land. God bless you all.'

Winston Churchill always recognised that his job as leader of the nation was to be its foremost servant. He paid particular attention to recognising the contribution of ordinary men and women, the service personnel, ambulance and fire fighting crews and many others who worked with the utmost dedication by simply doing their job. He went out of his way to recognise these 'ordinary' people in his speeches because he saw their achievements as *extra*ordinary. He understood that true contribution is never measured by rank or position, but by attitude. He was also deeply aware that leaders do not act alone but together with those who support them. One of the greatest assets that a leader can have is transparency. Churchill had it in spades. What you saw was what you got. When we are open and honest we tend to attract trust and loyalty. When we are opaque, we engender distrust and suspicion. Naturally, none of us is perfect. We all make mistakes. But people are a lot more willing to forgive our errors of judgement if they believe we are not hiding something. 'Your brand is what people say about you when you are not in the room', Jeff Bezos, CEO and Chairman of Amazon, is supposed to have observed. Heraclitus, the Greek philosopher, put it another way, 'Hide our ignorance as we will, an evening of wine soon reveals it.' Transparency breeds trust and we can only do that if we have developed the humility and selflessness to risk being open.

Creating our own pathway

> 'Read, every day, something no one else is reading. Think, every day, something no one else is thinking. Do, every day, something no one else would be silly enough to do. It is bad for the mind to continually be part of unanimity.'
> **Christopher Morley, American Writer and Poet**

When we make a commitment to becoming a strategic leader we are also acknowledging the need to move beyond the limited belief systems that are so embedded in our world. As Albert Einstein pointed out, we can only resolve the big issues and challenges in our world today if we transcend the level of thinking that created them. Naturally, this is the complete opposite of what most of want to do. It is *so* much easier to stay close to comfortable and familiar territory. This includes the way in which we think about and tackle problems. Normally, we seek the easiest and most familiar tactics to resolve difficult issues. In practical everyday matters, this offers many benefits including the ability to operate automatically without the need to engage too deeply. Strategic leadership, on the other hand, is the very opposite. It is the ability to see the bigger picture and act from the deepest part of who we are. Neither can be done unconsciously and both require discipline and work. To be able to see the whole requires us to go beyond conventional thinking. To truly understand who we are is the journey of a lifetime. We have to move to a new plane with a fresh perspective. As United States Senator, James William Fulbright, remarked, 'we must dare to think unthinkable thoughts.' As a result, strategic leaders are often called upon to create their own paths, building a trail where none currently exists. We do this not only for ourselves but also for those who wish to follow us.

Trailblazing a new pathway may sound exciting but it is not for the faint hearted. It inevitably brings us into conflict with those who think more traditionally. As we begin to challenge conventional thinking, by learning to *'think small'*, *'go slowly'*, work with the power of relationship and let go of the need for control, we inevitably threaten others who see the world differently. Leaders who are ahead of their time, who see things that are invisible to others, will often experience persistent opposition from the mainstream. They struggle to gain acceptance for their ideas. They find themselves being taken gently (or not so gently) aside by their friends and advisers to be told that they are 'naïve', 'foolish', 'unrealistic', 'out of touch with the real world', 'fanatical' or even 'dangerous' and 'unethical'. In short, they swim upstream in a world that doesn't understand them. Entrepreneurs also do this, refusing to see barriers or accept obstacles in their way. As a result, they often find it difficult to access conventional funding sources and support. Instead, they find new ways of doing things. They work around the system. They make their dreams happen by taking the road less travelled.

Perhaps this sounds obvious. In many ways it is. After all, we don't change the world by following opinion polls. However, living with this tightrope is quite a different matter from theorising about it, especially when there is often little or no safety net to support us. What counts when the chips are truly down is often a combination of the steely determination of a leader and the support and commitment of the team around them. This bond is born out of trust and it is most often earned and forged through 'trial by fire'. Ironically, the tougher the conditions and challenges are, the stronger the opportunity to forge enduring relationships. We may believe that we are trusted, but we will never know until we are tested to the satisfaction of those around us. Do we walk the talk? Will we stand up for what we believe when it is against our personal interests to do so? Are we committed to serving the greater good or merely serving our own needs? It is in the tough choices that we make during the difficult times that most people find the answer to these questions. Leaders understand that trust is the most precious of commodities because it is something that can be very easily lost but is extraordinarily difficult to gain. The leadership journey is exciting and exhilarating and the rewards are substantial. But the path requires more than just commitment and perseverance. We will also need courage and stamina and, at times, blind faith too.

The value of consistency

'The only constant is change,' is almost a mantra in today's society, although it is actually attributable to the Greek philosopher, Heraclitus! We are only too aware that things are constantly changing in the world around us. If we look closely, however, we find that successful business leaders know what to change and what to leave alone. The central purpose and mission of a business is part of its core identity. It is usually closely linked to its unique proposition and we tinker with this at our peril. Failing businesses often tamper with their core identity, desperately seeking to emulate the success of others, with a regularity that is sometimes reminiscent of a chameleon. When we see this happening to a business we are inevitably witnessing its death throes. With its 'soul' ripped out, the enterprise often has nothing left to sustain it. Sometimes it dies dramatically but most often it withers away, exiting the world 'not with a bang but with a whimper', a sad reflection of its former glory. Strategic leaders are consistent in the face of success or failure. They stand for something and this is directly linked to what the organization stands for. Core purpose and meaning become the central point of stability within change. It is a key part of the sacred bond of trust that joins leaders to those who support them. Trust is one of the fundamental keys to successful change. 'Trust is at the heart of the matter', said Charles Handy, one of the most influential living management thinkers. 'That seems obvious and trite,' he continues, 'yet most of our organizations tend to be arranged on the assumption that people cannot be trusted or relied upon, even in tiny matters.'

Consistency and constancy are essential if we are to succeed as leaders. Dr Hazelwood, Head teacher of St John's school in Marlborough, was committed to achieving a new school on a single site. But not at any cost. The new school is merely the physical representation of the values that underlie the learning and caring ethos and have made St John's the best performing state school in Wiltshire. Normally, school mission statements are rarely a good place to look for real values. They tend to be crafted by committee and are rigidly politically correct, which results in vapid generic statements of intent. The St John's mission statement is more interesting. Naturally, the school seeks to be 'innovative and dynamic' and to be recognized for excellence in both learning and teaching. Given that it is highly committed to the International Baccalaureate, it is not surprising to find a reference to being 'full participants in the global community.' But the line I find so revealing is that it seeks 'to provide all learners with the confidence and capability' to do these things. Not just capability, which is assumed in a learning environment, but personal confidence. Knowing the school as I do this strikes me as a very accurate representation of its core values. It is a dedication to bring out the very best in each student, no matter where they stand in terms of academic ability and achievement, together with the confidence to go out into the world and *be* the very best they can. This ethos remains constant and it is the glue that binds the school together.

The Economist is seeing its industry turned upside down by technology. There is no question that these are challenging and uncertain times for the newspaper industry as news, media and information migrate online, together with advertising revenues. *The Economist* has always been a premium publication, well-know for the high quality of its journalism and dry wit. The writers compact large quantities of information into a lively style that is both highly informative and engaging, a very hard act to pull off in practice. It also has remarkably broad coverage, extending beyond world news, politics and business to science, technology and the arts, as well as publishing regular in-depth reports that are often definitive in their own right. In short, it is passionate about what it does. It does not compromise. Not surprisingly, there is a limited market for such in-depth journalism. This kind of coverage is never going to suit everyone. *The Economist* currently has a circulation of 1.6 million copies, half of which are sold in North America. It has even made a joke of its limited appeal with its slogan in the early 1990s, '*The Economist* – not read by millions of people.' Its 'snob appeal' has earned it two appearances in *The Simpsons*, evidence, if any is needed, of what a durable brand the publication has developed. In short, it will always be in a niche market. The secret to its success is that information is a global product and *The Economist* aims to be definitive in its chosen niche. What the publication offers most of all is consistency in writing style and analysis and there are few equals in the market segment that it occupies. This is a global 'niche' well worth fighting for.

Like all publications, *The Economist* will to continue to change as the digital age becomes more embedded into our everyday lives. It has already built a strong online presence, which is tightly integrated with the physical publication. It has long been a mantra in the media and information industries that 'content is king', which is a way of saying that good quality content is always in the shortest supply. The vast increase in online content may, ironically, simply reinforce this. 'Content is not just king,' observed Rupert Murdock, Chairman and CEO of News Corporation in early 2010, 'it is the emperor of all things electronic.' It is the uniqueness of content that is ultimately the arbiter of its value. *The Economist*'s consistency and refusal to water down its proposition is its greatest strength, despite its relatively narrow appeal. It is good and it is dependable. And there is a strong premium in the media and news market place for dependability. As a result, it is likely to be a feature of our digital world in 20-30 years. There are many others in the newspaper business that would dearly love to be able to say that with certainty.

The Economist is not alone in demonstrating the value of consistency in business. We see this quality in many of our best business leaders. Timothy White was editor-in-chief of *Billboard Magazine*, the American music trade magazine, from 1991 until his death in 2002. A former rock journalist he stamped his authority on *Billboard* with his insistence on definitive music journalism and his inquisitive, philosophical mind. When he became editor-in-chief in 1991 the magazine was close to its first century in business and was in need of change. Timothy did this by focusing on the creative side of the business as well as evolving the proposition to meet the impact of new technologies. He was a man of huge personal integrity and he used his prolific writing abilities to build *Billboard*'s reputation for premium content and maintain its independent focus. He had an encyclopaedic knowledge of the industry and music in general. His knowledge and appreciation of music, particularly of less commercial genres, deeply impressed artists. Brian Wilson, of the Beach Boys, once commented that Timothy 'knew more about me than I knew about myself.'

When Timothy White died of a heart attack in 2002 tributes poured in from artists. Brian Wilson called him 'the best friend an artist could ever have', and Angelique Kidjo went further, calling him her 'spiritual guide musically.' However, the tribute that best sums up what he stood for, both at *Billboard* and within the broader music industry, was the one by the highly respected country artist, Emmylou Harris. She wrote: 'Timothy White didn't write about artists. He didn't write about himself. He wrote about what he loved: music. And I'm honoured to have had him write about the music that came through me.' It was the consistency and commitment to this passion that maintained *Billboard* as the indispensible 'bible' of the music industry during his tenure as editor-in-chief. Consistency matters for a premium trade magazine that people in the industry rely on for information. It matters a lot. Timothy had his own take on the importance of content. One of his articles was titled, *'Don't Call It Content – It's Substance Or Nothing'*.

Waitrose

Like all successful retailers, Waitrose has a clearly defined proposition that means something very tangible to customers. If we were to use contemporary marketing terminology we might talk about 'the Waitrose experience', which would be a combination of the high quality product range, excellent customer service and the overall ambience of the stores. Thankfully, Waitrose does not talk in these terms. In the simplest terms, it has established a premium brand that consumers trust. There is only one way of doing this and that is by consistent execution day in day out. The foundation of a good retailer is attention to detail and it is in the little things that Waitrose excels. The acid test is consumer trust. Waitrose is regularly voted as Britain's favourite supermarket. It was voted Britain's best shop for the second year running by *Which Magazine* in 2009 and it currently holds awards by the *Telegraph Magazine Shop Awards*, *BBC Watchdog* and *Good Housekeeping Magazine*. Attention to detail works. But Waitrose is not just a superbly executed up-market proposition. There is an understanding in its brand promise that high quality products and personable service is delivered at fair value. It is explicitly committed to 'give customers quality food that is honestly priced and represents excellent value.' This commitment becomes harder to meet for a relatively smaller chain in recessionary times when consumers are naturally more price conscious and demand more for less.

Waitrose currently has just over 4% of the grocery market in the UK and is the sixth largest supermarket. Tesco, in comparison, is the mighty behemoth in the industry, with a market share of over 30% and enormous purchasing power with suppliers, not surprising as it accounts for one pound in every eight spent in the country. Many retailers in such a fiercely competitive environment would be tempted to react by subtly degrading quality and service in order to meet price expectations. Waitrose behaves very differently. It is acutely aware of the need to be price competitive and has rolled out its 'Essentials' range quickly in response to changing economic conditions. At the same time, it continues to adhere rigidly to its commitment to quality food and service. This commitment lies at the heart of its brand and is 'non-negotiable'. It extends to all Waitrose products, not only those in the premium segment. The chain continues to pioneer local sourcing policies for fresh fruit and vegetables and it has developed close supplier relationships with individual producers and farms. It actively links quality assurance to ethical and environmental concerns through its 'LEAF' mark ('linking environment and farming'), fair trade products and the Waitrose Foundation. But its commitment extends much deeper than this. Waitrose supports the growing move to eat more seasonal products, showing much greater consideration for the environment by reducing supply miles. It also reinforces the knowledge that our parents knew but we seem to have forgotten. Regional products taste differently and for those who appreciate good food it is these subtle nuances in taste that define the eating experience. Most of all, the store acts as a guarantee that the quality of food, and increasingly the fairness and ethics of food supply, is taken seriously throughout the supply chain.

Waitrose has moved quickly in the area of 'responsible' sourcing on the assumption that consumers will pay a premium for food that is ethically produced and sourced. Ethical food polices are now part of the explicit Waitrose promise to customers. The chain is 'dedicated to offering quality food that has been reasonably sourced,' it says, 'combined with high standards of customer service.' This is a welcome guarantee, but to be worth something it must also be reliably and consistently executed. Waitrose delivers on both. It has developed an enviable reputation based on product innovation, operational excellence and consistent delivery. In wines, for example, its rigorous quality control and tasting process has enabled the chain to establish itself as a serious contender in an overcrowded and competitive marketplace. Part of the reason that Waitrose achieves these high standards is because it views itself as more than a 'supermarket'. It fashions itself as providing the convenience of a conventional supermarket but 'with the expertise and service of a specialist shop.' Expertise, by its nature, needs to be devolved in a large food store. It means developing, supporting and rewarding many people across the business in order that they can become experts in their areas. This brings with it the advantages of distributed intelligence, not least close customer contact at the operational level, producing timely and valuable feedback. As a result, Waitrose generally attracts high quality people to work for it, who share a genuine pride in being part of the enterprise. This, in turn, results in a better in-store ambience and quickly becomes a virtuous cycle.

There is something else that is very interesting about Waitrose, especially given its success. Its Managing Director, Mark Price, is quite different from some of the larger-than-life leaders we have looked at so far in *Freedom from Fear*. He has a much lower profile and is focused on achieving the broad strategic aims of the business, to double revenue and market share by 2016. But this is not at any cost. When he was interviewed by Matthew Naylor at the National Farmers Union annual conference in February 2009, he talked mostly about maintaining and extending commitments to quality, ethical sourcing and, most of all, strengthening relationships with British Farmers. 'We realize that a long term sustainable relationship with farmers is more important,' he said, 'than riding the spot markets or doing something on the hoof.' Given the community orientation of both Waitrose and the John Lewis Partnership this underplayed role is entirely consistent with the values of the business. Not all leaders are out there attracting attention. Some are just quietly getting on with their job and doing so exceedingly well. Waitrose is thriving because it is adapting rapidly to changes in its business environment without compromising its standards. It knows what business it is in and it sticks to it. The same is true of many other successful retailers who operate in fiercely competitive markets.

Peter Boizot founded Pizza Express in 1965 and one can scarcely imagine a more competitive and fickle marketplace. Yet, it survives and prospers today, nearly 50 years after it first started out. Like Waltrose, it has mastered the ability to constantly update its proposition without compromising its deep commitment to quality and service. The Pizza Express Club, which is a membership club for its most loyal customers, allows it instant feedback on restaurant experiences. It uses the information to improve its proposition constantly, without changing the sacrosanct aspects of its dining experience (which apparently include the availability of 'dough balls' on its starter menu!). This is the mark of any good retailer, but identifying what is sacrosanct in a retail offer can be desperately difficult in practice. Just ask a few retailers! It requires the ability to be open and learn quickly from mistakes. It is as much a 'gut feeling' as it is the result of intellectual analysis. In many smaller entrepreneurial ventures this 'gut feel' actively reflects the core values of the founder. It is also evident in the uncompromising standards of Pret A Manger, which has revolutionized the concept of the 'sandwich shop chain'. Yet again, it is the consistency of the customer experience that is paramount. Both Pizza Express and Pret A Manger have enviable records of operational excellence and innovation, constantly evolving their menus to make the customer experience more interesting and exciting. This is much harder to achieve than it looks. Both propositions are thriving and boast strong customer brand loyalty. Execution matters in retail. It matters a lot. But the trick is to know what to change and what to keep the same and that is almost an art form.

Surviving the journey

> *'The miracle is not to fly in the air,*
> *Or walk on the water,*
> *But to walk on the earth.'*
> **Chinese Proverb**

Wilma Mankiller was principal chief of the Cherokee Nation, the

290 Freedom from Fear

first women in that position. Under her leadership the tribe expanded from 55,000 to over 150,000 members and she greatly increased the financial resources under its control. When she first ran for office, however, she was opposed by the entire tribal council because no woman had led such a large tribe before. She persevered until she won them over, re-establishing the traditional values and culture of the Cherokee, which emphasises a balance between the two genders. Her life was one of struggle and determination, given meaning by her passionate belief in her mission to restore the Cherokee's lost faith in themselves. Her name came from her birthplace, Mankiller flats in Oklahoma, and she never lost that connection, despite moving to San Francisco at the age of ten at the behest of the US government when a local airbase wanted to expand onto Cherokee land. In 1976 she returned to her home and set about her life mission of restoring a sense of 'oneness' to the Cherokee Nation by encouraging self-reliance and chipping away at the desolation that had occurred when the tribal lands had been subdivided into allotments in 1907. She refused the patronage of well-meaning white people on many occasions, because she knew that the loss of community and spirituality was an inside job for the Cherokee.

Wilma Mankiller's leadership journey may have been born out of her belief in a better future but it was also intensely practical. She arranged for one settlement to put in its own water line connected to the main supply 16 miles away. She established tribally owned businesses and community development projects and revived the Sequoyah High School in Tahlequah. This didn't happen quickly. It took years of hard work, when she slogged away, taking one step at a time. She once commented that 'we've had daunting problems in many critical areas but I believe in the old Cherokee injunction to 'be of good mind.' Today it's called positive thinking.' It may have been built one piece at a time. But over the course of her lifetime, Wilma's contribution has made a very big difference to the Cherokee people. When she died in 2010 Barrack Obama spoke of her 'vision and commitment to a brighter future' and concluded that she had 'served as an inspiration to women in Indian Country and across America.' Wilma put this in her own words, 'Prior to my election,' she said, young Cherokee girls would never have thought that they might grow up and become chief.' This alone is quite a testament to her legacy.

I am ending this chapter with Norma Mankiller's leadership journey because no aspect of it could possibly be described as 'fortuitous' or 'easy'. It was a long hard slog but it also made a profound difference for people of the Cherokee Nation. She wasn't a perfect person. No leader ever is. But her achievements were considerable. For many of us, our day-to-day experience of leadership will be just like Norma's, a long hard slog. It is often only many years later, when we begin to see some of the difference that we have made.

Our life's work

'A lot of managers work long and hard simply to make the inevitable happen... They just preside over the inevitable. Yet management is about making things happen that otherwise wouldn't, about making ordinary people produce extraordinary results.'

Sumantra Ghoshal

Naturally, it can be interesting and even inspirational to read other people's stories. But at the end of the day our leadership journey is our own. Along the way we develop, or build upon, the leadership characteristics that underlie our ability to stay on course: persistence, resilience, fortitude, humility, selflessness, consistency and, most of all, courage. We may be lucky to be imbued with some of these qualities by nature. That is good because it means that we can hit the decks running. However, the chances are that we will have to learn them as we go along. We need not worry. Events are likely to give us plenty of practice in sharpening our skills. At first, we may be in a rush but we would be wise to be patient. Everything comes when it is most needed, although not necessarily in the way that we imagine or would most like! The truth is that we grow into leadership. It takes time. Normally it takes a lifetime.

11
CREATING A NEW EARTH

*'To hear the sea
Lift, and gently fall
Is to feel the earth
Breathe, and all is well.'*
Jane Miles

Looking for the key

The Sufi tradition often uses stories to pass on wisdom and some of the best-known tales are those of Mulla Nasruddin, who plays the same role in Sufi literature as the wise fool does in its Western counterpart. In one such story, Nasruddin is searching for a key outside his house. After a while a man stops and asks the Mulla, 'What are you looking for?' 'My key,' replies Nasruddin. Soon many people have joined in the search and there is quite a crowd outside the front of the Mulla's house. Some time passes in busy activity until another man, hoping to focus the search, asks, 'Where exactly did you drop it?' 'In my house', comes the reply from the Mulla. 'Then why are we searching for it in the street?' asks the man. 'Because there is more light here than in my house', replies Nasruddin.

Sufi stories can be understood at many levels and this one is no exception. At a basic level, the tale reminds us that we need to go the root of a problem if we wish to resolve it, which is not necessarily the place that is either most familiar or comfortable. At a deeper level, the story draws our attention to the nature of the spiritual journey. The 'key' is symbolic. It is not found in the external world but inside us. In practice, most of us would much rather search on the outside, where the terrain is known and we feel secure, rather than enter into our own 'darkness'. Yet, this is where the key to understanding who we really are lies. We might also see the story on a third level. We are at a 'key' moment in our history. The challenges and issues that we face can no longer be resolved at the same level of consciousness that created them. We are being asked to go to a deeper level of awareness, recognising our interrelationship with the whole. This is the root of both strategic thinking and strategic leadership. For some of us, this may be part of a spiritual journey and we will see it through this lens. For others it may not be. But for all of us it is the key to our future.

The snow leopard

In March 2010, a hunter captured a snow leopard, one of the rarest creatures on earth, in the Wakhan Mountains of Afghanistan. He bundled the animal onto a truck and drove it to Feyzabad for a quick sale. The hunter was undone when he became greedy and began to shop around after realising just how much his captive might be worth. After the creature was rescued, Mostapha Zaher, Director General of the National Protection Agency in Kabul, contacted the Afghan President, Hamid Karzai, and a four-day international rescue mission began. Richard Fite, a veterinarian adviser to the US Agriculture Department in Northern Afghanistan, tended to the creature for three days and its health appeared to be on the mend. He gave the go-ahead to fly the animal back to Wakhan in a US helicopter so that it could be released back into the wild. The next day, bad weather grounded the chopper and, sadly, by the morning afterwards the leopard had died. 'My guess,' said Richard, 'and it is just that – is that it died from shock.' This is not just unfortunate. There are only an estimated 3,500 to 7,000 snow leopards left on the planet and the animal is a powerful symbol of Afghanistan's untamed wilderness. What has been lost is more than simply one beautiful creature in a country that has already been decimated by turbulence and war. Dave Lawson, the Country Director of the Wildlife Society in Kabul, comments that 'a lot of these mountain people have respect for wildlife'. One villager told him that 'God put these animals here for us to look after.' When the snow leopard died it was a loss felt throughout Afghanistan, by both villagers and those at the highest levels of power alike. One Afghan elder openly wept as he watched the body of the animal being carried out. The snow leopard is not simply a lone creature; it is symbolic of the identity of the Afghan people.

To some of us the loss of a single creature, no matter how rare or beautiful, is unfortunate but no more than that. Surely the world can live without snow leopards, even if the worst-case scenario should come to pass and they were to become extinct? Are there not more obvious and urgent problems to resolve in this war-torn area? As always with strategic thinking, the answer lies not in 'either/or' but in both. We need to shift to a higher level of awareness. Those who were touched by the snow leopard in some way, such as the Afghan Elder and the President, know this intuitively. Far from being a distraction from more 'important' things, simply looking into the eyes of such a magnificent creature is enough to remind us of the sacred unity that binds us all. It is this knowledge that will help us to heal and resolve the bloodthirsty human conflicts that rage across the globe, including those in Afghanistan. Ultimately, all living things on earth are bound together in a common endeavour. As the I-Ching remarks, 'Without the breath of the tiger there will be no wind, only clouds, and certainly no rain.'

We cannot simply 'think' our way to this deep truth using our minds. That will only take us so far. We also need to 'feel' and 'know' our way to this connection. This means using our full human consciousness: heart, mind, body and soul. We move towards combining the power of the mind with the wisdom of the heart. We begin to express ourselves using the language of the soul. At this level, there are no 'big' or 'small' issues because we look at them all as being equally important. This makes no sense at all to our intellect or to our ego, which see us as separate from the world. But when we recognise the interconnectivity of all things we begin to understand that the way we relate to even the tiniest part of the whole will affect everything. Even the smallest of acts changes the entire fabric of the universe. This is our true power and destiny. It is by making this connection that we can change the world by focusing our attention on one 'small' thing at a time.

The call to sanity

During our journey together in *Freedom from Fear* we have looked at the scale of some of the major issues and challenges that face us. Many of the most serious are systemic in nature and are not conducive to resolution through simple linear measures. Despite all our efforts to conserve water, food and energy – the basic necessities of life – we continue to squander all three. In 2006, for example, American food retailers wasted some $20 billion of perishable food in their supply chains (equivalent to 8-10% of the total food chain). This could be reduced dramatically by better supply chain technology, tighter control of 'shrinkage' and improved data collection and forecasting. US 'shrink rates' are currently double those of European firms, partly because American retailers value large displays and the widest possible range of products. Unfortunately, too much choice tends to overwhelm customers and the result is a high percentage of wasted products. There are valid cultural differences between European and American consumers but the opportunities for waste reduction are immense, both for sustainability and increased profitability. And this is merely the tip of the iceberg. At a broader level, consumption of basic human requirements remains deeply unequal, as does the use and enjoyment of the earth's resources in general. This is not just a question of equity. Our unintelligent over-consumption is now threatening the health of the planet as a whole. Even the legitimate headway that we have made towards combating global poverty and inequality is now at risk because of economic and environmental turbulence. The time has come to think differently.

In practice, we are *all* subject to the three great illusions, those of independence, size and control. These almost invisible belief systems are not only deeply entrenched within our society but are also infinitely subtle. Many of our 'solutions' to deep-seated issues, for example, do not recognise the deep interconnectivity between the natural and human worlds. We also consistently overestimate our ability to 'control' complex systems, resisting the understanding that we need to work *with* natural systems rather than to seek to dominate them. If we see ourselves in competition with the natural world, it is a fight that we are destined to lose. To win *is* to lose. In 2010, to no-one's surprise, the United Nations reported that government agreed targets to reduce the rate of biodiversity loss had not been met. Between 1970 and 2006 the abundance of vertebrate species fell by a third and nearly a quarter of all plant species are currently threatened with extinction. Such savage reductions should focus the attention of even the most sceptical of observers. Even our response to the global financial crisis has been principally for government to throw money at it. This limited, if partially necessary, reaction has served to shift the epicentre of the crisis from banking to sovereign debt. Until we begin to identify the underlying systemic factors that have led to the financial crisis we will not be able to work towards resolving it. Neither will we be prepared for the further waves of financial turbulence that are yet to come. At the very minimum, a sustainable economic solution entails a radical reassessment of our current ideas and policies on retirement, tax, the role of the state, including the balance of rights and responsibilities of government and citizens, the nature of risk and who should bear it and much more besides.

One of the direct results of the rapid increases in government debt is a transfer of wealth from future generations to the current one. Few of us seem aware of the consequences of such an enormous transfer of resources. In very simple terms, we are living beyond our means and taking the money from our children and grandchildren in order to sustain our excesses. If we then consider our failure to tackle environmental, demographic, social and community issues (the cost of which will fall on future generations) we can begin to appreciate the full extent of the transfer of wealth and resources that our current policies imply. This is not just unethical and unjust. It is a collective failure to take responsibility. If we then address the destructive potential of our current lifestyle it becomes a form of collective insanity. As Goethe caustically observed, 'We do not have to visit a madhouse to find disordered minds; our planet is the mental institution of the universe.' This is the challenge that we face when we begin to create a New Earth by thinking differently and adopting the mantle of strategic leadership. As we have seen, we will need persistence, resilience and fortitude for our journey, not to mention plenty of courage.

Strategic thinking as the foundation for change

'The time to start worrying is when you think you've got it all figured out.'
Stephen Cottrell, The Bishop of Reading

We have looked at many examples of strategic thinking in action in *Freedom from Fear*, including the five organisations that we have revisited throughout this book: Apple, Starbucks, Waitrose, National Trust and the work of the Prince of Wales. Together with the case studies in *The Strategic Mind*, these illustrate the seven disciplines of strategic thinking in a wide variety of contexts and show how they translate into the ability to make a significant, sometimes radical, difference in this world. The disciplines are often counter-intuitive because they challenge some of our most cherished beliefs about the world in which we live. Taken together, they enable us to shift the way that we think to develop a much broader and more holistic view. This is the foundation in strategic thinking that enables us to make a significant difference as leaders in our world. We have seen it practiced by leaders from all areas of life throughout this book.

The seven strategic disciplines begin with *'know your own story,'* because knowing ourselves, what we stand for and where we come from, is the solid bedrock for acting out of the deepest part of ourselves. When we combine this with the ability to *'dream'*, it reminds us of who we *can* be when acting that way. Our dream becomes the purpose and vision, 'the prize', which provides us with the energy to continue our journey as leaders. When we *'think small'* and *'go slowly'* we directly confront the illusion of size and reframe our thinking in the longer term. *'Serve others'* is a reminder of the interconnectedness of life. We exist in relation to others, not independently of them. This makes us more aware of the illusions of independence and control and how these powerful belief systems limit our ability to perceive new possibilities and opportunities. Following the discipline to *'be simple'* allows us to direct our energies in a purposeful manner, avoiding fragmentation and distraction. And, finally, to *'reflect'* is the process of consciously putting aside time to access our inner wisdom and guidance. It allows us to access the 'space between our thoughts', the quiet wisdom deep within us. It is the source of insight, inspiration and creativity and the key to thinking 'outside the box'. Reflection is not only the core strategic discipline; it is also the hardest to put into practice. Ultimately, we all find our own unique path. When we combine reflection with lessons born of direct experience we are able to develop an awareness of our inner belief systems, which colour and influence the way we see the world around us. This awareness is critical to all of us who aspire to be leaders. 'The most important thing you can do to change the world,' says author, Shakti Gawain, 'is to change your own beliefs about the nature of life, people, reality, to something more positive... and begin to act accordingly.'

To think strategically is to think outside the box and there is often a price to be paid when we do so. In one of Scott Adams' insightful Dilbert cartoons, our office hero moves his chair outside his cubicle to think creatively. He is immediately reprimanded by his boss with the comment, 'you're a fire hazard. Do your thinking inside the box.' The response is often much worse than that, especially when we threaten the assumptions and beliefs of others by thinking and acting differently. As Abbot Anthony, a fourth century ascetic monk, remarked, 'A time is coming when people will go mad, and when they meet someone who is not mad, they will turn to him and say, "You are out of your mind," just because he is not like them.' This is the price we sometimes have to pay for rebuilding our house on more solid foundations, for moving beyond the current spiral of ignorance. This is the way that we will create a New Earth.

The strategic disciplines in action

Strategic thinking is a holistic practice and it makes little sense to attempt to prioritise the individual disciplines. There is no 'order of importance', although the ability to reflect, to put some space between thought and action, is the foundation of the ability to think holistically. In practice, we will all favour some of the disciplines of strategic thinking over others. Some will simply come more naturally to us, while others will take more effort to develop and integrate into the way we think. It is good to know, therefore, that each discipline can make a profound difference on its own, given the right context and circumstances. There are countless examples of leaders who are making a profound difference today by working with one or more of the strategic disciplines.

It is not only charities that are recognising the critical importance of relationship and interdependence within our world. Commercial businesses are broadening their propositions to serve the wider needs of communities, thereby linking sustainability and profitability. Will Allen runs a community food centre in urban Milwaukee. It is about the size of a large supermarket and it houses 20,000 plants and vegetables, thousands of fish and other animals, including goats, chickens, ducks, rabbits and bees. 'Everybody,' Will says, 'regardless of their economic means, should have access to the same healthy, safe, affordable food that is grown naturally.' His enterprise is part of a movement in America's low-income neighbourhoods to provide a healthy food alternative in areas deprived of regular grocery stores. In doing so, people like Will Allen are also making a powerful contribution to reducing greenhouse gases by shortening supply chains. Will's motto is simple and clear, as all good business propositions should be: 'Grow. Bloom. Thrive.'

Veta La Palma is a Spanish fish farm located on an island in the Guadalquivir River, ten miles from the Atlantic Ocean, which produces 1,200 tons of sea bass, bream, red mullet and shrimp every year. It is another excellent example of a commercial business working in harmony with the environment around it, to the benefit of both. It was created when the wetlands in the area were re-flooded, which reversed a previous decision to drain the land to raise cattle. Unlike so many other fish farms it has been founded on ecologically sound principles and it is now a refuge for migrating aquatic birds, including many endangered species such as egrets, spoonbills and pink flamingos. Miguel Medialdea, the biologist at Veta La Palma, summarises the positive link between human intervention and the environment. 'The point isn't to make use and conservation compatible,' he says, 'The point is to use in order to conserve.' 'Because of our artificial intervention,' he concludes, 'the natural environment is improved.' When the farm started there were just 50 species of birds. Now there are 250. He shrugs as a pink flamingo grabs a sea bass. 'They take about 20% of our annual yield,' he observes, 'But that just shows the whole system is working.'

Both Will Allen's community farm and Veta La Palma are examples of strategic leadership at its best, simultaneously making a profound difference to local communities and to the world at large. They are also commercially viable businesses, which highlights another interesting aspect of strategic thinking, its paradoxical nature. We learn to see the world not as 'either/or' but potentially both. The same truth is seen in the work of Temple Grandin, a Doctor of Animal Science at Colorado State University. Temple has become a powerful advocate in both the animal welfare and autism movements. Born with autism she did not talk until she was four years old. She vividly remembers being picked upon and teased at school because she was different. Today, Temple speaks about what it means to be hyper sensitive to everything in her environment and has become a source of inspiration and support for autistic children and their parents. This same sensitivity has led to her becoming a consultant in animal behaviour to the US livestock industry. Using 'her unique window into the minds of animals,' she has promoted the humane handling of livestock and the treatment of animals with dignity. Temple has instigated many improvements to reduce the stress of animals due for slaughter. 'I think using animals for food is an ethical thing to do,' she says, 'but we've got to do it right. We've got to give those animals a decent life and we've got to give them a painless death. We owe the animal respect.' Her work has enlarged the field of possibility in the way we think about both autism and animal welfare. It has also led to significant tangible improvements in the treatment of animals that is based on a more sustainable approach to living in harmony with our natural world.

Naturally, charitable organisations also perform a vital role in society by achieving communal aims that would be difficult under either private or public ownership. They are a critical conduit for building and maintaining community assets. The National Trust's 'Brecon Beacons' appeal, for example, aims to restore footpaths in this very special place of outstanding beauty, in order to limit further erosion and destruction. This work is expressly for the benefit of future generations rather than meeting the current needs of walkers. This is the principle of *'serving others'* in action. In the case of Westonbirt, the great arboretum in Gloucestershire, we might say that it is building its future 'one tree at a time'. Westonbirt, which is owned by the Forestry Commission, has over 18,000 trees from all over the world. It is a beautiful setting for finding peace and tranquillity and a wonderful place to reconnect with nature. The arboretum's objective is to become a 'truly national centre for learning about and appreciating trees' according to Simon Toomer, its new Director. This includes its important scientific role of studying how different tree species and ecologies perform as our climate changes.

The Wiltshire Wildlife Trust is another good example of a broad community remit. It looks after 44 nature reserves in Wiltshire and works with local communities, schools, businesses and public bodies to achieve its community aims. It is also actively working on educational issues such as reducing the county's eco-footprint. Charities such as the National Trust, the Royal Society for Protection of Birds ('RSPB') and the Woodland Trust, support individual projects to protect landscapes and areas of outstanding beauty and importance that will benefit people who are yet to be born. The RSPB, for example, is currently managing a project at Titchwell Marsh in Norfolk, which aims to protect the site against coastal erosion for another 50 years. This work will inform other projects where human settlements are threatened in a similar way. Knowledge accumulation and transfer play a vital role in these projects, which ultimately benefits society as a whole. Historically, we have not been very adept at 'joining up the dots' and applying this kind knowledge to other areas in life. By doing so, we are opening up a vast reservoir of untapped possibility and opportunity.

Power of a dream

Rob Parsons, Executive Chairman of Care for the Family, has a dream. It is the same dream that drove him to set up the charity over twenty years ago. In November 2009, he set that dream out in full because he believes that dreams are not only important, they are also contagious. 'Let me confess,' he writes, 'that it is a big vision and some may dismiss it as no more than a 'pipe dream'. 'But in setting the bar of this dream high, even in the process of *trying* to fulfil it, we will touch the lives of millions of people for good.' The dream of Care for the Family includes seeing 'a day when every child has the best possible chance of growing up in a secure home,' and 'every family has somewhere to turn to when things get tough.' Other aspects of the dream are more tangible and relate to the capabilities and support that Care for the Family will be able to give to families in need: support that will help them through times of crisis and help to break the cycle of family breakdown. It is a mission that involves travelling *alongside* families in distress, being there when the support is most needed.

Raffi Cavoukian, better known simply as Raffi, also has a dream. After a highly successful career as a children's entertainer (when he sold over ten million albums and almost defined the genre of children's singer-songwriter), he founded *Child Honouring*, a vision for creating a humane and sustainable world by addressing the universal needs of children. He describes child honouring as a philosophy that 'adopts a children-first approach to healing communities and restoring the environment. 'It is a novel idea,' he admits, 'organizing society around the needs of its youngest members.' But it is one that would turn our world upside down, in the most positive of senses, by putting stewardship and sustainability at the core of what we do. Both Rob Parsons and Raffi work tirelessly to bring their visions into reality. They both realise how profoundly energizing a powerful dream can be. Rob Parsons points to the words of Michelangelo who said, 'The greater danger for most of us lies not in setting our aim too high and falling short, but in setting our aim too low and achieving our mark.' Both leaders recognise how ambitious their dreams are, so they build incrementally, step-by-step. They *'go slowly'* to build sustainable foundations for the future that they envisage. They *'think small'*, paying great attention to detail along the way, so that those foundations are strong for years to come. They are both completely committed to making the world a better place, long after they have left the world themselves.

The mantle of leadership

'Our deepest fear is not that we are inadequate. Our deepest fear is that we are powerful beyond measure. It is our Light, not our Darkness, that most frightens us.'
Marianne Williamson

Learning to think strategically is the foundation for tackling many of the world's most intractable problems. The questioning of accepted truth is an essential prerequisite of the role of any leader. However, strategic leaders not only think differently, they have the courage to commit that insight into action. During *Freedom from Fear*, we have looked at the process of developing the courage and commitment to become a leader and the characteristics that leaders commonly display in order to achieve their aims: persistence, resilience, fortitude, humility, selflessness and consistency. We have considered *what* leadership means (*'taking responsibility'*), *where* it is exercised (developing the ability to see the big picture), *with whom* (acting on behalf of others) and *how* leaders operate in the day-to-day (with simplicity, clarity of purpose and learning to '*go with the flow*'). We have also followed the internal journey that leaders embark upon. It is only when we venture inside ourselves that we discover our full power. We are then able to harness the courage and inner strength to stay constant when our journey gets tough, as it will invariably do from time to time. Finally, we have looked at leaders acting in almost every conceivable area of human endeavour, sometimes with positional authority, often not.

It is tempting to finish *Freedom from Fear* with a grand leadership story, something big and uplifting, which leaves us feeling inspired and motivated on our own personal journey. But I believe that this would be wrong. A better future does not lie in the hands of a few charismatic individuals with big aspirations, no matter how inspiring they may be. It lies with us. We will create a New Earth through a multitude of 'small' acts, which together will make our world a better place. Each and every decision that we make from a deeper state of awareness is a sacred, precious moment. Let us celebrate each one. A new world awaits us if we have the courage to follow our calling and the tenacity to stick with the journey. The stories that follow are about leaders who have already made a significant difference in the world. But they are only part of the way through their leadership journeys. This is where most of us are too. Our stories are still unfolding.

Leadership in action

David Waters is Chairman of the Great Bustard Group, a charity that is hoping to reintroduce these charismatic birds back into the United Kingdom after an absence of nearly 180 years. Ever since David first witnessed the courtship display of the male bird he was hooked. It was an 'incredible sight,' he says, 'I knew Britain was missing a jewel in its crown of biodiversity.' Great bustards were once common in Britain, until hunters finally wiped them out. The birds have also suffered devastating declines internationally and are on the 'Red List' of the International Union for Conservation of Nature as a globally threatened species. With the global population now estimated at just 35,000, the Great Bustard Group is also involved with practical conservation measures for the birds in the Saratov Oblast region of South West Russia. Project costs come to about £130,000 a year, with most of the money raised from private donations, so it helps that awareness has been raised by the decision to place the great bustard at the centre of the Wiltshire flag. Great bustards can weigh up to 20 kilos and are the heaviest flying birds in the world, so they make quite an impact when seen, especially the two who were spotted flying over Stonehenge in the summer of 2009!

David set up the Great Bustard Group in 1998 with the aim of achieving a healthy self-sustaining population of the birds on Salisbury Plain using chicks from Saratov in Russia. He was undeterred by the fact that previous plans to reintroduce the great bustard had failed. 'Many people in Wiltshire are so enthusiastic about the bird,' he says, 'it's a testimony to how special it is.' Simply gaining permission from the Russians, however, was an arduous feat in its own right. It took years of negotiations and 33 different licences, before permission was finally granted. David recalls this process as a 'long and lonely struggle,' but he continues, 'I refused to believe that it was impossible because although previous attempts were made no one had ever tried anything quite like this so there was no proof that it couldn't be done.' The first great bustard was introduced on Salisbury Plain in 2004 and in 2009 two chicks hatched, 'Rhubarb' and 'Crumble', the first great bustards born on British soil since 1832. As Salisbury Plain is the largest undeveloped area of grassland in Europe, it is ideal environment for the birds and hopes are high for the future. For David, this is only the beginning of his dream. 'It has been a hard struggle to get this far,' he says, 'I am exhausted and nearly broke, but to see great bustards breeding after an absence of 177 years is brilliant.'

The bottled drinks market is not for wimps. With companies such as Nestlé and Coca Cola operating in the segment it is fiercely competitive. Selling bottled water in this market adds a new dimension in complexity, as increased environmental awareness has taken its toll on demand for bottled water, particularly in restaurants. Most consumers now prefer their water from the restaurant tap (63% according to a survey in 2009). This does not, however, deter Reed Paget. He is the founder and CEO of Belu (pronounced 'blue'), a non-profit maker of environmentally sound bottled water, sourced from Shropshire in the United Kingdom. Reed founded the company in 2004, with the aim of 'helping the environment not lining investors' pockets'. Our collective future,' he adds, 'depends on properly managing the finite resources of the Earth.' Reed practices what he preaches. Belu donates all its profit to clean water projects, with a commitment to 'deliver clean water to one person for one month' for each bottle it sells. It was the first drinks company in the world to become carbon-neutral in 2006. The company uses a wide variety of eco-friendly practices, such as local sourcing, smart manufacturing and distribution systems and the use of 50% recycled glass in its bottles. Belu has notched up some other impressive industry 'firsts', including compostable bottles made from corn (which can be recycled back into soil in just eight weeks) and the use of PVC-free liners in its bottle caps. It is currently supporting projects in India, Mali, Madagascar and Bangladesh as well as working alongside 'Thames 21', London's leading waterways charity, to reduce the rubbish content in the River Thames before the Olympics in 2012. The pioneering work of the company has been recognised by the outside world and Reed has garnered a host of awards including *The Independent's* 'Social Entrepreneur of the Year' and an 'O$_2$ Inspiration Award'.

Working as a social entrepreneur is not easy. In addition to all the normal challenges associated with running an entrepreneurial business, Belu has to meet its community and society objectives and ensure adequate funding for the company, without having a formal profit objective. Simply running the business and moving it forward can be painstakingly difficult. It took 32 rounds of funding to raise $2.5 million and Belu is still undercapitalised. Venture capitalists have shown little interest in the company, despite its obvious success in both marketing and environmental terms. As a result, it is over-reliant on a limited number of 'angel investors'. 'I probably would have more success robbing banks,' observes Reed, 'than getting funding from those [venture capitalist] sources.' Nevertheless, by 2008 sales had reached $4 million and the business was breaking even, with the hope of a small profit. It is also inspiring others. New businesses such as Frank Water, One Water and Thirsty Planet have entered the market. Reed sees this as a good thing. 'Part of my intention,' he says, 'was to prove that business could be used to make things better. If we can't encourage our industry to make the environment a core part of its thinking then we've failed.' He hopes that the success of Belu will 'convince businesses that investing in long-term sustainability is not only good for the planet but smart for business too.' This is particularly symbolic for a company selling water. As *The Economist* pointed out in its survey on water in May 2010, 'the world's most expensive commodities are worth nothing in the absence of water. Fresh water is essential for life, with no substitute. Although mostly unpriced, it is the most valuable stuff in the world.'

It is not just leaders in the developed world that are changing the rules of the game. Entrepreneurs in emerging markets are becoming leaders in 'frugal innovation', the ability to develop new products that are tough and easy to use yet affordable for those with limited income. To do this they are redesigning products to reduce costs not by just 10% but up to 90%. In some cases, emerging market companies are re-engineering entire business processes. In many ways, they are following their entrepreneurial peers in the rich world, who have long grasped the irony that ample resources can often be a curse to innovation. If many people are surprised with the speed and agility of emerging market businesses this does not include the management thinker, C.K. Prahalad, who died in April 2010. In his book, *The Fortune at the Bottom of the Pyramid: Eradicating Poverty Through Profits*, he sought to correct two fundamental misconceptions; that the poor are not important to business and that the profit motive cannot be used to eradicate poverty. Mr Prahalad has preached for some time that the developing world is not 'an also-ran' but a 'vortex of innovation and creativity.' His views are remarkably prescient. Business leaders in emerging markets are not just replicating and re-engineering products and business processes developed elsewhere. They are increasingly thinking outside the box, bringing new technologies and approaches to established industries ranging from health care to banking. This creativity is also being applied to other areas such as environmental issues, where developing nations are increasingly taking the initiative. Strategic leadership knows no national, gender or racial boundaries, just as it is not constrained by class, income or personality characteristics.

The unique role of business

'In any great organisation it is far, far safer to be wrong with the majority than to be right alone.'
John Kenneth Galbraith, Canadian-American Economist

There are those who argue that business should have nothing to do with societal issues. The economist, Milton Friedman, was one of them. He believed that there is only one social responsibility for business, 'to use its resources and engage in activities designed to increase its profits so long as it stays within the rules of the game, which is to say, that it engages in open and free competition without deception and fraud.' Many environmentalists and social activists also see a deep divide between the commercial sector and communal issues. Some see business as the 'natural enemy' and view the profit motive as the underlying cause of much of humanity's suffering. At the very least, this is not helpful, given the scale of some of the challenges that confront us. In reality, many of the world's most intractable problems can only be resolved if we learn to work together. Strategic leaders need to move beyond this 'us' and 'them' thinking, which fails to see the deeply intertwined nature of our world. Thankfully, this is exactly what the best leaders in the commercial world are doing right now. By going beyond the traditional remit of business they appear to be taking no heed of Milton Friedman's advice. At a deeper level, however, the exact opposite may be true. What if we took Milton Friedman's viewpoint and substituted the word 'resources' for 'profit'? What if we then extrapolated his underlying logic to every one of us? His statement could then be rephrased to state that every one of us has the responsibility to act as a steward for those resources that are under our control (leaving the world better off than when we found it) by doing what we are best suited to do (the unique selling proposition in business) without self-deception or trickery. If we all acted in this way, we would create a New Earth instantaneously.

We become strategic leaders when we act from the deepest part of ourselves (the inner journey) in the name of the whole (the external recognition). This is exactly what our best business leaders are doing. Steve Jobs, CEO of Apple, is not an early adopter of 'green values', despite asking former Vice President, Al Gore, to join Apple's board of directors as long ago as March 2003. However, his contribution to resolving some of the world's most intractable problems is immense. As we have seen, Apple is at the forefront of a major change in the way that we use technology and this has profound, and I believe very positive, implications for our society. That is Steve Job's unique role. Howard Schultz, CEO of Starbucks, expresses his unique contribution through his belief that the coffee chain can be a force for good, supporting both those who work for the company and the communities within which it operates. Naturally, there are many detractors who see the world of 'big business' and social community as opposites. In some ways, this is good because it keeps Starbucks 'on its toes'. But it won't stop Howard Schultz from pursuing his mission and we should be thankful for that. Waitrose is deeply engaged in a quest to bring back a human scale to food retailing, linking good, healthy eating with ethical and supportive relationships with suppliers. As we have seen, the Prince of Wales and the National Trust (both of which operate commercial activities) are even more directly involved with some of the biggest and most difficult challenges that we face today.

All these leaders make mistakes. We *all* make mistakes. What marks strategic leaders out as different, however, is that they are at the forefront of change in their areas of expertise. Each one of them

310 Freedom from Fear

is playing a critical role in challenging the limiting belief systems that characterise our world and is pushing out the boundaries of possibility within their endeavours. Most importantly of all, each of these organisations has a proven capacity to act. This is the very definition of strategic leadership: the ability to make a profound difference by making our dreams a reality. This is not easy stuff. Drilling down and truly understanding what we do exceptionally well, whether as an individual or an organisation, is difficult. It is much simpler for commercial organisations to undertake a variety of 'good deeds', under the auspices of 'corporate social responsibility', than it is to link these activities directly to the very essence of what the organisation is all about. Yet, Waitrose (the 'Waitrose Foundation'), Innocent Drinks (the 'Innocent Foundation') and Pret A Manger (The 'Pret Foundation') are doing just this. Each one of these organisations is having a profound impact in its own way, simply by doing what it is best at, in the name of the broader community. At the end of the day, business is an integral part of our world and it will play a critical role in determining our future.

The challenge for not-for-profit organisations

The challenge for not-for-profit organisations is slightly different. Many have an overt mission that is community oriented, or provide services within the public sector. Many people make a positive choice to work for a not-for-profit organisation precisely because it allows them to serve others in a way that speaks to a deeper part of themselves. Unfortunately, thinking strategically within non-commercial organisations presents its own difficulties. The public sector is highly politicised, often with a very short-term decision-making horizon. This makes strategic thinking difficult for anyone who is not in a very senior position (or, better still, within the political system itself). Sadly, without the discipline of the profit motive, many public sector organisations prove to be very poor stewards for the resources allocated to them. Although making public services 'more efficient' and 'cutting waste' are political mantras, there is very little talk of improving the *effectiveness* of service provision. Effectiveness is concerned with doing the 'right' thing, rather than improving the way we do an existing activity. As Anthony T. Dadovano observes, 'a good leader is not the person who does things right, but the person who finds the right thing to do.' Unfortunately, it is in precisely this area that political issues dominate decision-making. And, there is good reason for it. Making strategic decisions involves risk and making trade-offs. Neither are very palatable in a public sector environment. Unfortunately, both are central to strategic decision-making.

There is another challenge in the public sector that is equally difficult to tackle. Bureaucracy (derived from the word, 'bureau', meaning an office) is a set of procedures, regulations and structures put in place to manage an activity. It developed in the early nineteenth century as a centralised tool to ensure that the legitimacy of those in power was under-pinned by a respect for the rule of law. This is obviously a good thing. In theory, power is no longer exercised on a self-interested and ad hoc manner. A sense of fair 'due process' replaces random and self-serving decision-making. Unfortunately, bureaucracy tends to build on itself unless it is constantly monitored. The public sector is particularly vulnerable to adding layers of administrative activity, much of which contributes very little to the provision of 'front line' services. In reality, 'back office' and 'front line' services are inextricably intertwined, which makes it even more difficult to reduce the deadly hand of 'complexity creep'. The end result, ironically, is often a public service that is inward looking, rather than one that is focused on serving society. This is the exact opposite of what we would hope to achieve.

Charities and voluntary organisations have their own challenges too. There is no question that they tend to be highly focused on the area where they can make a big difference. As we have seen, many charities are making a profound and very positive contribution to our world. This can, however, translate into an organisational culture that is unhealthily rigid and one that tolerates subtle (and often not-so-subtle) abuses of power. Sometimes, the 'cause' overrides our sense of humanity. It would be lovely to minimise these practical issues, whether we work in the commercial sector or within a not-for-profit environment, but it is advisable to work with realistic assumptions. This does not mean, however, that we are powerless. Far from it. Strategic leadership begins with what is in front of us. We start, as with many of the case studies and stories in this book, with small, practical steps. We build strong foundations and then we take it one step at a time. The problems facing commercial and not-for-profit organisations may be different but the challenges facing our world are the same. We can only resolve them by tearing down the division between different organisational structures and learning to work together. It is time to move beyond the 'us' and 'them' thinking that has so bedevilled our world and begin to create a new one.

Reality of the leadership journey

*'Stretching his hand up to reach the stars, too often man forgets
the flowers at his feet.'*
Jeremy Bentham

David Waters, Chairman of the Great Bustard Group and Reed Paget, CEO of Belu, make very good case studies in strategic leadership. In many ways, they are achieving their aspirations despite near 'impossible' odds, at the same time as moving the boundaries of our knowledge forward by doing things differently. Both stories are also unfinished. They are works-in-progress and we don't know what the final outcome will be. That is the way it is with most leadership journeys. Such stories make impressive magazine articles. They are tales of success, fought against the odds, which is always a good starting point for a good story. The leaders are frequently outsiders, often coming from humble beginnings to beat the system anyway. When we know a little more about leadership, however, we can sense the difficulties that they have had to endure along the way. It is very easy to 'airbrush out' these complexities in a magazine article. In reality, many social entrepreneurs struggle simply keeping their businesses afloat. It is not just a question of overcoming challenges in order to thrive. It is more often a case of having to overcome a relentless series of life threatening events just to survive. This is not a journey for the fainthearted or those who are seeking reasonable balance in their lives. It is almost always '24/7' and can grind down even the most passionate and committed of leaders. There are always many 'dark nights of the soul' on any leadership journey, times when we begin to feel that the task ahead of us truly is impossible. Sometimes we even begin to doubt our own sanity. I sometimes tell my students that 'all leaders are bonkers' and I am only half-joking. Strategic leadership often involves going *beyond* the sensible point into the unknown. That can be a very isolated and lonely place indeed.

Leadership is not a solitary pursuit because it implies influencing and moving others. As nineteenth century US President, John Quincy Adams, observed, 'If your actions inspire others to dream more, learn more, do more and become more, you are a leader.' Yet, it can certainly *feel* like a *very* solitary place when the path to travel on is not yet defined and we have to build one from scratch. What courage and determination does it take for San Suu Kyi, Myanmar's opposition leader to continue her opposition to the repressive ruling Junta in that country? This is not a simple question to answer. In 1995 a journalist asked her whether she saw any hope for her country. 'I do not hope,' she replied, 'I persevere.' Fifteen years later she is an object lesson in perseverance. Her story is unfinished but there is no doubt about her status as a leader, regardless of how her journey should end. And endings can sometimes be surprising. When Rosa Parks sat in a bus seat designated for whites only on December 1st 1955, she apparently meant to do no more than demonstrate against the unfair treatment of blacks on the bus. Instead, her courageous act was followed by a boycott of all Montgomery's buses for over a year, which was swiftly followed by similar measures in other cities. Her case finally went to the Supreme Court, which ruled that bus segregation was illegal. And, that was just the beginning. With Martin Luther King as its spokesman, a movement of non-violent protest took hold in the United States with far reaching consequences for the advancement of equal rights both within and outside the US. It is the possibility of real change on this scale that motivates leaders, even if there are times when they need to rely on blind faith alone.

The magic of working together

'From the pain come the dream
From the dream come the vision
From the vision come the people
From the people come the power
From this power come the change.'
Peter Gabriel

It is difficult to write a book about leadership without focusing on individual leaders. After all, it is *within* us that the leadership journey begins. But leaders change the world by working with others. Things happen because of the symbiotic relationship between the leader and their supporters. This is obvious. I suspect, however, that most of us would prefer to be seen as a 'leader' rather than a 'follower'. Apart from the more tangible benefits of being perceived as a leader (advancement, recognition, success, special status and material rewards to name but a few) we are also in *control* of the process. And, that feels good to most of us. The truth is, however, that we are both leader and supporter depending on context. Either way, we have a *very* important role to play. By adding our support to others we help to make real change possible in ways that *we* may not even have dreamt of. There is also something very healthy about taking the time to support others. It keeps our ego in check. There is nothing that prevents us from fulfilling our aspirations as leaders more quickly than our ego. As soon as we start to talk about 'my' achievements, or hear ourselves using the pronoun, 'I', rather too frequently, we know we have lost the plot. Sooner or later we will fall flat on our face. Working with, and for, others is the best recipe to keep us grounded. Ironically, the world's greatest leaders rarely worry about whether they are recognised by the external world. They merely get on with the job.

And it is by working together, one small act at a time, that real change happens in all areas of life.

We are faced daily with a barrage of negative media attention on the daunting challenges that face our world. 'Good news' stories are hard to come by. As the old saying goes, the only thing better for the media than bad news... is *very* bad news. As a result, we may be missing the quiet revolution that is currently taking place, one that should give us great heart and hope for the future. This is the kind of revolution that happens at grassroots level and is just as alive at the parish village fete as it is in the National Trust or within our schooling system. We are becoming a nation of volunteers. We work for 'Thames 21', removing plastic bags, shopping trolleys and traffic cones from London's historic river. We support charities such as 'Trees for Life', which is helping to restore part of the Caledonian Forest in the Scottish Highlands ('Caledonia' is the Roman name for Scotland, meaning 'wooded heights'). We work on parish councils or help out in schools because we know that it will make a difference to the community. We join 'friends' organisations because we know that many community institutions would struggle without tangible support from within the community. We help others to achieve their dreams by giving up our time and resources in whatever way we can. It is one of those ironies in life that at the very same time that the media is pronouncing the death of community, it is being reborn, stronger than ever. Community is dead. Long live community.

Making fear our friend

'Life is difficult. This is a great truth, one of the greatest truths. It is a great truth because once we truly see this truth, we transcend it. Once we truly know that life is difficult – once we truly understand and accept it – than life is no longer difficult. Because once it is accepted, the fact that life is difficult no longer matters.'
Dr M Scott Peck, American Psychiatrist and Author

Fear plays a useful part in our lives. It motivates and energises us when danger is imminent. But, as we have seen, it is designed to be a protective mechanism in the short term. When we live out of balance we store up problems that are essentially long term in nature. We experience anxiety, stress, worry, apprehension and a vague sense of dread. We then feel powerless and debilitated. Naturally, there are many different ways of reacting to this. Some of us attempt to reinforce our control in those areas of our life where we can, while others hide by blocking out uncertainty or retreating from it through one addiction or another. It is normal to seek to minimise, ignore or override these 'negative' feelings. Yet, there are some of us who choose to confront challenges head-on and act despite the uncertainties involved. These are the leaders amongst us. It is not that they don't feel fear or are 'free' of it. Far from it, they are just as susceptible as the rest of us. But, they learn to work positively with their fears and apprehensions, using the energy to provide the drive to achieve their aspirations. Ironically, by working with and accepting our fear, we are able to rise above it. When we do this something surprising happens. Fear becomes our friend. We begin to hear its call when we have previously shut it out. We are no longer frightened by fear itself. We learn to embrace our fears for the long term and, in doing so, we become more deeply aware of our part in the whole. In short, we make fear our friend. That is the nature of true freedom.

Creating a New Earth

'Thousands of candles can be lit from a single candle and the life of that candle will not be shortened.'
The Buddha

Mississippi is the poorest state in the United States, measured in terms of per capita income. It also has one of the highest rates of charitable contributions. Challenges often bring out the best in us. As Nancy Gibbs, editor at large for *Time Magazine*, points out, 'To suffer alone is a tragedy; to struggle together is an opportunity.' There are no real boundaries for human creative endeavour. It is easy to be fearful about the future. If we use the past as a guide to how the future will turn out, we have every reason to be. But we are not living in the past. We are living in the now. And within that moment lies our future. The challenges in front of us are daunting. That does not mean that we should be daunted. Each and every one of us has the capability to be a leader, in our own unique way. We can be supporters and followers too. We shouldn't mind too much which role we happen to be playing at any particular point in time. Above all, strategic leadership is being in a position of service to others. We act, not on behalf of ourselves, but as a servant for the community and we do so by expressing the deepest part of ourselves.

It doesn't matter where we are in our lives. We start our leadership journey with whatever is right in front of us. It need not be 'big' or 'important' in the eyes of others. The work of Steve Gascoigne, a photographer based in the Isle of Wight, is stunning. So too are the images taken by Welsh photographer, Janet Baxter, who lives in Cardiganshire. Both these special people capture nature in unique and inspiring ways, allowing us to see the beauty, mystery and sheer awe of the natural world. They open a gateway into nature, so that we can reconnect to our place within the totality of life. This is personal leadership in action because the work of Steve and Janet is a direct expression of the deepest part of who they are. It is strategic because it directly confronts our assumptions of separateness, independence and control. It allows us to reframe our perspective a little, learning new ways to see and act, thus glimpsing at opportunities and possibilities that were previously hidden to us. There is no telling where this will take us. We all have the ability to do the same in our own unique ways. The journey to strategic leadership will change us, and our world, in ways that we can scarcely imagine when we first begin. As Buckminster Fuller once remarked, 'There is nothing in a caterpillar that tells you it's going to be a butterfly.' I wish you well with your new pair of wings.

SOURCES

Foreword

Paul Kimmage, *'Andy Ripley, the most extraordinary human being I had ever met'*, Sunday Times, May 23rd, 2010

Andy Ripley, Althone Friary, June 10th 2007

Prologue

William Beebe (*'The Bird: Its Form and Function'* 1906, BiblioBazaar 2010) from Lee Durrell, *'Remembering Gerald Durrell'*, BBC Wildlife Magazine, Oct 2009

Alison Benjamin and Brian McCullum, *'A World Without Bees'*, Guardian Books, 2009

Stephen Moss, *'Bees in the balance'*, National Trust Magazine, Summer 2010

'Bzzzt, it's back, The short-haired bumblebee', The Economist, Sep 17th 2009

'Why bees are the most invaluable species', The Guardian (guardian.co.uk environmental blog), Nov 2008

'Take part, keep the bees buzzing', BBC website, bbc.co.uk, May 2010

'An Innocent spotter's guide to bees', Innocent Drinks juice carton

Ted O'Donoghue and Matthew Rabin, *'Choice and Procrastination'*, UC Berkeley Department of Economics, April 25th 2000

'New-year irresolution, How to combat the natural tendency to procrastinate', The Economist, Jan 2nd 2010

Rob Parsons, *'The Sixty Minute Father, An Hour to Change Your Child's Life'*, Hodder & Stoughton, 1995

Introduction

Karine Polwart, *'Faultlines'*, from the album, *'Faultlines'*, Neon, 2004

Richard Corliss, *'Avatar Ascendant, Why James Cameron's megahit is rewriting the rules and the record books'*, Time Magazine, February 8th 2010

Stephen Cottrell, Bishop of Reading, Author Evenings, Mustard Seed, Marlborough, Wiltshire, 2010

John Tucker, International Centre for Families in Business, personal interviews, 2009-2010 *(see also www.icfib.com)*

'Schumpeter, Remembering Drucker', The Economist, Nov 21st 2009

M. Scott Peck, 'The Different Drum, Community Making and Peace, A Spiritual Journey Toward Self-Acceptance, True Belonging, and Hope for the World', Touchstone, 1987

David Lorimer, 'Radical Prince, The Practical Vision of the Prince of Wales', Floris Books, 2004

Jules Pretty OBE, 'Modern city, stone age mind', Natural World Magazine, Winter 2009

Stacey O'Brien, 'Wesley, 'The Story of a Remarkable Owl', Constable & Robinson Ltd, 2008

'Tuna fishing, Changing tides', The Economist, Nov 21st, 2009

Krista Mahr, 'Rare Tuna, How our appetite for its flesh is killing off one of the oceans' most magnificent creatures', Time Magazine, Nov 9th 2009

Kevin Hall & Colleagues, National Institute of Diabetes and Digestive Diseases, Nov 2009, as reported in 'Science News' (www.sciencedaily.com) and other online sources

'Environment, A hill of beans', The Economist, Nov 28th 2009

'What We Believe', and related web pages, eBay website, (www.ebay.com), 2010

'World's Most Admired Companies', Fortune Magazine, CNNMoney.com, 2010

Joan Borysenko, 'It's Not the End of the World', Hay House, 2009

'The Age of Stupid, Why Didn't We Save Ourselves When We Had The Chance', Dogwoof Ltd, 2008

Steve Jobs, 'Commencement Address at Stanford University, June 12th 2005', Stanford University website (http//news-service.stanford.edu/news/2005/June 15/jobs)

'Schumpter, The cult of the faceless boss', The Economist, Nov 14th 2009

Master Sgt. Rogers Traehan, 81st Medical Support Squadron first sergeant, Keesler Air Force Base, 'Leadership has no rank; anyone can be a leader' (www.keesler.af.mil), Nov 2009

Chapter 1

David Harmer, *'Our Tree'*, *'Earthways, Poems on Conservation'*, Selected by Judith Nicholls, Oxford University Press, 1993

Aretha Franklin, *'10 Questions, 'The Queen of Soul talks about giving Detroit a little respect. Aretha Franklin will now take your questions'*, Time Magazine, Mar 1st 2010

'Detroit's future, Thinking about shrinking', The Economist, Mar 27th 2010

'Lexington, Farmers v greens', The biggest obstacle to a climate-change bill is rural America', The Economist, Nov 14th 2009

'Biodiversity, Fewer Creatures great and small', The Economist, Oct 18th 2009

*'Poverty Facts and Stats, Global Issues (www.globalissues.org), May 2010

'How to feed the World, The Economist, Nov 21st 2010

'Water, Sin aqua non', The Economist, Apr 11th 2009

'Water for farming, Running Dry', The Economist, Sep 20th 2008

'Shutting Down the Oceans, Act I: Acid Oceans', Institute of Science in Society, ISIS press release (available at www.i-sis.org.uk/AcidOceans.php), Jul 26th 2006

Bryan Walsh, *'A River Ran Through It'*, Time Magazine, Dec 14th 2009

'The IPCC's 2035 prediction about Himalayan glaciers', Skeptical Science (www.skepticalscience.com), Jan, 21st 2010

'Glaciers and the IPCC, Off-base camp', The Economist, Jan 23rd 2010

'Climate change, A heated debate', The Economist, Nov 26th 2009

Peter Taylor, *'Cool inconvenient truths expose flawed CO2 model'*, Caduceus Magazine, Issue 767, 2009

'How long till the lights go out', The Economist, Aug 8th 2009

'Falling fertility, How the population problem is solving itself', The Economist, Nov 6th 2009

'Bugs are under threat!', 'buglife' (the Invertebrate Conservation Trust) advertisement, BBC Wildlife Magazine, Oct 2009

'Iraq and the kirkuk conundrum, A hint of harmony at last', The Economist, Dec 5th 2009

Gary Zukav, *'The Dancing Wu Li Masters, An overview of the New Physics'*, HarperOne, 2001

'The potato, Spud we like', The Economist, Feb 28th 2008

Christopher Redman, *'King of the carbs, A new history traces the potato's unlikely path from toxic tuber to dietary staple'*, Time Magazine, Mar 3rd 2008

John Reader, *'Propitious Esculent, The Potato in World History'*, William Heinemann Ltd, 2008

Richard Stengel, *'Person of the Year, Ben Bernanke*, Time Magazine, Jan 4th 2010

'Economics focus, Measuring what matters', The Economist, Sep 19th 2009

Pierre Pradervand, *'What is True Wealth?'*, Cygnus Magazine, 2009

Stephan Faris, *'A Better Measure, Our obsession with gross domestic product is unhealthy – and misleading'*, Time Magazine, Nov 2nd 2009

'Gross national happiness', Wikipedia, Dec 24th 2009

Edmund Conway and Andrew Porter, *'UK economy overtaken by Italy'*, Daily Telegraph (www.telegraph.co.uk), Oct 23rd 2009

'Clustering, The phenomenon whereby firms from the same industry gather together in close proximity', The Economist, Aug 24th 2009

'Cities and commercial life, Location, location, location', The Economist, June 16th 2001

Joe Baker, *'Big stuff, little place'*, YorkU Magazine, York University, Toronto, 2009

'Struggling giants, What the world's biggest carmaker can learn from other corporate turnarounds', The Economist, Dec 12th 2009

'Briefing Toyota, Losing its shine', The Economist, Dec 12th 2009

'Toyota's overstretched supply chain, The machine that ran too hot', The Economist, Feb 27th 2010

Bill Saporito with Michael Schuman and Joseph R. Szczesny, *'Toyota's Tangle, How the world's biggest carmaker went wrong – and how to set it right'/'Toyota's Blown Engine,'* Time Magazine, Feb 22nd 2010

'Bill Saporito, *Spotlight, Toyota's Recall'*, Time Magazine, Feb 15th 2010

Alex Altman, *'Spotlight, Toyota Hearings'*, Time Magazine, Mar 8th 2010

Hans Greimel, *'Akio Toyoda savors flavor of excitement'*, Automotive News (www.autonews.com) Nov 16th 2009

Barbara Kiviat, *'Global Business, Reassessing Risk, Wall Street failed spectacularly in managing it. A new approach is emerging: human judgment'*, Time Magazine, Dec 22nd 2008

'Lexington, Law v common sense', The Economist, Jan 17th 2009

Martin Lindstrom, *'Business Books, Buying on the Brain'*, Time Magazine, 2009

Martin Lindstrom, *'Buy*ology: Truth and Lies About Why We Buy'*, Broadway Business, 2008

'Economics focus: Waist banned, Does a tax on junk food make sense', The Economist, Aug 1st 2009

'A mortgage from Tesco?', The Economist, Oct 4th 2008

'Stop the Barbaric and Senseless Badger Cull', Badger Watch and Rescue leaflet, Dyfed, 2009

'Press freedom and the internet, Barbra Streisand strikes again', The Economist, Oct 17th 2009

'Buttonwood, Bribing the markets', The Economist, Oct 31st 2009

'Buttonwood, Covered in shame', The Economist, May 3rd 2007

Michael Elliott, 'The Moment, 04/06/09 L'Aguila', Time Magazine, Apr 20th 2009

Justin Fox, 'The Curious Capitalist, From Makro to Freako. With economists under fire, maybe it's time for them to return to what they do best: the little stuff', Time Magazine, Oct 26th 2009

'America, Europe and the management of danger, A hazardous comparison', The Economist, Mar 1st 2008

'Dangerous dogs in Denmark, Shoot the puppy!', The Economist, Aug 20th 2009

Simon Jenkins, 'We must support the Kensington road revolution', Evening Standard, Jul 21st 2009 (www.thisislondon.co.uk/standard)

Bryan Walsh, 'Eat Your Greens', Time Magazine, Mar 2nd 2009

'Europe, Portugal's drug policy, Treating, not punishing', The Economist, Aug 29th 2009

Chapter 2

'Farewell to WW1, From memory to history', The Economist, Dec 19th 2009

Sue Palmer, 'The Head's View, A way with nature', View Magazine, Oct 2009

'The joy of dirt', The Economist, Dec 19th 2009

Lisa Abend, 'Save the Planet: Eat More Beef', Time Magazine, Jan 25th 2010

Russell Louis 'Rusty' Schweickart, extract from a speech to a gathering on 'Planetary Culture' in the summer of 1974 (full text available at http://thoughtwax.com)

M. Charlene Porter, 'New York Firefighters Remember September 11, 2001', www.america.gov, June 2010

Andrew Farrow, The Prince's Charities (www.princescharities.org/stories) and www.liveyourpotential.co.uk, June 2010

Graeme Sims, 'The Dog Whisperer: How to Train Your Dog Using Its Own Language', Headline, 2009

Steve Jobs, 'Steve Jobs speaks out... on his management style', Fortune Magazine, CNNMoney.com and www.cnn.com, Mar 2008

Lynn A. Robinson, 'Intuition in the News', Intuitive Consulting Inc. www.lynnrobinson.com, Mar 2010

Ted Oakes, 'The Bear Whisperer', BBC Wildlife Magazine, Oct 2009

Lee Durrell, 'Remembering Gerald Durrell', BBC Wildlife Magazine, Oct 2009

Jane Goodall, '10 Questions, Jane Goodall will now take your questions', Time Magazine, Sep 21st 2009

Professor Michael Fitzgerald, Trinity College, Dublin, 'Age of autism', Communication Magazine (National Autistic Society), Winter 2009

Chapter 3

A. A. Milne, 'The House at Pooh Corner', Methuen Books, 1989

'Mikhail Gorbachev and the fall of the wall, The man who trusted his eyes', The Economist, Nov 7th 2009

Jimmy Carter, 'A Village Woman's Legacy', Time Magazine, Mar 31st 2008

'Rain Forests, The Burning Issue', The Prince's Rainforests Project 2009 (Free Guide) and www.rainforestSOS.org, 2010

Roland Gribben, 'The Prince's Trust's boss battles the recession', The Daily Telegraph (www.telegraph.co.uk), Apr 15th 2009

Barbara Kiviat, 'Starbucks Can Smell Growth', Time Magazine, Mar 1st 2010

Susan Berfield, 'Starbucks: Howard Schultz vs. Howard Schultz', Business Week, Aug 6th 2009 (www.businessweek.com)

Andrew Clark interviews Howard Schultz, 'Starbucks boss: we're not all froth', The Guardian, Mar 20th 2009 (www.guardian.co.uk/business)

Karlene Lukovitz, 'Starbucks' Financial Performance Perking Up', MediaPost News (www.mediapost.com), Nov 10th 2009

'The Book of Jobs, Hope, hype and Apple's iPad'/'Steve Jobs and the tablet of hope', The Economist, Jan 30th 2010

Josh Quittner, 'Apple's Vision Of the Future', Time Magazine, Feb 8th 2010

Lev Grossman, 'Wise Guy', Time Magazine, Dec 1st 2008

Lev Grossman, 'Jumping to Conclusions', Time Magazine, Jan 10th 2005

Mary Chapin Carpenter, 'The Long Way Home', from the album, 'Time * Sex * Love', Sony Nashville, 2001

Enneagram Institute, 'Introduction to the Enneagram' (www.enneagraminstitute.com), Mar 2010

Simon Parke, 'The Enneagram, A Private Session with the World's Greatest Psychologist', Lion Hudson plc, 2008

'Miep Gies', The Economist, Jan 30th 2010, Sony Nashville, 2001

Chapter 4

Joni Mitchell, 'Both Sides Now', from the album 'Clouds', Reprise Records, 1967

'Buttonwood, Law of easy money', The Economist, Aug 13th 2009

Jon Moen, 'John Law and the Mississippi Bubble: 1718-1720', Mississippi History Now (http//:mshistory.k12.ms.us), Mar 2009

'Lightweight Dinosaurs, Not so terrible', The Economist, Jun 27th 2009

'Rapid Transit: York's Bridget Stuchbury finds songbird species worth crowing about', YorkU Magazine, York University, Toronto, Summer 2009

'The Industrial Revolution Explained, Supply and demand', The Economist, May 23rd 2009

Robert C. Allen, 'The British Industrial Revolution in Global Perspective', Cambridge University Press, 2009

Janis Ian, BBC Radio 2 documentary on Janis Ian narrated by Mary Black, circa 2000

'Obituary, Alison Des Forges', The Economist, Feb 23rd 2009

James Gleick, 'Chaos, Making of a New Science', Penguin Books, 1988

'Economics focus, A new fashion in modeling', 'The Economist, Nov 2007

Roman Frydman, Edward S. Phelps and Michael D. Goldberg, 'Imperfect Knowledge Economics: Exchange Rates and Risk', Princeton University Press, 2007

Maddy Harland, 'Celebrating the Marginal', Cygnus Books Magazine, 2009

Nassim Nicholas Taleb, 'The Black Swan: The Impact of the Highly Improbable', Penguin, 2008

Wikipedia (Sainsbury's, ASDA, Morrisons and Tesco results), April 2010

Charles Handy, 'The Age of Unreason: New Thinking For A New World', Random House, 2002

'The Lure of Lichen', National Trust Magazine, Autumn 2009

'Climate change, No hiding place?', The Economist, Jan 9th 2010

National Trust Annual Report, 2008/09

'Hold steady!', National Trust Magazine, Spring 2010

'Millennium Seed Bank Project Kew, A global network for plant conservation', Royal Botanic Gardens Kew booklet, Summer 2009

'Kew's Millennium Seed Bank', Information Sheet_MSB001, Summer 2009

Henry David Thoreau, *'Selections From The Journals'*, Dover Publications, New York, 1995

Chapter 5

Karine Polwart, *'Daisy'*, from the album *'Scribbled in Chalk'*, Hengri Music, 2006

Craig Reynolds, *'Boids, Background and Update'*, www.red3d.com/cwr/boids (*see www.red3d.com/cwr for information on Craig Reynolds*), Mar 2010

Margaret Evans, *'The Sense of a Goose'*, Cygnus Magazine, 2009

'Efficient aviation, V for victory', The Economist, Dec 5th 2009

Margaret Silf, *'Sacred Spaces, Stations on a Celtic Way'*, Lion Books, 2001

'A biography of Friedrich Engels, A very special business angel', The Economist, Aug 15th 2009

'Volunteering, A service nation', The Economist, Apr 11th 2009

Lev Grossman, *'Wise Guy'*, Time Magazine, Dec 1st 2008

Lev Grossman, *'Jumping to Conclusions'*, Time Magazine, Jan 10th 2005

Malcolm Gladwell, *'Outliers: The Story of Success'*, Penguin, 2009

Rob Parsons, *'The Sixty Minute Family: Experience the magic of traditions'*, Care For the Family Magazine, 2009/2010

Carol Thatcher, *'Below The Parapet, The Biography of Denis Thatcher'*, Harper Collins, 1996

'A poll on trust, What's good for General Motors', The Economist, Feb 2010

'Social networks, Primates on Facebook', The Economist, Feb 28th 2009

'Business-networking websites, Insider out', The Economist, June 25th 2009

Rick Jarow, *'Creating the Work You Love: Courage, Commitment and Career'*, Inner Traditions Bear and Company, 1996

Laurie Beth Jones, *'Jesus, CEO, Using Ancient Wisdom for Visionary Leadership'*, Hyperion, 1992

Martyn Joseph, *'Please Sir'*, from the album *'Being There'*, Sony Music, 1992

St John's School, Marlborough, '*St John's News*', School Magazine, May 2009

Waitrose literature and website materials (www.waitrose.com) and View Magazine, '*Princely partnership*' and '*Grape expectations*' ('The Waitrose page'), 2009/2010

'*Leckford Estate*', www.waitrose.com/ourcompany/leckfordestate, 2009/10

'The Pret Foundation Trust', www.pret.com, 2009/10

'The Innocent Foundation', about the foundation', www.innocentfoundation.org, 2009/10

Ikujiro Nonaka, '*The Knowledge-Creating Company, How Japanese Companies Create the Dynamics of Innovation*', Oxford University Press, 1995 and '*The Knowledge-Creating Company*', Harvard Business Review on Knowledge Management, Harvard Business Press, 1998

'*Economics focus, Commons sense*', The Economist, Aug 2nd 2008

Garrett Harding, '*Tragedy of the Commons*', Science Magazine, 1968 (*see The Garrett Hardin Society @ garretthardinsociety.org*)

'*Elinor Ostrom*', Daylife, www.daylife.com, Mar 2010

David Lorimer, '*Radical Prince, The Practical Vision of the Prince of Wales*', Floris Books, 2004

Chapter 6

Gary Snyder, '*For the Children*', '*Turtle Island*', W.W. Norton & Co., 1974

Susan Berfield, '*Starbucks: Howard Schultz vs. Howard Schultz*', Business Week, Aug 6th 2009 (www.businessweek.com)

Andrew Clark interviews Howard Schultz, '*Starbucks boss: we're not all froth*', The Guardian, Mar 20th 2009 (www.guardian.co.uk/business)

'*Peter Mandelson Has Christian Bale Moment Over Starbucks*' '*Downward Spiral*' *UK Jibe*', Bad Idea Magazine, www.badidea.co.uk

Satish Kumar, '*Opinion, Satish Kumar: Trees are the answer*', National Trust Magazine, 2009

'*Spin, science and climate change*'/'*The clouds of unknowing*', The Economist, Mar 20th 2010

'*Airdrie Savings Bank, Boring, stolid, small and safe*', The Economist, Nov 13th 2008

Airdrie Savings Bank website (www.airdriesavingsbank.net), 2009

'*Flat pack*', The Economist Technology Quarterly, Mar 6th 2009/10

'The diner rolls on, Burger's revenge', The Economist, Nov 13th 2003

Action for the River Kennet ('ARK') (www.riverkennet.org), Mar 2010

'Help Us Create A Spectacular Wetland', Langford Lakes appeal letter, Wiltshire Wildlife Trust, Oct 2009

Chapter 7

Kit Wright, 'Acorn Haiku', Judith Nicholls, 'Earthways, Poems on Conservation', Oxford University Press, 2000

'Wesley Autrey, From New York subway rider to all-American hero', Time Magazine, Time 100 Heroes and Pioneers, May 14th 2007

'Biography for Wesley Autrey', IMDb, www.imdb.com, Oct 2009

'Obituary, Marek Edelman', The Economist, Oct 10th 2009

Wikipedia, 'Marek Edelman', Oct 2009

Benny Gallagher & Graham Lyle, 'A Heart In New York', from the album, 'Heart On My Sleeve, The Very Best of Gallagher & Lyle', A&M, 1991 (song: 1977)

'The Concert in Central Park', Wikipedia, March 2010

'A Passage to Bristol', Bristol Indymedia, wwwbristol.indymedia.org, Mar 2010

Richard Stengel, 'To Our Readers, The Rules of Leadership', Time Magazine, Jul 20th 2009

Simon Burke, personal interviews, 2000 – 2010

'Who does business trust?', Fortune Magazine, CNNMoney, http://money.cnn.com, Dec 2009

'Apple Reports Fourth Quarter Results'/'Apple Reports Third Quarter Results'/'Apple Sells Two Million iPads in Less Than 60 days', Apple 'feed', Apple.com, 2009/2010

'How Apple's App Store got to 1.5 billion downloads', Fortune Brainstorm Tech, CNNMoney (http://brainstormtech.blogs.fortune.cnn.com), July 2009

'Face value, Sauce of success, The Economist, Apr 11th 2009

Kikkoman website, www.kikkoman.com, Jan-Mar 2010

Bill Graham, Schulich International Alumni Association, Schulich School of Business, York University, Toronto, Canada, letter dated Oct 28th 2009

'Business Education, Which MBA?', The Economist, www.economist.com, Oct 2009

'Out in Front', York University, Toronto, Canada, booklet (taken from Report on Business Magazine, Jan 2007)

Mamdouh Shoukri, President and Vice Chancellor, York University, Toronto, Canada, 'Our Global Reach', YorkU Magazine, York University, Feb 2010

Mamdouh Shoukri, President and Vice Chancellor, York University, Toronto, Canada, 'Sustaining York', YorkU Magazine, York University, Oct 2008

Nancy Gibbs, editor at large, Time Magazine, 'The Message of Miracles', Time Magazine, Apr 10th 1995

'Savings and the poor, A better mattress', The Economist, Mar 13th 2010

John Madeley, '100 Ways to Make Poverty History for a Fiver', Canterbury Press, 2005

'Change the World for a Fiver', We Are What We Do (a project of community links, www.community-links.org), Oxfam, 2004

Archie Duncanson, 'Ecology Begins at Home, Using the Power of Choice', Green Books, 2004

Bruce Cockburn, 'Child of the Wind', from the album, 'Nothing But a Burning Light', Columbia/Sony Music, 1991

Chapter 8

Jane Miles, 'No Added Sugar, Poems by Jane Miles', St Andrew's Press of Wells, 2006

'Obituary, John Thorbjarnarson', The Economist, Mar 20th 2010

'John Thorbjarnarson, A Crocodile and Alligator Expert, Is Dead at 52', New York Times, (www.nytimes.com), Mar 7th 2010

Richard S. Tedlow, 'Denial: Why Business Leaders Fail to Look Facts in the Face – And What to Do about It', Portfolio, 2010

Thich Nhat Hanh and Anh-Huong Nquyen, 'Walking Meditation', Sounds True, 2006

Jon Kabat-Zinn, 'Full Catastrophe Living: How to Cope with Stress, Pain and Illness Using Mindfulness Meditation', Piatkus Books, 2001 and 'Full Catastrophe Living', Cygnus Magazine, 2008

Malcolm Gladwell, 'Outliers: The Story of Success', Penguin, 2009

David Lorimer, 'Radical Prince, The Practical Vision of the Prince of Wales', Floris Books, 2004

'A distant voice from another dimension is crying out for recognition', The Online Community for Intelligent Optimists, Ode Magazine, www.odemagazine.com, May 2010

Temenos Academy, www.temenosacademy.org, Mar 2010

Richard H Thaler and Cass R Sunstein' 'Nudge – Improving Decisions about Health, Wealth and Happiness', Penguin, 2009

Dr David Freemantle, Customer Service Magazine, circa 1990's

Dan Millman, 'No Ordinary Moments, A Peaceful Warrior's Guide to Daily Life', HJ Kramer Inc., 1992

Steve Jobs, 'Commencement Address at Stanford University, June 12th 2005', Stanford University website (http//news-service.stanford.edu/news/2005/June 15/jobs)

Chapter 9

Anaïs Nin, as quoted by Dan Millman in 'Living On Purpose: Straight Answers to Universal Questions', New World Library, 2000

Stephan Faris, 'Heroes of the Environment, Craig Sorley', Time Magazine, Oct 6th 2009

Michael Elliott, 'Heroes of the Environment, Van Jones', Time Magazine, Oct 6th 2009

Martha Tancock, 'Peace Bridge', YorkU Magazine, York University, Toronto, Canada, Summer 2005

'Building a Dream', Dream Magazine (Honda Automotive Customer Magazine), 2009

'Simon Usborne, 'Lord of the butterflies: Clive Farrell has turned his Dorset estate into an insect-filled fantasia', The Independent website (www.indpendent.co.uk) and Butterfly World website (butterfly-world.org)

New World Encyclopedia, 'Soichiro Honda', www.newworldencyclopedia.org, 2009

Warren G. Bennis and Robert J. Thomas, 'Crucibles of Leadership', Harvard Business Review, Sep 2002

Martha Tancock, 'Still Running', YorkU Magazine, York University, Toronto, Canada, Oct 2009

Martha Tancock, 'To The Rescue', YorkU Magazine, York University, Toronto, Canada, Feb 2010

Bartlett Arboretum website (www.BartlettArboretum.com)/Wikipedia, 'Robin Lynn Macy', Mar 2010

'Songs From the Garden', Robin Lynn Macy, Bartlett Arboretum, 2008

National Trust Annual Report 2008/09, Magazine, Summer 2010 and literature (brochures and information leaflets), 2009/10

Susan Enan, '*Bring on the Wonder*', from the album, '*Plainsong*', Feast Music Group, 2009

Robert K. Greenleaf, '*The Servant as Leader*', Greenleaf Center, 2008

Robert K. Greenleaf & Larry C. Spears, '*Servant Leadership, A Journey into the Nature of Legitimate Power & Greatness*', Paulist Press International, 2002

Piero Ferrucci, '*What Our Children Teach Us, Lessons in Joy, Love and Awareness*', Simon & Schuster, 2002

Chapter 10

A. A. Milne, '*The House at Pooh Corner*', Methuen Books, 1989

Samuel Beckett, Worstward Ho, Grove Press, 1983

John Tucker, International Centre for Families in Business, personal interviews, 2009-2010 (*see also www.icfib.com*)

Rob Parsons, '*The Heart of Success, Making it in business without losing in life*', Hodder & Stoughton, 2002

Ani DiFranco, Billboard Magazine, circa late 1990's/early 2000's

Tucker Zimmerman, '*The Taoists Tale*', 1975

Eckhart Tolle, '*This too, will pass*', Cygnus Magazine, 2009

Eckhart Tolle, '*A New Earth, Create a Better Life*', Penguin, 2009

Lev Grossman, '*Inside Steve's Pad*'/'*The tale of the tablet*', Time Magazine, Apr 12th 2010

Stephen Fry, '*How Jobs works*' and '*On the Mothership*', Time Magazine (and website – www.time.com), Apr 12th 2010

Apple feeds (www.apple.com) and CNBC (www.cnbc.com)

Greg Hurst, '*Lesson in willpower as headmaster and team raise £25m to rebuild entire school*', The Times, Dec 5th 2009

St John's School, Marlborough, '*St John's News*' (school newsletter) and website (www.stjohns.wilts.sch.uk), 2009/10

Rupert Murdoch, News Corporation earnings call, Feb 2nd 2010.

The Economist website (www.economist.com)/Wikipedia, The Economist, 2008/10

'*Remembering Timothy White*', Billboard Magazine, July 13th 2002

Timothy White, '*Don't Call It Content – It's Substance Or Nothing*', Aug 4th 2001

Charles Handy, '*Trust & The Virtual Organization*', Harvard Business Review, May-June 1995

John Lewis Partnership website (www.johnlewispartnership.co.uk) Waitrose website (www.waitrose.com) and partnership brochures, information leaflets, 2009/10

Matthew Naylor, 'Matthew Naylor interviews Waitrose CEO Mark Price', YouTube video (www.youtube.com), Mar 2010

LEAF (Linking Environment and Farming), www.leafuk.org

'Wilma Mankiller', The Economist, Apr 24th 2010/Wikipedia, 'Wilma Mankiller', May 2010

Sumantra Ghoshal, Interview in Management Today, Dec 1996

Fiona Jebb, 'UK: The Gurus – Sumantra Ghoshal', Management Today (www.managementtoday.co.uk)

Chapter 11

Jane Miles, 'No Added Sugar, Poems by Jane Miles', St Andrew's Press of Wells, 2006

Tim McGirk, 'Postcard: Kabul', Time Magazine, Apr 5th 2010

'Supply-chain management, Shrink rapped', The Economist, May 15th 2008

Stephen Cottrell, Bishop of Reading, Author Evenings, Mustard Seed, Marlborough, Wiltshire, 2010

'St Anthony the Abbot', Catholic Online (www.catholic.org/saints) and 'Antony of the Desert' (www.goodnews.ie)

Rob Parsons, 'The power of a dream', Care For the Family Partners Newsletter, Nov 2009

Van Jones, 'Heroes: Will Allen', Time Magazine, May 10th 2010

Lisa Abend and Isla Mayor, 'Going Green, Net Profits', Time Magazine, June 15th 2010

Marc Hauser, 'Heroes: Temple Grandin', Time Magazine, May 15th 2010 (source of the 'unique mind' quote)

Wikipedia, 'Temple Grandin', June 2010

'The Brecon Beacons appeal', National Trust website (www.nationaltrust.org.uk), Apr 2010

Simon Toomer, Director of Westonbirt, 'A New Direction', 'Westonbirt, The National Arboretum' newsletter, Winter 2009

Wiltshire Wildlife Trust Annual Review, 2008/09

RSPB, 'Impact' Magazine, Titchwell Marsh Appeal news, Winter 2009

Raffi Cavoukian's website (www.raffinews.com) and Centre for Child Honouring (www.childhonouring.org), 2009/10

Raffi Cavoukian, Sharna Olfman, Editors, 'Child Honouring, How to Turn This World Around', Praeger, 2006

Milton Friedman, 'The Social Responsibility of Business is to Increase its Profits', The New York Times Magazine, Sep 13th 1970

Steve Marshall, 'Great bustard is back and breeding', Wiltshire Life, Aug 2009

Clare-Marie Dobing, 'Free as a bird', Wessex Water Magazine, 2009

Great bustard group website (www.greatbustard.org) and BBC website, 'Springwatch 2010' (www.bbc.co.uk/meettheanimals/greatbustard), 2010

Adam Smith, 'Bottled Up', Time Magazine, Aug 2009

Joe Lutrario, 'Spotlight on… Belu Water', Restaurant Magazine (website: www.bighospitality.co.uk), July 2009

Belu website (www.belu.co.uk), Mar 2010

Thames 21 website (www.thames21.org.uk), Mar 2010

'Water, The world's most valuable stuff', The Economist, May 22nd 2010

'Schumpeter, the guru of the bottom of the pyramid', The Economist, Apr 24th 2010

'The world turned upside down, A special report on innovation in emerging markets', The Economist, Apr 17th 2010

'Myanmar's evil junta, The paucity of hope', The Economist, May 1st 2010

'Obituary, Rosa Parks', The Economist, Oct 29th 2005

Peter Gabriel, 'Fourteen Black Paintings' from the album, 'Us', Real World, 1992

Janet Baxter's website (www.cymriccards.co.uk), 2009/10

Steve Gascoigne's website (Available Light Photography, www.availablelight.cc), 2009/10

Nancy Gibbs, editor at large, Time Magazine, 'The Recession's Big Test', Jan 19th 2009

M. Scott Peck, 'The Road Less Travelled: A New Psychology of Love, Traditional Values and Spiritual Growth' (Classic Edition), Rider & Co., 2008

General sources

Christopher Booker, 'The Seven Basic Plots, Why We Tell Stories', Continuum, 2004

Simon Parke, 'The Beautiful Life, Ten New Commandments Because Life Could Be Better', Bloomsbury, 2007

Paul Hawker, 'Soul Survivor, A Spiritual Quest Through 40 Days in the Wilderness', Lion Books, 2000

Stephen Cottrell, 'Do Nothing to Change Your Life', Church House Publishing, 2007

Pierre Pradervand, 'The Gentle Art of Blessing', Cygnus Books, 2003

Scott Adams, Dilbert cartoons, United Feature Syndicate Inc., Various dates

Note: The author has done his best to acknowledge all sources used in this work. In the event that something has slipped through inadvertently without due acknowledgement it is entirely unintentional and the author offers his apologies. Quotes have been sourced above if they are not freely available in the public domain. Other quotes are readily available from multiple online sources.

INDEX